Faith–Based Initiatives and the Bush Administration

The Good, the Bad, and the Ugly

Jo Renee Formicola,
Mary C. Segers, and Paul Weber

ROWMAN & LITTLEFIELD PUBLISHERS, INC.
Lanham • Boulder • New York • Oxford

ROWMAN & LITTLEFIELD PUBLISHERS, INC.

Published in the United States of America
by Rowman & Littlefield Publishers, Inc.
A Member of the Rowman & Littlefield Publishing Group
4501 Forbes Boulevard, Suite 200, Lanham, Maryland 20706
www.rowmanlittlefield.com

PO Box 317
Oxford
OX2 9RU, UK

British Library Cataloguing in Publication Information Available

Library of Congress Cataloging-in-Publication Data

Formicola, Jo Renee, 1941–
  Faith-based initiatives and the Bush administration : the good, the
bad, and the ugly / Jo Renee Formicola, Mary C. Segers, and Paul Weber.
    p. cm.
Includes bibliographical references and index.
  ISBN 0-7425-2304-7 (hardcover : alk. paper) — ISBN 0-7425-2305-5
(pbk. : alk. paper)
  1. Federal aid to public welfare—United States. 2. Federal aid to
human services—United States. 3. Church charities—Government
policy—United States. 4. Church charities—United States—Finance. 5.
1946-7. United States—Social policy—1993– I. Segers, Mary C. II.
Weber, Paul, 1937– III. Title.
HV95.F59 2003
361.7'5'0973—dc21

                                                            2003005704

Printed in the United States of America

♾^TM The paper used in this publication meets the minimum requirements of
American National Standard for Information Sciences—Permanence of Paper
for Printed Library Materials, ANSI/NISO Z39.48-1992.

Faith–Based Initiatives and the Bush Administration

To Hugh, who gave new meaning to the terms colleague, collaborator, and friend.
To Jerry, Suzanne, and Jean-Paul, with love.
To Don and Laurel, good friends for many years.

Contents

Acknowledgments

*W*e wish to thank all those who made this book possible. First, we wish to thank all those individuals—named and unnamed—who freely offered information, expertise, analyses, and opinions. Most critical among these was John DiIulio, former Assistant to President Bush and Director of the Faith-Based Initiative in the White House, who shared his time, energy, and files with us. Second, we wish to thank our respective institutions. Seton Hall University provided Jo Renee Formicola with a summer grant that made research, travel, and secretarial services possible, in addition to release time from teaching and student assistants such as Kristin Weis who helped with the bibliography and endnotes. Special thanks to George Kelly who helped with research for the completion of the manuscript. Mary Segers wishes to acknowledge Andrew Buchwalter, chair of the Philosophy Department of the University of North Florida in Jacksonville. His invitation to give a public lecture on the faith-based initiative started her on the path to research in this area. He assembled clergy and social workers "in the field" of faith-based social services who provided invaluable information on their concrete experiences. She is also grateful to Professor Julie Ingersoll of the University of North Florida for stimulating conversations about the policy. Finally, she owes a debt of gratitude to her students in the "Ethical Issues and Public Policy" course at Rutgers University (Newark) in spring 2002. They invited El-Rhonda Williams Alston, then director of the New Jersey Office of Faith-Based Initiatives, to her class to explain the New Jersey program in detail. Paul Weber wants to thank Gary Gregg, director of the McConnell Center for Political Leadership, a truly compassionate conservative, for his support of this research (even though he does not share his conclusions), and Charles Ziegler, chairman of the Department of Political Science, for his encouragement and financial support. Finally, we all wish to thank our families, who continue to support us in completing another long, yet fulfilling, project.

Preface

$\mathcal{I}$n January 2001, Jo Renee Formicola and Hubert Morken were completing their book, *Religious Leaders and Faith-Based Politics: Ten Profiles*, when President George W. Bush announced his new faith-based initiative. Both welcomed the news and interpreted it positively. They saw it as the beginning of a special relationship with those faith-based leaders that provided social and charitable services. They viewed it as the long overdue administrative—and possible financial—recognition of the extraordinary work of religious volunteers who were making a difference in their communities. And they believed it would augment the Clinton public policy to change welfare as it had existed in the past. Just as importantly, Formicola and Morken also believed, quite optimistically, that the new chief executive could make a strategic and meaningful difference in how the federal government would provide needed help to the under-served in society.

Morken retired, but Formicola continued to follow the progress of the faith-based initiative, realizing that it was a critical beginning: a new approach to the dynamic interplay between politics and religion and its impact on public policy. In November 2001, Formicola presented a paper at the Northeast Political Science Association on the "Catholic Response to the Faith-Based Initiative," and Mary Segers, as the discussant, critiqued it. They decided to collaborate, revise, and publish the paper together; and soon decided to pursue a contract to write a book on the broader aspects of the president's plan.

In the course of their research, Formicola and Segers realized they also needed a constitutional law scholar who could address the church-state implications of the initiative. They contacted Paul Weber, a highly regarded scholar and friend, and soon he was on board to work on the project with them.

Weber likes to tell people that in his day job he teaches constitutional law and civil liberties. In all seriousness, however, that led him to be interested in several initiatives of the Bush presidency as well as the increased activism of the Rehnquist Supreme Court. He realized that both could bring substantial changes to his field of study and to the country. Therefore, when Jo Formicola and Mary Segers invited him to join them in writing this book, he jumped at the chance. He saw it as an opportunity to research in depth and think through the implications of faith-based initiatives. If nothing else, he knew it would help keep his teaching on the cutting edge—no mean task these days.

All three of the authors came at the faith-based initiative from different perspectives. Originally, Formicola was convinced the initiative could work, and supported its aims. She believed that religious groups, which played such a significant part in charitable services, had been shut out of the quest for funds—too long and unfairly. But, gradually, she realized that politics, rather than concern for the under-served, would play the critical role in the legislative passage and administrative implementation of the president's plan. She feared that partisan considerations would overtake the policy process.

Segers was more skeptical at the start. She saw the faith-based initiative in political context—as a way President Bush could both secure his Republican party base of conservative evangelicals and expand that base to include minority and Catholic voters. She worried that focusing on the eligibility of faith-based organizations for federal contracts would detract from the primary purpose of welfare reform—that is, to free the poor from poverty, rather than to bring religion back into public life. She was concerned that the dependence of faith-based institutions on government funding of their social programs would undermine their independence and their critical, prophetic role in society. Finally, she did not think taxpayer (public) funds should be used to support religious proselytization and religious discrimination in hiring.

Weber began the project with great curiosity, a modicum of hope, and many questions. But he had little knowledge and few solid convictions. He liked the prospect of trying fresh approaches to enduring problems. He was deeply impressed by the sincerity and concern for the needy by those who wrote and advocated for compassionate conservatism. He was in awe after reading somewhere that President Bush wanted to redo the New Deal—and this time get it right. Wouldn't it be ironic and wonderful, Weber wondered, if substantial progress could be made in further reducing poverty and increasing the personal competence and confidence of the needy through the initiatives of a proudly conservative administration?

Thus, to look at the president's plan from the perspectives of "the good, the bad, and the ugly" seemed most appropriate, since the authors each seemed to gravitate toward one of those views. And, as might be expected, in the course of their research and writing, each of the authors changed their minds about the faith-based initiative. Formicola became much more realistic, realizing the potential political, partisan, and legal pitfalls that could occur in the implementation of the faith-based initiative. She accepted the fact that government needs "proxy-networks" and must provide grants and funding to religious and secular social providers in order to meet the growing demands for needed services. And she now believes that the concrete nature of the collaboration between the public and private sectors must be more strictly and clearly defined in order to reach a similar goal: helping the under-served in society. She also realizes that strict separation of finances alone cannot completely eliminate preaching and assure total equality in the social services workplace, but she remains optimistic about what the faith-based initiative can accomplish.

Segers became less opposed and more focused on what it would take for concrete programs to work. On one hand, she was impressed with the doubts expressed by faith-based providers during the meeting at the University of North Florida. The directors of Catholic Charities and Jewish Family Services questioned whether or not the policy would provide enough federal funds to handle the increasing needs of the poor in the Jacksonville area in a time of economic recession. An Anglican woman priest questioned whether President Bush's conservatism could be truly compassionate. The African American director of a prison ministry for women with children worried whether or not her small organization could meet the requirements of federal paperwork and feared that her faith-based organization was "being set up to fail." On the other hand, the New Jersey case (described in chapter 1) showed that at the grassroots, a little government funding could make a big difference in the ability to provide needed social services to the disadvantaged. Segers became increasingly aware of the disjunction between the national debate about the constitutionality of the faith-based initiative and the local needs of providers. She began to think that perhaps the theoretical strictures about church-state separation are less urgent when the practical operation of these programs is considered.

Weber had the most objections to start and ended up reinforcing his original concern: that the faith-based initiative was an effort—at least on the part of some—to undo, rather than redo, the New Deal. During the course of his research, he began to see the initiative not as a conservative approach to helping the needy, but as a radical step toward abandoning them. He concluded that it was a deliberate effort to undermine America's cherished separation of church and state. Whether this was done in good but naïve faith, or simply as a calculated effort to provide government support for a traditionally conservative base, he still does not know. He became alarmed that religious groups receiving tax-raised funds could now discriminate in hiring, firing, and delivering services. He became concerned that, in the absence of substantially increased funding, faith-based initiatives would radically increase competition among religious groups and open the door to religious fraud. These were both outcomes that could undo decades of cooperation and building public trust that have made the United States the most religious nation in the free world. But even after coming to those conclusions Weber was deeply influenced by Formicola's optimism and Seger's caution. He retains a sliver of hope that more good than evil can come out of faith-based initiatives.

Whether the authors themselves have overreacted or reached an accommodation between their research and ideologies remains for the reader to determine. It is our hope, however, that this volume stimulates the reader to ask questions and to find creative solutions to the policy quandary of President Bush's faith-based initiative.

Introduction

President Bush's Faith-Based Initiative

Mary Segers

$\mathcal{O}$ne of the most controversial policies of President George W. Bush's administration is his "faith-based initiative." No other issue has sparked as much passion, discord, and suspicion as his proposal to make it easier for faith-based groups to obtain federal money to provide social services to the nation's needy. The televangelist Pat Robertson did not want the Hare Krishnas to get public funds because, frankly, their theology was wrong.[1] Jews did not want Southern Baptists to get federal dollars because Baptists might use that money to fund their campaign to convert Jews.[2] The editors of *Commonweal* worried that taxpayer monies might go to someone like David Koresh of the Branch Davidians or to the Nation of Islam, whose leaders are known for their anti-Semitic diatribes.[3] Thoughtful citizens wondered whether the government, in deciding who gets money, might also be deciding what is or is not a legitimate religion.

The controversy itself is indicative of how divisive religion can be, especially when mixed with politics. President Bush's faith-based initiative raises serious issues of religious autonomy, government intervention, and public accountability. The complexity of modern American society is such that churches, temples, and mosques are inevitably part of the social fabric of a welfare state. In the normal course of everyday life, religious institutions are subject to government regulations such as fire codes, employment laws, and tax laws like everyone else. But to make religious organizations dependent on

1

Uncle Sam for money to fund their community programs or to suggest that they compete for federal contracts seemed, initially at least, to raise more questions than answers.

It took at least a year for the Bush White House to clarify what it meant by its "faith-based initiative." The proposal floundered in Congress. The initiative fared better in the executive branch, where the president could invoke executive powers to create agencies and order them to implement existing laws. By the end of his second year in office, the president had done just that—operationalized a controversial policy through executive fiat. But his policy is almost certain to be challenged in the courts.

This book is a study in religion, politics, and public policy. Its purpose is to explain the president's faith-based initiative and to describe the controversy surrounding it. The intent of the authors is to provide a brief history of the Bush policy, to set it in larger historical context, and to discuss its pros and cons. The book is divided into three parts: the good, the bad, and the ugly. In chapter 1, on the "good," Jo Formicola discusses the ideas that influenced President Bush in his formulation of the faith-based initiative, as well as the initiative's many positive features. The chapter also examines the New Jersey faith-based initiative to illustrate the advantages of such a policy in action. In chapter 2, on the "bad," Paul Weber reviews common criticisms of the policy, analyzes the constitutional and legal difficulties of the initiative, sets the policy in the historical context of church-state jurisprudence, and discusses concrete problems of policy implementation. In chapter 3, on the "ugly," Jo Formicola and Mary Segers explore the political conflicts that have shadowed the Bush initiative from its inception. Based on interviews with key participants in the policymaking process, they describe conflicts within the Bush administration and the debate in the House and Senate over the plan. In the final chapter, conclusions, all three authors summarize what went wrong in the first two years of the president's faith-based initiative and suggest what the future of the policy might be.

As political scientists, Jo Formicola, Mary Segers, and Paul Weber have collectively spent much of their scholarly careers researching and writing about religion and politics. Each has a particular view of President Bush's faith-based initiative; however, each has tried to be objective in the analysis presented here. What the authors can do is indicate why the president's initiative is, and should be, of great interest to all Americans.

First, the faith-based initiative is intriguing to those who study the role of religion in American society. Throughout American history, faith-based organizations have established an exemplary record of community service. Building communities at the local level and contributing practically to the infrastructure of civil society— churches, temples, and mosques have been doing these tasks for a long time. The debate over the faith-based initiative recognizes this role, and what religion does in American society. At the same time, the debate reminds Americans of the reasons why constitutional church-state separation exists in the United States. In the case of the president's proposal, his policy has met with a mixed reaction from religious groups. It has been opposed by most mainline Protestants, such as the United Methodist Church, the president's own denomination, and by most reform and conservative Jewish groups. Most evangelical Protestants and Orthodox Jewish groups are in favor of the initiative, while African American denominations have been split. The U.S. Catholic Bishops Conference supports the faith-based initiative with some reservations. The diversity of denominational views about the president's plan helps to explain why the debate about faith-based initiatives has been so passionate. It should also alert the public to the potential for sectarian strife, one of the reasons for the long American tradition of church-state separation.

Second, the faith-based initiative is of great interest to legal scholars interested in church-state jurisprudence and in the degree to which government can fund religious charities. As will be seen, issues of religious proselytizing and religious hiring raise First Amendment issues. In reality, the Bush initiative represents a strategic change in thinking about church-state relations and signifies a move away from strict separation toward greater accommodation of religion by government. No wonder constitutional lawyers and church-state scholars are so deeply interested in the president's proposal.

Third, the faith-based initiative is critical to those who study politics because of the full involvement of all three branches of the federal government in this policy. To date, the proposal has failed to gain full legislative approval in its original form, has met with modest success in the executive branch, particularly in the White House and parts of the federal bureaucracy, and is beginning to be challenged in federal courts. No doubt, the prominence of congressional deliberations in the first year of the president's initiative has contributed to the passionate public debate documented by the media. By contrast, bureaucratic implementation has gone on quietly and has attracted less media coverage. Those interested in the influence of government structure upon the shape of public policies can find plenty of research possibilities here, where the separation of powers between three coequal branches of government has had controversial policy results.

Finally, the faith-based initiative is of concern to all citizens because it addresses a fundamental question for all Americans: How do we care for the poor and the needy? In 1996, the federal government, moving away from "welfare as we knew it," handed the responsibilities of welfare back to the states, imposed time limits on recipients, and ended aid to families and dependent children as a right or an entitlement. Throughout the prosperous late 1990s, the welfare rolls steadily declined. But demand for the social services of churches and nonprofit agencies increased as the recession of 2000–2003 brought economic hardship. This challenges all citizens to think about what safety net is in place for the disadvantaged. Should government subsidize *religious* providers of social services such as soup kitchens, after-school childcare, inner-city prison ministries, substance-abuse programs, and the like? In fact, government already subsidizes some faith-based organizations that provide social services, such as the Salvation Army, Catholic Charities, Jewish Family Services, and Lutheran Services in America. These religiously related organizations agree, however, to be incorporated separately from their churches, to keep separate books, to refrain from evangelizing, and to follow federal nondiscrimination standards in hiring. President Bush's faith-based initiative changes many of these conditions for the receipt of federal contracts and grants—and that is why his policy is so controversial.

In this introductory chapter, the authors will set the policy in context, provide a brief history of its political fortunes in the first two years of the Bush administration, and outline briefly its positive and negative features.

PRESIDENT BUSH'S FAITH-BASED INITIATIVE:
A BRIEF OVERVIEW

On January 29, 2001, nine days after his inauguration, President George W. Bush introduced a major public policy initiative, one proposing to provide government funds for churches that offer social service programs to the needy. Calling this "faith-based initiative" the cornerstone of his agenda of "compassionate conservatism," the president sought to encourage contributions to religious organizations and, at the same time, encourage those groups to take on a wider range of social services using funding from the federal government. Bush acknowledged the central responsibility of government for public health and welfare and said "government will never be replaced by charities and community groups." However, he stated,

> When we see social needs in America, my administration will look first at faith-based programs and community groups, which have proven their power to save and change lives. We will not fund the religious activities of any group, but when people of faith provide social services, we will not discriminate against them.[4]

To implement this new policy initiative, the president signed two executive orders. The first created a new office called the White House Office of Faith-Based and Community Initiatives, to which Bush appointed John DiIulio, a political science professor from the University of Pennsylvania, as director. The second order established centers at five cabinet agencies—Justice, Housing and Urban Development, Labor, Education, and Health and Human Services—to ensure greater cooperation between government and church-related social service programs.

The president described his initiative in these terms:

> We're in the process of implementing and expanding "charitable choice"—the principle already established in federal law that faith-based organizations should not suffer discrimination when they compete for contracts to provide social services. Government should never fund the teaching of faith, but it should support the good works of the faithful.[5]

Bush was correct in saying that the idea of charitable choice was not new. It first appeared as a little-noted provision in the 1996 welfare reform law,[6] and was actually sponsored by then-Senator John Ashcroft (R-MO). One of Ashcroft's goals in proposing Charitable Choice was "to encourage faith-based organizations to expand their involvement in the welfare reform effort by providing assurances that their religious integrity would be protected." Calling it a constitutionally permissible partnership between government and the churches, Ashcroft had argued that charitable choice would protect the rights of faith-based providers, as well as the religious liberty of the individuals they serve.[7]

In the furor about welfare reform, charitable choice did not garner much attention. It was a bit of a "sleeper." During the Clinton administration, federal administrators largely ignored this provision. Nevertheless, both Al Gore and George Bush supported the idea in the 2000 presidential campaign. Once elected, President Bush made charitable choice a top priority and created the White House Office of Faith-Based and Community Initiatives to implement it.

Stated briefly, Charitable Choice is a legislative provision designed to remove unnecessary barriers to the receipt of certain federal funds by faith-based organizations that provide social services. Charitable Choice rests on four principles:

1. *Level playing field.* Faith-based providers are eligible to compete for funds on the same basis as any other providers, neither excluded nor included because they are religious.
2. *Respect for the integrity of faith-based organizations.* Allowing them to retain control over the definition, development, practice, and expression of their religious beliefs protects the religious character of faith-based providers. Neither federal nor state government can require a religious provider to alter its form of internal governance or remove religious art, icons, scripture or other symbols in order to be a program participant.
3. *Protection of clients.* In rendering assistance, religious organizations shall not discriminate against an individual based on religion, a religious belief, or refusal to actively participate in a

religious practice. If an individual objects to the religious character of a program, a secular alternative must be provided.

4. *Church-state separation.* All government funds must be used to fulfill the public social service goals, and no direct government funding can be diverted to inherently religious activities such as worship, sectarian instruction, and proselytization.[8]

George W. Bush made assistance to faith-based organizations a centerpiece of his presidential campaign. The initiative is of great personal importance to him. He often speaks of the power of religious conversion in helping him to overcome substance abuse, and he connects his own experience with the work of religious providers seeking to transform lives. Having made the faith-based initiative a central campaign pledge, Bush acted on this even before his inauguration.

In December 2000, president-elect Bush met with about thirty ministers and other religious leaders to discuss ways to expand the roles of religious and charitable organizations in federal welfare programs.[9] He attempted to begin a dialogue with them[10]—a conversation on "how best to help faith-based programs change people's lives," and on "how best government can encourage . . . faith-based programs . . . [to] perform[ing] their commonplace miracles of renewal."[11] But, his motives were immediately questioned, with some in the media claiming that Bush was simply attempting to reach out to African Americans through their clergy, since so few blacks had voted for him.[12] Others, such as the Rev. Jesse Jackson, who had not been invited to the meeting, contended that "I know the subplot: This is an attempt to play one group against the other."[13]

In reality, Bush's actions signaled more than a reprioritizing of public concerns and more than the establishment of a new governmental infrastructure for the funding and delivery of charitable and social services in the United States. Indeed, his proposals reflected a *strategic* change in White House thinking about the relationship between church and state—from a traditional one based on *separation* to a new one characterized by *collaboration*. The new relationship might be defined by what students of the law would call a "zone of accommodation," or what approving politicians would call government action for the "common good," or what some political scientists would call a type of "prophetic politics."[14]

However, the Bush administration's faith-based initiative ran into rough weather almost from the start. Opponents from both the left and the right increasingly criticized the president's actions on a number of grounds. Ralph Neas, president of People for the American Way, claimed that Bush's new faith-based plan had constitutional difficulties that put "church and state on a direct collision course."[15] Even some Bush supporters, such as the Rev. Pat Robertson of Regent University and the "700 Club" and Marvin Olasky, author of the book that influenced Bush, *The Tragedy of American Compassion*, verbalized their fears. They argued that by accepting government financing, religious programs would invite government meddling into their mission and message.[16] Other members of the Christian Right argued that the president's proposals could provide tax dollars to Hare Krishna and Scientology social agencies. Jewish organizations were concerned that the Nation of Islam, an anti-Semitic organization, would receive government funds. The Southern Baptist Convention's North American Mission Board urged its ministries to "proceed with caution."[17] And Dr. James Dobson, spokesperson for the evangelical organization Focus on the Family, was cool to the notion early on. Fourteen liberal and moderate Baptist leaders issued a statement urging rejection of the initiative, and about 350 leaders with the Jewish Council for Public Affairs interrogated the new head of the White House Office on Faith-Based Initiatives, John DiIulio, at a meeting in Washington.[18] Some Congressional critics complained that the plan amounted to government funding of discrimination. Rep. Chet Edwards (D-TX) said that he did not "want Bob Jones University to be able to take federal dollars for an alcohol treatment program and put out a sign that says no Catholics or Jews need apply here for a federally funded job."[19] His words seemed to portend such fears. Indeed, it came as no surprise to many policy opponents that the Salvation Army, a few months later, sought an exemption from local laws that forbade discrimination based on sexual orientation.[20] The matter of religious exemption from federal and state antidiscrimination laws has been controversial from the start.

Nevertheless, in March 2001 the president's faith-based initiative received legislative form through the introduction of H.R. 7, known as the Community Solutions Act of 2001.[21] J. C. Watts (R-OK) and Tony Hall (D-OH) introduced the bill in the House with forty-four co-sponsors. It detailed and enlarged on several federal tax incentives for charitable giving and individual development accounts. First, Section 101 allowed taxpayers who do not itemize any of their deductions on their income tax form to, first, be able to take the standard deduction for charitable contributions and, second, to be able to itemize and deduct their charitable contributions. Second, Section 102 permitted withdrawals of funds from traditional and Roth individual retirement accounts (IRAs) for charitable distributions, while permitting them also to be exempt from inclusion in the calculation of their taxable gross income. Third, Section 103 sanctioned an augmented deduction for charitable contributions of food inventory to the poor. Fourth, the bill allowed the establishment of individual development accounts (IDAs) for eligible individuals,[22] permitting them to receive a matching contribution of up to $500 per year from a qualified entity, such as a bank, a foundation, or the federal, state, or local government. The monies could be used for higher education, first-time home buying, business capitalization, rollovers, and death benefit payouts.

While the bill passed with significant support in the House,[23] its introduction in the Senate faltered and eventually died. The House of Representatives passed H.R. 7, the Community Solutions Act, in July 2001, by a vote of 233 to 198. Senators Rick Santorum (R-PA) and Joseph Lieberman (D-CT) had reported optimistically in the spring that they were "moving full steam ahead in drafting legislation,"[24] that would mirror the bill that had been approved in the House. However, during the Senate hearings, a variety of problems emerged that gave Senator Lieberman second thoughts on the faith-based initiative.

First, the Salvation Army made a request to the White House to support a hiring exemption with regard to homosexuals, which, according to Lieberman, put "a cloud over the president's intention to expand a faith-based initiative."[25] Indeed, he thought it "might terminally wound [the bill] in congress," especially because it was also a "kind of an end run" around the lawmakers.[26] Second, Democrats in both the House and the Senate were split on the bill. Some legislative constituencies, such as the Congressional Black Caucus, and vocal Congressmen like Representative Barney Frank (D-MA) attacked the bill on its discriminatory possibilities. The American Association of University Women also brought pressure to bear on the legislators. Certain religious groups continued to oppose it as well, particularly the United Methodists and the Baptist Joint Committee. Taking all this into consideration, Lieberman decided not to cosponsor the Charitable Choice section of the legislation, claiming that it was unconstitutional. Senate Majority Leader Tom Daschle (D-SD) also made it clear that he would not even place the bill in its present form on his agenda. Finally, Lieberman maintained that the White House was not dealing with the legal issues—and without a response on the matter, he would not move it forward. Instead he asked the Government Accounting Office (GAO), the research arm of Congress, to study the possible effect of these programs on the First Amendment. Effectively stunting the movement of the bill, Senator Lieberman left the matter in limbo, with Senator Santorum having to admit that "this is a hot button issue"[27] and that the entire matter would probably have to be revisited later. In July, Lieberman met with the president and decided that he would prefer to write his own version of a faith-based bill to be considered later.

In August, John DiIulio resigned as head of the White House Office of Faith-Based and Community Initiatives. Claiming that he was keeping his pledge to leave after six months in office, he stated that he needed to take care of his health and family responsibilities. His departure, nonetheless, came at a time when the White House faced a major political battle: trying to save the president's "signature social issue."[28] Reportedly, DiIulio found it difficult to deal with senior White House aides who "increasingly cut him out of strategy sessions about how to win passage of the initiatives."[29]

To summarize, after a promising beginning, the White House Office for Faith-Based and Community Initiatives had a rocky first year. The office was "hindered by classic organization problems: shifting priorities, lack of autonomy for the director, the absence of internal White House coordination, and inflated expectations."[30] In its haste to establish this new entity, the Bush administration encountered unanticipated criticism from civil libertarians, even from leaders of religious right groups. These criticisms prompted the Senate to delay action on the bill despite early passage by the House of Representatives. Finally, the events of September 11, 2001, effectively placed President Bush's faith-based initiative on the back burner. The war on terrorism clearly took precedence over domestic policy proposals.

THE RETURN OF THE FAITH-BASED
INITIATIVE IN 2002

Undeterred, President Bush signaled renewed interest in faith-based social services in his State of the Union Address in January 2002. In February, he appointed James Towey, former secretary of health and rehabilitative services for Florida, an advocate for the aging and the man who worked as legal counsel for Mother Teresa's ministry for twelve years, as the new director of the Office of Faith-Based and Community Initiatives.[31] The president also announced an agreement with Senators Lieberman (D–CT) and Santorum (R–PA) on a considerably revised bill to provide federal money to religious charities and other nonprofit organizations. The new Senate bill, the Charity Aid, Recovery, and Empowerment Act, proposed new tax breaks to encourage charitable giving and included extra money for a social services grant program. But the bill eliminated the most contentious element of Bush's original proposal, the "charitable choice" provision allowing religious groups to favor members of their own faith in hiring. The bill thus represented a significant compromise on what had been a central proposal of Bush's "compassionate conservative" presidential campaign.[32]

In addition to deleting the Charitable Choice provisions in the Senate measure, the context and purpose of the White House's original faith-based initiative had changed. The Senate proposal was declared an emergency measure in response to the events of September 11 and the recession. Senator Lieberman described it as an effort to meet human needs resulting from those events. Since government could not meet all those needs, the bill empowered a whole range of charitable organizations, including faith-based groups, to do that.[33] Moreover, the White House recast its faith-based initiative to emphasize volunteer service. The new director of the White House Office of Community and Faith-Based Initiatives, James Towey, now answers to John Bridgeland, who was named by President Bush to head all volunteer efforts through the White House.[34]

Thus, the president's original faith-based initiative has changed significantly. It morphed from an emphasis upon charitable choice and federal funding of religious groups into a tax deduction bill promoting charitable giving to religious and other nonprofit groups in the wake of the September 11 attack on the World Trade Center and the Pentagon.

The new bill, popularly known as the CARE Act, was introduced in the Senate in February 2002. In addition to Senators Lieberman and Santorum, co-sponsors included Senators Hillary Clinton (D-NY), Sam Brownback (R-KS), and Orren Hatch (R-UT). Ultimately, the bill had eighteen Republican and ten Democratic sponsors. It was referred to, and ultimately approved, by the Senate Finance Committee. But the Senate in 2002 was distracted by corporate scandals, debates about homeland security, resolutions authorizing the president to take military action against Iraq, if necessary, and by political campaigns for reelection. As a result, the CARE Act languished in the Senate until after the 2002 Congressional elections.

It was finally considered in the waning days of the lame duck session at the end of the 107th Congress. In that session, the House and Senate quickly passed bills on homeland security and terrorism insurance. But the CARE Act stalled once again. This time, five Democratic senators introduced amendments to the legislation to improve church-state safeguards and employment protections. Senator Richard Durbin (D-IL) objected that the bill had never been considered in hearings of the Senate Judiciary Committee. He said he supported the bill's goals but was concerned about possible abuses by religious groups. He argued that Democratic amendments would help to ensure that religious groups taking federal funds "would not discriminate, proselytize, defy local regulatory laws or keep sloppy books."[35] Senator Jack Reed (D-RI) was concerned that religious groups using federal dollars not discriminate in whom they hire. He proposed amendments barring government funds from use for proselytizing, and safeguarding state laws, such as those protecting the rights of homosexuals.[36] Republicans, led by Senator Santorum, countered that the CARE Act added nothing new to the 1996 law on charitable choice, so the Democrats were raising false church-state and discrimination issues. When senators could not resolve these differences, the clock ran out and the bill died.

A PROVERBIAL PHOENIX RISING FROM THE ASHES

Despite the failure of faith-based legislative proposals in Congress in 2002, President Bush would not give up on his signature program. On December 12, 2002, he announced that he would use his executive powers to clear the way for federal aid to flow to religious charities, even if they discriminate in their hiring practices on religious and moral grounds. In a speech to more than a thousand religious and charitable leaders in Philadelphia, Bush said he was issuing an executive order requiring that federal agencies not discriminate against religious organizations in awarding money to community and social service groups for programs to assist the needy. He also signed a separate executive order establishing faith-based offices in the Department of Agriculture and the Agency for International Development (USAID), joining similar offices already established in five other cabinet departments. Finally, he directed the Federal Emergency Management Agency (FEMA) to allow religious nonprofit groups to qualify for aid after disasters like earthquakes and hurricanes in the same way that secular nonprofits can qualify.[37]

As if to underscore the president's intent, the Department of Housing and Urban Development, in January 2003, issued new federal regulations regarding public funding of church construction. The new rules (in the draft-and-comment stage) would allow religious groups for the first time to use federal housing money to help build facilities where religious worship takes place, as long as part of the building is also used for social services. Under this proposal, a church could erect a building using federal money to create a homeless shelter in one part and private money to create a sanctuary in another part.

The proposal, published January 6, 2003, in the Federal Register, covers programs that administer about $7.7 billion a year to communities. The Bush administration defended its proposal on grounds that it would end discrimination against religious groups in the disbursement of Housing and Urban Development (HUD) funds. Critics, civil rights advocates, and legal experts criticized the policy shift, saying that it moved the government dangerously close to financing the building of houses of worship in violation of the separation of church and state. According to Christopher Anders, legislative counsel for the American Civil Liberties Union (ACLU), the new proposal takes "federal money that is serving the neediest of the needy in our society and diverts it to the bricks-and-mortar constructions of churches and sanctuaries and other places of worship."[38]

Thus, the president's faith-based initiative is being implemented through the executive branch at a rapid pace. Relying primarily on his executive powers, then, the president has been able to order the federal bureaucracy to implement Charitable Choice.

In February 2003, another turnabout occurred. Senator Santorum reintroduced the Care Act in the 108th Congress, but this time without the Charitable Choice provision. Four months later, in April, it was changed into a virtually new measure and co-sponsored with Senator Lieberman. As before, the bill offered tax incentives for charitable donations and tax breaks for faith-based social services. But now, the Care Act provided financing for technical assistance to those religious groups seeking federal funds and an increase in social service monies to be distributed through block grants. Most importantly, and in an expedient shift, the bill eliminated the provision that would have allowed faith-based groups to discriminate on the basis of religion in matters of hiring. Passed by a 95-5 vote, the far-reaching ramifications of these major changes now await House debate and possible, future, presidential action.

ADVANTAGES AND DISADVANTAGES OF THE BUSH FAITH-BASED INITIATIVE

A standoff now exists on what could be a new way of providing social and charitable services in the United States. Any hope for future legislative passage seems to be tied to both the positive and negative features of the faith-based initiative.

The strength of the effort is essentially related to the fact that Charitable Choice and the faith-based initiative both emphasize that government, the private sector, religious groups, and individuals all have a duty to help those in need. The faith-based initiative enforces the positive role of religion in society, recognizing that in many cases churches, synagogues, and mosques are the only institutions able to "suffer with" the poor and act as the "voice of the voiceless" in a world that equates check-writing with charity. At the same time, the initiative respects the role, mission, integrity, and autonomy of religious groups. Although it allows denominations to hire individuals who subscribe to their spiritual points of view, it also requires total respect for the religious or nonreligious views of the beneficiaries of publicly funded religious agencies. Thus, religious belief is not a prerequisite for faith-based assistance in the construct of the faith-based initiative. The policy stipulates that if an individual client objects to the religious character of a social program, a secular alternative must be provided. The faith-based initiative also takes the insularity out of individual problems; it provides a support group and volunteers; it builds coalitions and the social structure of society. This is what is known as developing "social capital."[39] Economists argue that government and private funding sources should invest in social capital, as it were, and provide "venture funds" to rebuild the inner cities, rural areas, and places where revitalization and new energy are needed.

The faith-based initiative is also a way to get the poor on the political agenda. The focus of politics—that is, "who gets what, when, and where"—must now give pause to the needs of the under-served in society. In reality, the debate about what actually happens and what is needed with regard to charity is often very different from what is said in the halls of the capitol and what goes on in soup kitchens, prisons, AIDS clinics, and homeless shelters. Clearly, the efforts of those committed to the poor in society need some kind of assistance to keep their work on track in the real world.

Finally, the faith-based initiative serves the purpose of capacity building and empowering of the poor. It helps faith-based organizations to continue their work, to compete for government funds, to manage them, and to enhance the services that they currently provide.

While these are all noble objectives, the president has one more point that he makes whenever he talks about the faith-based initiative: That those religious groups who provide needed social services also have the ability to change the lives and spirit of those who come under their care. As Bush stated, "This initiative recognizes the power of faith in helping heal some of our nation's wounds. I have faith that faith will work in solving the problems."[40]

The drawbacks, however, are also formidable. Opponents of the faith-based initiative point out that the principles and legislation that have been considered thus far do not even have a clear-cut definition of what a faith-based organization is. They claim the empirical evidence does not support Bush's contention that faith-based social services are more effective than secular programs in reducing dependency and changing people's lives. They are concerned that religious groups will compete with each other for funds rather than work in a cooperative way to deal with the immediate problems within their communities. They ask if anti-Semitic religious groups, such as the Nation of Islam, would be eligible for funds. They note that, realistically, there are "no shekels without shackles"—that churches receiving government monies will become overly dependent upon public funds and will be stifled by bureaucratic red tape and restrictive regulations.

Others argue that the faith-based initiative breaches the wall of separation between church and state. They say it creates an entangling alliance and in many cases may end up funding specific religious or theological views. They worry about governmental enforcement of the ban on religious proselytizing. While the Bush administration has insisted that faith-based organizations must not use Uncle Sam's dollars to proselytize, "just how Washington will ensure that down in the basement of some church a little prayer will not be required before a little food is doled out is hard to see."[41] One also cannot overlook the charge that the faith-based initiative may foster discrimination by allowing religious groups to refuse to hire individuals of different faiths who do not subscribe to their religious views. This concern about religious hiring is a major stumbling block to the success of the initiative. It is actually a very complex issue because, as Paul Weber notes later in this book, religious groups are exempt from some, but not all, of the antidiscrimination provisions of federal law.

To date, there are two challenges in federal courts to these potentially negative aspects of the Bush faith-based policy. The first concerns religious proselytizing and indoctrination. On January 8, 2002, federal district judge Barbara Crabb ordered Wisconsin's Department of Workforce Development to stop funding Faith Works, a Milwaukee agency that assists men with alcohol or drug-abuse problems. The agency operates within a Christian framework, providing religious counseling as well as Bible study, chapel services. and daily prayer time. In her ruling in *Freedom from Religion Foundation v. McCallum*, Judge Crabb held that a state grant to Faith Works "constitutes unrestricted, direct funding of an organization that engages in religious indoctrination" in violation of the church-state provisions of the First Amendment.[42] Interestingly enough, the grant struck down by Judge Crabb came from the Wisconsin governor's discretionary portion of federal funds allocated through the Temporary Assistance to Needy Families (TANF) program. This decision was the first federal court decision striking down federal aid to religious groups under the controversial "charitable choice" provisions of the 1996 welfare reform law.

The issue of religious hiring is also in federal court. A lawsuit filed in Georgia raises the precise legal question at stake in the Bush faith-based initiative: Do religious institutions that are ordinarily free to discriminate in hiring on the basis of religion lose that freedom by accepting government money? In this case, the United Methodist Children's Home, a foster home in Decatur, Georgia, terminated a job interview with Alan Yorker, a Jewish psychological therapist, because he was not a Christian. Yorker is joined in this lawsuit by another therapist,

Aimee R. Bellmore, who was fired when the home learned that she is a lesbian. In papers filed in the case, the Methodist foster home said she had been fired because "her religious beliefs were not in conformity with those required" and because she did not subscribe to the home's religious doctrines, including one that does not "condone the practice of homosexuality." The case is complicated, involving both employment discrimination and religious discrimination. The issues at stake in this case turn on whether government money alters the uneasy accommodation between religious liberty and civil rights. It is this problem that made House passage of H.R. 7, the Community Solutions Act, difficult in 2001 and ensured Senate defeat of the CARE Act in 2002. [43]

Finally, critics who question the constitutionality of the Bush faith-based initiative worry that it violates the religious freedom clause of the First Amendment. This criticism takes seriously religious conviction as well as the rights of believers and nonbelievers to religious freedom. Derek Davis has stated this objection clearly: "There are serious problems attending a framework of nondiscriminatory distribution of government benefits to religious institutions. . . . Every distribution of taxpayer dollars to a church, synagogue, mosque, or other religious organization is a violation of the religious liberty of taxpayers who would find objectionable the propagation of the form of religious belief represented by the recipient. In the words of Thomas Jefferson, 'to compel a man to furnish contributions of money for the propagation of opinions which he disbelieves and abhors is sinful and tyrannical.'"[44]

Given these arguments for and against the president's faith-based initiative, it is easy to see why there is so much controversy about his policy. Many, like Senator Joseph Lieberman, who defend the role of religion in public life are perplexed by the difficulties of this policy. These complexities raise challenges for all those of good faith who seek new ways to help the under-served.

HOW TO READ THIS BOOK: IT'S ABOUT CONTEXT, CONTEXT, CONTEXT

Understanding, and eventually evaluating, the Bush faith-based initiative needs to be done within the broad context of politics, personalities, the law, economics, religion, and a variety of other meaningful factors. These could also include commitments, political will, and timing—for each plays a role in agenda setting, policy development, and policy implementation. Thus, while context is often complex, it serves to give meaning to events and plays a decisive role in judgment. The authors pose some questions here that might help the reader to come to personal conclusions about the potential value or problems in the faith-based initiative:

1. *Policy questions.* Is the initiative about welfare reform? Is it about public means to stimulate philanthropy? Is it about tax change? Is it about new ways to fund charitable services? Is it a different way of looking at government responsibilities to the underserved? Is it about innovative collaboration for the poor? Is it about helping religious organizations? Is it about competition between government and private social service providers?

2. *Constitutional questions.* Is it part of a fifty-year debate about the meaning of the First Amendment religion clauses? Is this a resurgence of the religious rivalries of the nineteenth century? Will this open the door to newer, and perhaps more conservative, views of the Establishment Clause?

3. *Political questions.* Is it part of the Bush administration's efforts to secure its Republican base constituency, particularly the religious right, and to expand the party's support among minorities and Catholics? Is it a sincere attempt to instill compassion into conservatism? Will this give a political voice to the poor? Will Hispanics gain from this outreach? What will this mean for mainline religious groups? How will it affect other interest groups seeking to be heard on a variety of other issues?

4. *Pragmatic questions.* Can the faith-based initiative provide the services and changes that the president and his followers envision? What empirical proof exists? Are there any government studies under way to justify these programs? Can such programs succeed without new monies? Can religious groups provide needed social services without government training and monitoring?

These questions are but a few that the authors pose. They challenge their audience to keep these questions in mind and to formulate others as they critically read *The Bush Faith-Based Initiative: The Good, the Bad, and the Ugly* and attempt to come their own conclusions. Make no mistake: This policy is one that has the potential to change the relationship between religion and government as we know it, and to create a strategic change between the two major institutions in the United States. It requires thought. It requires critique. And, perhaps most importantly, it requires a creative solution to the question of how to help the under-served in America.

NOTES

1. Pat Robertson, "Mr. Bush's Faith-Based Initiative Is Flawed," *Wall Street Journal*, 12 March 2001, A15.

2. Rabbi David Saperstein, quoted in Thomas B. Edsall, "Jewish Leaders Criticize 'Faith-Based Initiative,'" *Washington Post*, 27 February 2001, A4.

3. The editors, "Church, State & Money," *Commonweal* 28, no. 4 (23 February 2001), 5–6.

4. "Text: Bush Pushes Faith-Based Plans," eMediaMillWorks, *Washington Post*, Monday, 29 January 2001. <www.washingtonpost.com/wp-srv/0npolitics/elections/bushtext012901.htm>

5. George W. Bush, Commencement Address at the University of Notre Dame, South Bend, Indiana, 20 May 2001. Reprinted in *Origins* 31, no. 3 (31 May 2001): 46–48.

6. Public Law 104–193, the Personal Responsibility and Work Opportunity Reconciliation Act of 1996, enacted 22 August 1996, Sec. 104.

7. Letter from Senator John Ashcroft, U.S. Senate, Washington, D.C., December 1996. This is the first page of a packet of materials on Charitable Choice prepared by Stanley W. Carlson-Thies, Director, Project on Government and the Religious Social Sector, The Center for Public Justice, Washington, D.C.

8. U.S. Department of Health and Human Services, The Center for Faith-Based and Community Initiatives, "What Is Charitable Choice?" 12 December 2002 (last revised). <www.hhs.gov/faith/choice/html>

9. Richard A. Oppel Jr. and Gustav Niebuhr, "Bush Meeting Focuses on Role of Religion," *New York Times*, 21 December 2000, A37.

10. Invitees included the Rev. Eugene Rivers of the Azusa Christian Community in Boston, Rev. Jim Wallis of Call to Renewal, and Bishop Joseph A. Fiorenza of Houston, who was also the president of National Conference of Catholic Bishops. Others included Rev. C. Welton Gaddy, executive director of the Interfaith Alliance, Rev. Floyd Flake, former congressman and pastor of the Allen AME Church in Queens, New York, Rev. Robert Sirico, president of the Acton Institute, and several local, senior ministers from churches in Texas.

11. Dana Milbank and Hamil R. Harris, "Bush, Religious Leaders Meet," *Washington Post*, 21 December 2000, A6.

12. Oppel and Niebuhr, "Bush Meeting Focuses," A37.

13. Oppel and Niebuhr, "Bush Meeting Focuses," A37.

14. Jo Renee Formicola and Hubert Morken, eds., *Religious Leaders and Faith-Based Politics* (Lanham, Md.: Rowman & Littlefield, 2001), 226.

15. Laura Meckler, "Bush Moves to Aid Faith-Based Groups," *Washington Post*, 30 January 2001, A1.

16. Laurie Goodstein, "Bush's Charity Plan Is Raising Concern for Religious Right," *New York Times*, 3 March 2001, A1.

17. Goodstein, "Bush's Charity Plan Is Raising Concern," A1.

18. Goodstein, "Bush's Charity Plan Is Raising Concern," A1.

19. Goodstein, "Bush's Charity Plan Is Raising Concern," A1.

20. "Charities Are Denied Bias Law Exemption," *New York Times*, 11 July 2001, A1. The article, without a by-line, also reports that after "a flurry of meetings and telephone calls," Bush senior aides claimed that they were unaware of the charity's request.

21. Introduced on 29 March 2001. It is explained in detail in Joint Committee on Taxation, *Description of Present Law and Certain Proposals Relating to Charitable Giving and Individual Development Accounts* (JCX-55-01). 13 June 2001.

22. This would apply to those who earned an adjusted gross income of $20,000 as individual tax filers, $40,000 for joint filers, and $25,000 for head of household filers.

23. "How Representatives Voted on Religion-based Initiative," *New York Times*, 19 July 2001, A16. It passed with a voice vote of 233 to 198. Voting yes were 15 Democrats, 217 Republicans, and 1 Independent. Voting no were 193 Democrats, 4 Republicans, and 1 Independent. Several members did not vote and, at the time, there was one vacancy in the House.

24. Elizabeth Becker, "Bill on Church Aid Proposes Tax Incentives for Giving," *New York Times*, 18 March 2001, A20.

25. Frank Bruni and Elizabeth Becker, "Charity Is Told It Must Abide by Anti[-]discrimination Laws," *New York Times*, 11 July 2001, A15.

26. Bruni and Becker, "Charity Is Told It Must Abide," A15.

27. Elizabeth Becker, "Senate Delays Legislation on Aid to Church Charities," *New York Times*, 24 May 2001, A22.

28. Elizabeth Becker, "Head of Religion-Based Initiative Resigns," *The New York Times*, 18 August 2001, A11.

29. Becker, "Head of Religion-Based Initiative Resigns," A11.

30. Kathryn Dunn Tenpas, "Can an Office Change a Country?" Report by University of Pennsylvania at a forum sponsored by the Pew Forum on Religion & Public Life, 20 February 2002.

31. Elisabeth Bumiller, "New Leader Picked for Religion-Based Initiative," *New York Times*, 2 February 2002, A14.

32. Elisabeth Bumiller, "Accord Reached on Charity Aid Bill after Bush Gives In on Hiring," *New York Times*, 8 February 2002, A19. The CARE Act would have cost $10.4 billion over ten years, mostly in tax incentives for families and corporations to give to charity. It also included $1.3 billion in block grants to social services. Under the act, religious groups could bid for social service grants.

33. Milbank, "Bush Endorses Compromise in Senate on Aid to Charities," A4.

34. Milbank, "Charity Bill Compromise Is Reached," A1.

35. Larry Witham, "Amendments Kill CARE in Senate," *Washington Times*, 15 November 2002. <www.washtimes.com>

36. Larry Witham, "Towey Says Faith-Based Bill 'Held Hostage' by Reed," *Washington Times*, 24 October 2002. <www.washtimes.com/national/20021024-3491772.htm>

37. Richard W. Stevenson, "Bush to Allow Religious Groups to Get Federal Money to Aid Poor," *New York Times*, 13 December 2002, A34. See also David Gibson, "President Revives His Faith-Based Initiative," *The Star-Ledger* (Newark), 13 December 2002, 1 and 15.

38. Eric Lichtblau, "Bush Plans to Let Religious Groups Get Building Aid," *New York Times*, 23 January 2003, A1 and A20. See also Associated Press, "New Faith-Based Initiative Draws Fire," *The Star-Ledger* (Newark), 24 January 2003, A9.

39. This term is taken from the work of Robert Putnam in *Bowling Alone* (New York: Simon & Schuster, 2000). Putnam was one of the early supporters of the Bush initiative.

40. Ron Hutcheson, "Bush to Bypass Congress on 'Faith-Based' Charities," *Knight Ridder Newspapers*, 11 December 2002, with philly@com. <www.philly.com/mld/philly/4718731.htm?template=contentModules/ printstory.jsp> (23 January 2003)

41. Richard Cohen, "As Buddhas Fall," *Washington Post*, 6 March 2001, A23.

42. Americans United, "Taxpayer Funding of 'Faith-Based' Social Services Violates Constitution, Says Federal Court," Press release, 9 January 2002. <www.au.org/press/pr010902.htm>

43. Adam Liptak, "A Right to Bias Is Put to the Test," *New York Times*, 11 October 2002, A30.

44. Derek H. Davis, "President Bush's Office of Faith-Based and Community Initiatives: Boon or Boondoggle?" *Journal of Church & State* 43, no. 4 (Summer 2001), 418.

1

The Good in the Faith–Based Initiative

Jo Renee Formicola

$\mathcal{I}$n 1986, George W. Bush spent a weekend with Evangelist Billy Graham. Although nobody really knows why the two men originally met or what happened at their encounter, Bush later admitted publicly that the meeting lit a religious "spark that . . . kindled into a flame."[1] He also said in later interviews that he became more dedicated to his faith, that his life became more focused, and that the time with Graham was life changing. Bush said it reconfirmed his beliefs in what he characterized as a "more powerful and personal way."[2]

When he returned home, the future governor joined a community Bible study group, began to read the scripture daily, and tried to turn his life around. One way he showed his profound personal change was in the fact that he stopped drinking. What is even more noteworthy, however, is that his commitment to God continues, and that it impels his public persona as well:

> I also recognize that a walk is a walk, I mean, it's a never-ending journey. And I've got a lot of imperfections like anybody else. And the more I got into the Bible, the more that admonition "Don't try to take a speck out of your neighbor's eye when

The author wishes to acknowledge the research, writing, and help of Mary Segers for the section on the New Jersey faith-based initiative as it appears in this chapter. She generously gave total access to her paper originally given at APSA in Boston, parts of which appear in her own words below.

you've got a log in your own" becomes more and more true, particularly for those of us in public life. And so my style, my focus, and many of the issues that I talk about, you know, are reinforced by my religion.[3]

The most important, and debatable, of these issues is, of course, the Bush faith-based initiative. It is predicated on the idea that everyone should be involved in social/charitable assistance. The president perceives help for the under-served as a public and private responsibility that should be carried out jointly—with government and non-profit resources—to provide care and bring about a personal change in the lives of those in need.

This is a *strategic* change in charitable public policy, for it rejects treating social programs as entitlements and clearly places an emphasis on personal responsibility. It accepts the fact that the government can play only a limited role in this equation and recognizes that social, charitable, and religious organizations can provide the help, values, and intangibles that make it possible to turn around those in the cycle of need. People who know George W. Bush say there is little doubt that the president is dedicated to this idea in his heart and that he is also politically committed to bring about this change in the myriad of social programs that exist in the United States.

The faith-based initiative began to emerge as a viable public policy after Bush was elected to his first term as governor of the Lone Star State in 1994. Under his leadership, Texas was one of the first states to partner with religious groups to achieve common, public objectives. The state welfare philosophy was based on seven principles: respect for clients, excellence of staff, quality of programs, wise use of public funds, accountability, equitable access, and willingness to collaborate. The latter meant that the Texas was committed to "initiate partnerships with other public and private organizations, local communities, and volunteers to help . . . achieve shared policy, funding, and service goals."[4] In keeping with that strategy, Governor Bush established alternative licensing procedures for faith-based programs soon after his election, and he created a pilot program of group homes for unwed teen welfare mothers. He supported Teen Challenge, an evangelical program designed to cure drug addiction through religious conversion. "He allowed both religious and non-religious groups to apply for social service contracts, abstinence education grants, and poverty-fighting initiatives."[5] Bush even turned to Chuck Colson, founder of Prison Ministries, and asked him to take over a jail unit in Fort Bend County. He simply asked Colson if his methodology worked and if it could make a difference. To Bush, "the real strength of the program [was] not only what happens inside the ministry, inside the wall of the prison, but most importantly or as importantly is what happens outside."[6] The governor also initiated and signed two critical bills: a Good Samaritan law that gave liability protection to health professionals who donated charitable care and another that required governmental agencies to develop welfare-to-work partnerships with faith-based groups in a way that respected the unique religious character of those groups.[7]

During his tenure as governor, Bush also examined the philosophical and ideological debates among academics and others who, like him, sought to justify and find innovative ways to bring together the public sector and faith-based organizations to solve social and charitable problems. Karl Rove, Bush's increasingly trusted political advisor, played the role of intellectual mentor, recruiting strategists and finding ways to engage those who espoused similar Bush views. Most of these thinkers believed that government alone could not provide—and was not providing—effective welfare. Some also argued that to solve the dilemma, faith-based organizations and government should work together to benefit the public good and the under-served.

Rove, through his various roles on the Bush gubernatorial team, seemed to be connected in a variety of ways to many academic, media, and political leaders who were striving to put either a more humane, stronger, or kinder face on the policies of the ideological right. Among those to whom Rove reached out were Marvin Olasky, Myron Magnet, Stephen Goldsmith, and John DiIulio. There were many others, but these men advanced new ideas that influenced the evolving Bush ideology and provided critical strategies to implement "compassionate conservatism," the eventual philosophical basis for the public policy known as the faith-based initiative.

MARVIN OLASKY: "COMPASSIONATE" ADVOCATE
IN COMPASSIONATE CONSERVATISM

Marvin Olasky, a professor at the University of Texas in 1990, was the author of seven books on public policy, history, and journalism even before he served as a Bradley Scholar at the Heritage Foundation in Washington, D.C.[8] The issue of *compassion* as a civic and personal virtue had begun to dominate his thinking and research, so his time at the conservative think-tank gave him a welcome interval to flesh out his emerging thoughts. Olasky was beginning to believe that welfare should be transformed from a government monopoly that simply provided for the material needs of the under-served, to a public/faith-based partnership that could also tend to the spiritual needs of the less fortunate.[9]

He subsequently published *The Tragedy of American Compassion* in 1992 in which he argued that "the way we help has an effect on the human spirit and human behavior."[10] Challenging the social consensus that had taken over the United States after the 1960s, Olasky maintained that human beings could see the totality of need better than the bureaucracies that compartmentalized those requirements. Therefore, he reasoned, individuals rather than governments should play a critical role in helping the under-served in society.

Olasky's book called for the return to the early American, compassionate model of charity. Based on the principle of *suffering with* the poor, his ideal paradigm consisted of individuals giving personal assistance and time to those in need and serving as role models, as well, to those whom they served. Olasky argued that charity should be tied to creating work and helping the needy to earn a living and develop self-respect. Most importantly, Olasky maintained that the early American model of charity was also based on a theological belief that God intervenes through His people to help others. Thus, to him, charity was about more than simply doling out money. The charitable experience, he believed, as practiced throughout U.S. history by churches and other social agencies, was supposed to bring about a moral change in those who were plagued by social ills.

Olasky noted, however, that by the end of the nineteenth century the nature of American charity began to change. Widows were considered the "worthy poor," but most others seeking assistance were often suspect. The idea of material redistribution, fostered by those in the Social Gospel movement and the survivalist ideas of the social Darwinists, began to advance the notion that the "unfit" should be eliminated from public aid. The idea that bad charity would drive out the good gave way to the practice of investigating applicants, of demanding work from the able-bodied, and of training charitable volunteers to decide who should receive aid. Missions, which made demands for confession and witness as precursors for charity, also emphasized personal responsibility and the need for the "fallen" to make internal change. Problems of communications and organizational structure began to overwhelm the private charitable agencies in the United States, as well. Settlement houses that had developed could no longer meet the growing demands for more and more aid. Finally, charitable agencies came to realize that only the government could provide the organizational expertise to control the distribution of financial assistance to help the growing numbers of the poor. Thus, according to Olasky, state relief became a bureaucratic obligation based on the civic need for equality and equity. And the renewal of character and the duty to bring about a change of the inner person who sought assistance then became a religious responsibility.

By the twentieth century, then, the U.S. government, out of necessity, began to get more and more involved with assisting those in need. Theodore Roosevelt began pensions for widows and mothers and established children's bureaus. Taft and Harding worked to provide public welfare, and in the process, advocates for private services for the poor began to be transformed into boards for individual fundraising. Money, rather than time, came to characterize the new definition of charity. Philanthropy overtook compassion and suffering with the poor.

During the depression, when financial need was the greatest in the United States, FDR and his innovative social programs embodied in the New Deal began to give new meaning to government charity. They emphasized collective need and paid less attention to the personal aspects of poverty. By the 1960s, Lyndon Baines Johnson moved the American model of charity to a totally new paradigm, according to Olasky. He contended that the Great Society, under Johnson, equated public charity with a right, or entitlement.

Olasky blamed this shift in thinking and the programs of the War on Poverty for the cycle of welfare abuse and the failed social problems that emerged later. He interpreted entitlements as an attempt to take the shame out of welfare and to excuse the poor from the personal responsibility for their lives. Olasky argued that consequently, government bureaucracies grew and welfare benefits simply became gifts. Such a policy, he contended, stifled social mobility and hurt private, charitable organizations.

His response? Individuals should return to the original American model of charity and become *compassionate* once again. Olasky called on people to form affiliations—that is, to strengthen family, religious, and social bonds. He argued for volunteers to take on narrow but deep responsibilities. He called for the renewal of work requirements to prevent fraud and to place an emphasis on the positive aspects of work. To him, jobs represented freedom, an escape from poverty. Thus, in Olasky's thought, compassion involved *suffering with* and helping those in need to turn their lives around. To him, compassion was "more than a noun; it was a process."[11] He challenged the public to share with the poor and to give up just sending checks to charities. He called for welfare recipients to work, and neighbors to help create a sense of community. Olasky demanded accountability while also calling for a rethinking of what it means to be made in God's image.

His ideas profoundly affected those in conservative intellectual circles. In 1993, Olasky became an adviser to gubernatorial candidate George W. Bush. And in 1994, William J. Bennett, former Secretary of Education under Ronald Reagan and founder of Empower America, a conservative think-tank, gave *The Tragedy of American Compassion* to fellow Republican Newt Gingrich for a Christmas present. The future Speaker of the House recommended it to the incoming Republican members of the Congress, and it is easy to see how Olasky's book had an impact on the Welfare Reform Act of 1996. Olasky, himself, took a leave of absence from the University of Texas to assist in the legislative battle for the Charitable Choice provision of the act as advanced by Senators John Ashcroft, Dan Coates, Rick Santorum, and Congressmen Steve Largent, J. C. Watts, and Jim Talent.

Olasky continued to advance his notion for a new social philosophy and public policy toward the under-served in his second book,

Compassionate Conservatism. Published in 2000, it contained examples of how private programs in Texas, Indianapolis, Philadelphia, and Minneapolis were providing charity and making meaningful changes in individuals' lives. Essentially, Olsaky showed that economics alone could not change lives, but that faith could. He argued that government had to focus on more than material well-being, that it needed to direct "armies of compassion" to overcome the basic problems in American society. With his thought much more refined, Olasky made clear that he wanted to reform welfare by creating a "triangular relationship" between the state, faith-based organizations, and charities.

The future president's seven-plus year relationship with Olasky portended his adoption of "compassionate conservatism" as a viable approach to public policy when he wrote the forward to *Compassionate Conservatism*. Tightly aligned with Olasky's views, Bush's notion of charity was now clearer: It was based on the philosophy that true compassion could provide prosperity as well as hope, and that the ideology of conservatism could advance a policy agenda to promote social progress through individual change. Bush disavowed spending public money to simply build bureaucracies to help the poor and insisted, instead, that compassionate conservatism was a philosophy that cared about people, an ideology that would help to bring lasting change into the lives of the under-served. He stated in Olasky's book:

> Government can do certain things very well, but it cannot put hope in our hearts or a sense of purpose in our lives. That requires churches and synagogues and mosques and charities. A truly compassionate government is one that rallies these armies of compassion and provides an environment in which they can thrive . . . Government will not be replaced by charities, but it can welcome them as a partner.[12]

MYRON MAGNET: "CULTURAL" CONSERVATIVE IN COMPASSIONATE CONSERVATISM

Myron Magnet is part of the cadre of "public intellectuals," many of whom work at think-tanks and influence the media and policymakers though their creative thinking and interpretations of political, social, and economic phenomena. A Columbia Ph.D. with a scholarly background in Dickens, Magnet is a member of the board of editors of *Fortune* magazine and a fellow at the right-wing Manhattan Institute for Policy Research. He is the editor of the Institute's magazine, *City Journal*, and the author of several books, of which *The Dream and the Nightmare*, published in 1993, became an important social commentary.

Magnet's book critiqued the liberalism of the 1960s, the sexual revolution of its elites, and their alternative lifestyles. In seeking personal liberation, Magnet argued, the "haves" also pursued political liberation, leading to the creation of a culture of irresponsibility, moral confusion, and a "no-fault social policy."[13] The elites, according to him, accomplished their cultural revolution but, in the process, led the poorest of the poor into a life of government dependence and poverty.

Magnet argued that the liberals created an "underclass" who were chronically poor. Characterized as urban minorities, most were unskilled workers trapped in cycles of crime, violence, and illegitimacy— people who passed on to their children "a self-defeating set of values and attitudes, along with an impoverished intellectual and emotional development, that generally imprison[ed] them in failure as well."[14]

Further, Magnet maintained that the underclass was signaled, in repeated court decisions, legislation, and public policy, that it was wronged, victimized, and in need of special treatment. He maintained that although the elites had acted out of a democratic impulse, they tried to expiate their responsibility to the poor by enacting the War on Poverty and Affirmative Action. They extended government welfare benefits, ordered school busing, built public housing projects, instituted job training and drug treatment programs and special education—all of which did not work, according to Magnet. He argued that the underclass accepted these benefits because it did not have the internal tools such as values, social skills, literacy, and a sense of affiliation to the larger society to rise above its cultural *malaise*, rather than to simply confront its economic problems.

Magnet opposed telling the poor that they were either racial or economic victims. He insisted that they be given hope, responsibility, and, in turn, self-respect and equality. In short, Magnet believed that the poor should be inculcated with the belief that they could determine their own destiny. As a result, he called for personal accountability and a clarification of the moral confusion in the American value system. He indicted the personal liberation of the 1960s elites that became the basis of political liberation, as "a move influenced by left-leaning media and political figures."[15] This, he argued, "withdrew respect from the behavior and attitudes that have traditionally boosted people up the economic ladder— deferral of gratification, sobriety, thrift, dogged industry, and so on through the whole catalogue of antique-sounding bourgeois virtues."[16]

The nation's social problems, according to Magnet, were not being solved by government efforts. He believed that the main one was illegitimacy and approved of church-related agencies that provided services to welfare mothers tied to clear moral values that stigmatized sex outside of marriage. He wanted to see safer neighborhoods and supported activist policing in poor neighborhoods. He argued that public education was a "great national scandal, despite huge expenditures"[17] and saw vouchers as a means to bring about a change in schools for minorities and the under-served.

He ended *The Dream and the Nightmare* by saying that :

> For the breakdown of the poor to be healed and the moral confusion of the Haves to be dispelled, we need above all to repair the damage that has been done to the beliefs and values that have made America remarkable and that for two centuries have successfully transformed huddled masses of the poor into free and prosperous citizens. The soul of American society . . . [is] an allegiance to a few fundamental ideas . . . everyone is responsible for his or her actions . . . freedom under the rule of law . . . that the public communal life is a boon . . . that everyone has equal rights . . . that we are free to shape our own fate.[18]

Magnet insisted eventually that compassionate conservatism could change the plight of the poor because it was an "effort to make these solutions central to national politics."[19]

Karl Rove suggested that George W. Bush read *The Dream and the Nightmare* while he was still governor of Texas, and began making

introductions between the governor and such writers several years before his presidential campaign. Magnet's "attack on the counterculture
struck a chord with Mr. Bush. 'It really helped crystallize some of my
thinking about culture, changing cultures' Bush said in [an] interview,
'and of part of the legacy of my generation.'"[20]

Magnet's later book, *The Millenial City: A New Urban Paradigm for
21st Century America*, gave examples of municipalities in the 1990s
that came back to life by rejecting welfare-state ideology. New approaches to crime, welfare reform, making government smaller but
more effective, and changing education though school choice were
his hopes for the future.

STEPHEN GOLDSMITH: A COMPASSIONATE
AND CONSERVATIVE POLITICIAN

Stephen Goldsmith is a politician rather than an academic, but he
was, in his own way, an innovative two-term mayor of Indianapolis
who demonstrated how public-private partnerships could work successfully in real life. He had been the Marion Country district attorney for thirteen years before becoming "Hizzoner" and was most
concerned about crime, children, and communities. Goldsmith was
the author of *Twenty-First Century America: Resurrecting Urban America*
and the founder of the Front Porch Alliance.

When Goldsmith was first elected mayor of Indianapolis in 1992
he stepped into a typical urban city: one competing against the suburbs, trying to hold the line on taxes, fighting crime, illiteracy, and illegitimacy, and a municipality in need of efficiency and productivity.
In 1993, he met Larry Mone, the president of the Manhattan Institute, and Myron Magnet, two public intellectuals who encouraged
him to write a book about urban policy, his strategies for success, and
his experiences in Indianapolis.

Goldsmith, as a mayor and an individual, was plagued by the
quandary of what was wrong with contemporary urban areas. He rejected the conventional wisdom and argued that teen pregnancy and
illegitimacy were made economically viable through the convoluted

welfare system. He went even further, saying the "government subsidized the breakup of the family."[21] He opposed the public monopoly on education and the justice system that dealt with youthful offenders only after they were essentially lost to crime. He felt that the War on Poverty was a failure, an attempt at a massive redistribution of wealth that neglected the "core responsibilities of public safety and infrastructure."[22]

His strategies for success were simple: "People know better than government what is in their best interest. Monopolies are inefficient and government monopolies are particularly inefficient. Wealth needs to be created, not redistributed. Government should do a few things well. Cities must not raise taxes or price themselves out of competition with excessive regulations"[23]

Based on these principles, Goldsmith set out to bring free market competition, innovation, and cost effectiveness to city government in Indianapolis. While he worked with suburban officials to help revive the urban economy, he also sought to bring about major changes in social programs. One of the things that he called for was competition among social service providers, a radical idea. It was tied to customer needs, new ideas, and a focus on outcomes. Perhaps, more importantly, social services were also to be based on partnerships between the public and private sectors.

Several joint efforts existed and were already making a difference: the Franklin Township Churches Association and its mentoring program; the African American Minister's Association, which adopted families in distress; and Faith and Families, which worked to help single parents. Goldsmith was convinced that "Communities of faith can do more to help strengthen families than any government agency can hope to accomplish."[24] He opposed the public monopoly on social services that pushed out charitable agencies from providing care to the needy and enforcing a sense of responsibility. Goldsmith accused government of "transforming charity into [an] intergenerational entitlement."[25]

He ended his book on *Twenty-First Century America* by arguing,

> Religion and religious institutions must play a critical role in the future of our cities, and government can assist in two ways. First,

public officials should use the bully pulpit to celebrate and encourage religious commitment without favoring one [religious]
tradition over another. Second, cities can undertake initiatives with
houses of worship . . . that strengthen communities while encouraging connections that promote religious involvement. . . .
Church-based groups are infinitely better suited than government
to help vulnerable individuals. Government is typically unable to
discriminate between the truly needy and those simply seeking a
handout. Government programs are also prevented from instruct-
ing those on assistance about the need to exercise moral judgment
in their decision making. They can offer the soup, but not the salvation.

In contrast, when church congregations help needy individuals, they do more than merely pass out checks to case numbers—
they help their neighbors, thereby strengthening the bonds of
community. And by making faith an integral part of that assistance, church based efforts provide needy individuals with a
source of strength and the moral impetus for personal change that
government simply cannot. . . . The proper role of government is
to support, not supplant, the involvement of religious institutions
in their communities. Government can accomplish more by
working with faith-based efforts than it can ever achieve by de-
railing them.[26]

To give credence to his beliefs, Goldsmith launched the Front
Porch Alliance in 1997, a cooperative partnership between the city
of Indianapolis, faith-based organizations, neighborhood groups, and
community members. Its task was to deal with local problems, and it
initially had to find ways to develop effective collaboration between
the public and private sectors. Starting with a Community Outreach
Team, the group met with local clergy, community leaders, and residents to get an understanding of issues and concerns from their perspectives. Helping to set priorities, the group received $100,000 from
the city of Indianapolis and another $125,000 from a Community
Enhancement Fund, supported by businesses seeking tax abatements
in the city. Eventually, the Front Porch Alliance established 800 partnerships with more than 400 religious and community organizations.[27]

The Front Porch Alliance was based on the premise that faith-based and other private agencies were critical for community revival. Goldsmith encouraged Indianapolis's government to bring the community into the public planning while actively supporting its work. Thus, the Alliance was about bringing together all those who were already involved and could make a difference. It fostered community renewal, provided benefits to families and children, carried out activities for the youth, and resulted in a "significant decrease in crime in eight targeted neighborhoods."[28]

During his tenure, Goldsmith also focused on market-based incentives to bring business to the city. He set a goal of $700 million to rebuild poor neighborhoods and revitalize downtown Indianapolis. His office claimed to have saved nearly $400 million, cutting taxes three times to stimulate the economy and decreasing the overall city budget from $450 million to $441 million within seven years.[29]

It was on a swing though Texas while he was promoting his book that Karl Rove had asked Stephen Goldsmith to come to Austin to meet Governor George W. Bush. The mayor spent the night at the governors' mansion, with the two men purportedly becoming quick friends due to Goldsmith's efforts to involve faith-based institutions, neighborhood volunteers, and government agencies to solve community problems. Touted by some at the time as Bush's "intellectual soul mate,"[30] Goldsmith impressed the governor with his commitment to downsize government and to cut taxes. Bush said of Goldsmith, "He and I share a conservative philosophy. I think both of us understand the need to empower and uplift the individual. We understand that there is a role for government [in this]."[31]

Goldsmith gave advice to Bush, and brought in more than 100 experts from academia, think-tanks, and consulting firms to help the presidential candidate develop positions on public policy during his run for the White House. As a result, Goldsmith became a critical part of the Bush team, was named Domestic Policy Advisor for the presidential campaign, and counseled the president on the establishment of the faith-based initiative after his election.

JOHN DIIULIO: THE THINKER IN THE
MIDDLE OF COMPASSIONATE CONSERVATISM

One of the academics that Stephen Goldsmith introduced to George W. Bush was John DiIulio. He had all the credentials—a Harvard Ph.D., connections from his former position as a professor at Princeton, and the credibility that went with holding the Fox Leadership Chair at the University of Pennsylvania. He had founded the Center for Research on Religion and Urban Civil Society at Penn and was a senior fellow at both the conservative Manhattan Institute and the liberal Brookings Institution, as well as a contributing editor to *The Weekly Standard*. He was the author, coauthor, or editor of a dozen books, of which *What's God Got to Do with the American Experiment*, with E. J. Dionne, played a part in meeting George W. Bush and having an impact on his faith-based initiative. DiIulio also had the demeanor and self-assurance that went along with the degrees, legitimacy, and recognition—like the commercial said, when he talked, everyone listened.

DiIulio was a pragmatist more than an ideologue. He was interested in results more than labels, and strategies for success rather than religious platitudes. What he sought to do, metaphorically, was to find the reason why a Boston police officer would comment on the importance of the clergy and say, "with [their] cooperation, we can turn our neighborhoods around. Without them, without [their] cooperation, we can't."[32]

DiIulio was impelled by the question of what made ministries so effective, or perhaps more to the point: What made them so much better at preventing crime than the government? What could the public sector learn from their tactics? And could the state work with faith-based organizations, legitimately, to help those in need?

DiIulio began by reframing the question of who should provide charity. He asked: Who was subsidizing whom? He argued that it was really religious groups, rather than government agencies, who worked with the most at-risk youth, took care of crime victims and the hungry, who ministered to prisoners and their families, and who did most of the volunteering in neighborhoods and communities.

They were successful, he concluded, because they were on the scene, providing help at once, where it was needed. They were also used to scrapping for resources, filling out all kinds of convoluted government reports and documents for funds, and pursuing all avenues to strengthen and expand their efforts for those in need.

DiIulio proposed that because of the depth of their commitment, if faith-based groups produced even the same civic results as the public sector at a smaller human and financial cost, they should be considered successful.[33] This success, DiIulio argued should be interpreted as a social "profit," a phenomenon that justified the investment of civic "venture capital" in religious, charitable agencies. Such investing, he held, would be relatively easy for corporate, philanthropic, private institutions, and individuals to carry out.

The difficulty he saw arose from the fact that inner-city churches, particularly black congregations, were "leveraging several times their weight in community service,"[34] and could not continue to turn the tide even with other private help. Therefore, DiIulio concluded that government support at all levels was necessary to make a difference. It was how the public sector should and could provide that help that became the challenge.

In 1999, DiIulio saw compassionate conservatism as having the "makings of a coherent public philosophy." He found it morally compelling and politically sound.[35] He maintained that it was consistent with the Founding Fathers' understanding of civil society and government, and in keeping with contemporary American thought. DiIulio based his reasoning on the traditional benevolence of civil society, the competition within social welfare bureaucracies at all levels, and the possibility of obtaining lasting progress against the worst social ills. All that was needed, he contended, was an intelligent, rigorous implementation of compassionate conservatism and the political will to create a new American century.

DiIulio's arguments were based in part on Catholic social thought, cost-benefit analysis, and capitalism. His notion of compassionate conservatism was actually a mix of subsidiarity, personal volunteerism, and government devolution. He believed in limits on state intervention and contended that the family, as the original cell of social life and the community and should care for its young, old, sick, handicapped, and the poor. At the same time, though, he supported what George W. Bush was beginning to say—that resources should be made available "through contracts, certificates, or grants on a competitive basis to all organizations—including religious ones."[36] Thus, small, social, and charitable groups could and would seek assistance for their social work from the government. Devolution, as a result, would occur naturally then—and with a difference. For not only would large "proxy networks,"[37] such as Catholic Charities, the Salvation Army, and Lutheran Services, be eligible to compete for federal funds but other faith-based organizations would also be encouraged to compete directly with public sector agencies for government funds. This competition, DiIulio felt, "could usher in a new era of results-driven public administration,"[38] precipitating reform, change, reward, or the deletion of programs that no longer worked.

Such ideas, of course, were in line with the thinking of George W. Bush. So, it was only natural that Goldsmith would invite DiIulio to Texas to brief the presidential candidate and his domestic policy team on public-private partnerships. Given the opportunity to help Bush further refine his thinking on the faith-based initiative, the central questions for Bush, were, as always, could public/private partnerships work and, if so, what needed to be done to make them work? DiIulio's answers must have been potent, for immediately after the election, he was appointed advisor to George W. Bush and first director of the Office of Faith-Based and Community Initiatives.

GEORGE W. BUSH: CHANGING
THEORY INTO PRACTICE

The president announced the policy of public/private collaboration at the White House within weeks of taking his oath of office. On January 30, 2001, with thirty leaders from a variety of faith-based organizations,[39] as well as John DiIulio and Stephen Goldsmith, looking on, George W. Bush signed the executive orders that gave form and substance to his notions of compassionate conservatism and created the Office of Faith-Based and Community Initiatives. Calling religious leaders "agents of change" and admitting that "I was lost and then I was found," Bush's announcement sounded like a revival to some.[40]

The faith-based initiative was centered on a number of Bush assumptions. First, it was based on the president's belief that "compassion is the work of a nation, not just a government"[41]—that is, that public issues are everyone's concern and business. Second, it was grounded in the confidence that it is possible to encourage faith-based programs without changing the mission of the agencies involved.[42] The president recognized that charitable organizations could be fully religious without compromising the nation's commitment to pluralism. Third, the chief executive maintained that although government might encourage a different way to use "proven" means to "change and save lives," that "government will never be replaced by charities and community groups" in its obligations to serve those in need.[43] Fourth, he held that government would not discriminate against faith-based groups that might compete with secular ones for charitable funds. According to him, there would be a level playing field, for all nonprofit as well as private associations, including religious ones. Fifth, George W. Bush believed that regardless of size, all religious organizations must be eligible to receive help from the government. And finally, he maintained that faith-based and community groups would always have a voice around the Bush policy table. He promised that his administration would host discussions on public matters without imposing government policy solutions on the participants.[44]

The timing of the president's announcement gave credence and priority to the faith-based initiative; it was one of the main issues that defined his campaign. Now it would be a critical part of his domestic agenda, and it would be up to his staff to implement his vision. John DiIulio knew it would not be easy, and after six months, he knew it would be almost impossible.

On July 4, 2000, though, President Bush was in Philadelphia, eating hot dogs with John DiIulio and spending an afternoon with some of the "Amachi" volunteers from the Presbyterian Church and those in their care. Amachi is a West African word that means "who knows what God has brought us through this child."[45] The term is also the name of a program that is a partnership between the Big Brothers/Big Sisters of America, the Pew Charitable Trust, and various local churches. Its purpose is to mentor the children of prisoners. It was a perfect day, the culmination of what John DiIulio had signed on to do—to articulate the president's notion of compassionate conservatism, to mold its various facets into a viable public policy, and to make a difference in the lives of those in need. But he also reportedly said earlier that "even if Bush wins big, spends political capital to govern accordingly, and attracts experts . . . to his administration, it will not be easy. The devil is in the boring administrative details."[46]

Clearly, then, DiIulio's interpretation and implementation of compassionate conservatism would—and did—play a significant part in creating the specifics of the faith-based initiative at first. Among those who both championed and challenged the public/private partnership policy, the main source of contention came over the basic premise of the Bush plan: that religion and government should work together, find a "zone of accommodation," and provide charitable care. Although its purpose seemed lofty, the faith-based initiative had the potential for collaboration *and* entanglement, and appeared to fly in the face of the First Amendment with its protection of religious exercise and prohibition against the establishment of religion. Any attempt to make a strategic shift in the principle of separation of church and state, long held, constitutionally protected, and legally defined over two hundred years, was suspect to many people of good will.

DiIulio and the president both supported a return to a more personal model of charity, one based on individual responsibility and character—in short, the kind that is practiced often by those religious agencies and volunteers who work closely with those in need. The help that they envisioned was more than financial; it was based on values and the hope that it could also be life altering. The president and DiIulio tried to calm the fears of those who saw faith-based organizations and their staffs as "missionaries" or "proselytizers" or individuals seeking to make converts with government money. And they sought to assure religious social providers, as well, that their missions would not be compromised or curtailed by working with government.

Bush had said during his presidential campaign that it was "destructive" to think "if government would only get out of the way, problems would be solved."[47] Instead he argued that government should look "first to faith-based organizations, charities, and community groups that have shown their ability to save and change lives."[48] In contrast to the conventional political wisdom, Bush posited that the job of government was to make *greater resources* available to religious groups to carry out their social charitable missions, and to rally local armies of compassion or volunteers to do this. During his campaign, and immediately afterwards, the president admitted that charities or volunteers could not replace the government's role in providing social services and acknowledged that government should fund religious activities. He promised not to favor religious institutions over nonreligious ones. He argued that he was interested in what is constitutional, but also in "what works." He promised to fund programs, rather than religious organizations. To Bush, the church–state issue could be overcome—and in a simple way. To him, the government only needed to fund organizations that provided results and achieved valid public purposes based on pluralism, nondiscrimination, evenhandedness, and neutrality.[49] Thus, the church–state issue was minimized in the minds of both Bush and DiIulio in favor of pragmatism, and forged in the belief that a viable public policy based on charitable public/private partnerships could withstand a potential legal battle based on civic results in the future.

DiIulio also tried to answer other mounting objections to the faith-based initiative as quickly as possible. Questions of hiring discrimination that had plagued the Salvation Army and evangelicals were interpreted as invalid. DiIulio argued that under Section 702, Title VII, of the Civil Rights Act of 1964 certain organizations were permitted to discriminate in employment decisions on the basis of their "beliefs and tenets." And he pointed out that secular agencies—as well as religious ones—often used such exemptions. Planned Parenthood, in particular, was used as a prime example; it could, and legally does, refuse to hire those who do not share its views about family planning. Thus, to DiIulio, equal treatment meant that churches, mosques, and synagogues had the same right to discriminate in their hiring practices as secular nonprofits. He said, "We will defend the right of religious organizations to hire staff who share the organization's core belief and tenets,"[50] but also promised to protect the civil rights of all those whom they served. All beneficiaries under the Bush plan, he contended, would be allowed to seek charitable services at secular agencies, if they so chose. It was uncertain early on whether or not all services would be paid directly with public funds, "voucherized," or subsidized with tax credits. No payment system had been worked out in the first months of the initiative, a fact that eventually became a major problem in its implementation.

Beside these legal and philosophical interpretations of compassionate conservatism, John DiIulio believed that the principles were alive and well in the policy arena in the guise of Charitable Choice. Part of the Welfare Reform Act of 1996, the Charitable Choice Provision, was already a matter of law, simply needing to be clarified, and then implemented, according to DiIulio. There were others, on both sides of the political spectrum, however, who opposed this simple view. Most on the left saw Charitable Choice as a breach in the wall of separation between church and state. Because it supported public-private partnerships, allowed the use of public monies by religious, charitable agencies, and allowed them to discriminate in the hiring of individuals who worked for them, liberals and others feared its civil rights and fiscal consequences. Many on the right wanted the faith-based initiative to go even further; to give tax credits, vouchers and benefits, if not direct public monies, to carry out their missions— which in all cases were religious as well as charitable. Thus, they lined up: the Americans United for Separation of Church and State, the American Civil Liberties Union, and others against the Catholics, the Christian Right, the National Association of Evangelicals, and others. DiIulio was the man in the middle.

He attempted to find common ground by implementing the president's three objectives concerning the faith-based initiative. First, he would work to boost charitable giving, both human and financial, by helping to craft new legislation in the future if it was, indeed, necessary. Second, he would conduct program audits in the five faith-based offices that the president had established in the Departments of Justice, Labor, Education, Health and Human Services, and Housing and Urban Development to see how they were going to implement public/private partnerships in their particular areas. And, third, he would make sure that religious "proxy networks" could compete equally with secular nonprofits for public funds. Additionally, he would put performance measures in place to allow qualified and faith-based organizations to seek government funding on the same basis as any other nongovernmental providers of social services.

But, even with these strategies in place, DiIulio could not overcome the growing problems and opposition to the president's faith-based initiative. Trumped by September 11, the economy and other policy issues, the initiative is still in limbo today. That does not mean, however, that its principles lack merit, or that it cannot work on the local level. Following is an example.

THE "GOOD" IN ACTION:
A CASE STUDY OF NEW JERSEY

Most citizens believe that that "local churches, synagogues, and mosques," together with "organizations such as the Salvation Army, Goodwill Industries, and Habitat for Humanity," are among the best organizations to solve the problems in their communities.[51] Speaking before the National Association of Evangelicals, John DiIulio gave some interesting data about religious, charitable assistance in 2001. More than 90 percent of urban congregations provide social services; their beneficiaries are often not church, synagogue, or mosque members, but they collaborate with secular nonprofits and they do not make religious services contingent on receiving assistance. The replacement value of their services is inestimable, but in Philadelphia, DiIulio's hometown, it is thought to be about $250,000 a year.[52]

The press is filled with stories of crime and disaster, and tells few accounts of successful social and charitable programs that could do even better if they received financial assistance from the government to carry out their work. There is little publicity about public/private partnerships that are already working, but there is one such case that deserves note: the efforts of the state of New Jersey.

In 1998, Governor Christine Todd Whitman, then beginning her second term, launched a faith-based community development initiative. It was two years after passage of the 1996 federal welfare reform law (the Personal Responsibility and Work Opportunity Reconciliation Act) that contained the Charitable Choice Provision, and three years before President George W. Bush established the White House Office of Faith-Based and Community Initiatives. Originally conceived as a division of the Department of Community Affairs in Trenton, the New Jersey Office of Faith-Based Initiatives is a partnership between state government and the private sector including J. P. Morgan–Chase Manhattan Bank, Public Service Gas and Electric (the state's largest utility), and the Center for Non-Profit Corporations. In the six years of its existence, the New Jersey Office has funded over 140 grantees in most of the state's twenty-one counties.

New Jersey provides a good example of a faith-based initiative, but it is not, strictly speaking, Charitable Choice. Instead, the Garden State follows traditional patterns of governmental funding of non-profit social service agencies, such as Catholic Charities and Lutheran Social Services. The New Jersey policy requires that a funded program be an incorporated entity, a 501-(c) (3) nonprofit group with a separate board of directors, separate bylaws, separate records, and a budget completely separate from the budget of the parent church, temple, or mosque. This is important because it ensures that no government funds will go into church coffers in violation of the federal and state constitutions. Moreover, the policy stipulates that faith-based groups cannot proselytize, and they must follow civil rights laws in their personnel practices. Because of these important qualifications, the New Jersey faith-based initiative has avoided the thorny First Amendment issues concerning religious establishment and religious freedom that have dogged President Bush's faith-based initiative.

Some provisions of the Garden State's faith-based initiative are similar to the federal government's program. For example, the New Jersey policy respects the integrity of faith-based organizations. They are allowed to retain control over the definition, development, practice, and expression of their religious beliefs. Neither federal nor state government can require a religious provider to alter its form of internal governance or remove religious art, icons, scripture, or other symbols in order to be a program participant. Second, the New Jersey program protects clients. In rendering assistance, religious organizations are not allowed to discriminate against an individual on the basis of religion, a religious belief, or refusal to actively participate in a religious practice. If an individual objects to the religious character of a program, a secular alternative must be provided. Third, like the federal program, New Jersey's faith-based initiative prohibits the use of government funding for inherently religious activities such as worship, sectarian instruction, and proselytization.

However, on the crucial issue of direct government funding of a faith-based organization, the New Jersey program differs from the federal government's concept of Charitable Choice. The Garden State insists upon separate incorporation of a church's social service organization, in effect erecting a wall of separation between a church's religious activities and its services to the needy. Under the New Jersey plan, there is to be no entanglement between churches and associated service organizations; only the latter are eligible for public funding. Moreover, New Jersey, unlike the federal initiative, requires that faith-based organizations receiving public funds must observe civil rights laws in their personnel practices, in accordance with the New Jersey State Constitution.

Although small in size, New Jersey is the ninth largest state in population and the most densely populated state in the nation.[53] The Garden State is part of the old, industrial Northeast, as evident in its major cities: Newark, Trenton, Elizabeth, Jersey City, Camden, and Paterson. In the past thirty years its demographics have changed, making New Jersey a virtual "microcosm of the United States, with urban, suburban, and rural areas, significant blue-collar ethnic areas as well as sizable black and Hispanic populations."[54] The state's population has reached almost 8.5 million, with a sizable growth of Asian and Arab populations. As a result, there is an increase in the number of Muslims and Hindus in the state, but Catholics are still the most prevalent religious group. There are also significant populations of the earlier immigrant groups: Italians, Irish, Polish, and other Eastern European nationalities. What all this indicates, of course, is the tremendous diversity of the state. This variety coupled with population density means that New Jerseyans must learn to live with one another peacefully, to cooperate, and to respect each other's religious beliefs.[55]

New Jersey adopted its first constitution in 1776; it was subsequently revised in 1844 and in 1947. It is the latest document that is still regarded as a model of sound governmental structure and a guarantee of fundamental rights. The Constitution asserts "natural and unalienable rights, among which are those of enjoying and defending life and liberty, of acquiring, possessing, and protecting property, and of pursuing and obtaining safety and happiness." Religious freedom, rights of conscience, and prohibitions against religious establishment as well as religious tests for political office are part of Article I.

The more salient and controversial issues in New Jersey politics concern the environment, urban and suburban sprawl, traffic congestion, education, and taxes. The state has a diverse and prosperous economy based on the pharmaceutical and insurance industries, tourism, agriculture, research, and telecommunications. Proximity to New York and Philadelphia means jobs and commuting for residents in the New Jersey suburbs. At least one quarter of those killed in the September 11 attack on the World Trade Center were New Jerseyans.

There has been no real controversy in the Garden State about its faith-based initiative. As indicated above, church-state issues and the complex relation between religion and politics have not been burning issues in New Jersey politics. Perhaps the social diversity of the state has something to do with this. Equally important, however, is the structure and format of the faith-based policy itself.

New Jersey's faith-based program is six years old and claims to be the first in the country. It antedates President Bush's initiative and differs from then-Governor George Bush's initiative in Texas, which used federal funding; New Jersey's program uses state funding and is supported also by private sources. In the first year of its operation, the state's office received requests for information about the Faith-Based Initiative from Texas, Missouri, Maryland, and Florida.

As mentioned previously, Christine Todd Whitman proposed the New Jersey Faith-Based Community Development Initiative while running for reelection in 1998. She had asked various clergy, including many black pastors, for ideas and assistance in shaping new urban initiatives, particularly since the initial effects of the 1996 welfare reform were resulting in people being pushed off welfare rolls and having to turn to local churches for assistance. As a result, clergy asked Governor Whitman for state aid to help them meet the rising demand for social services. On January 20, 1998, having eked out a narrow reelection victory, the governor stated in her inaugural address:

> Talking bricks and mortar isn't enough. Our cities also need another kind of renewal; a renewal of faith, hope, and confidence. That's why I've launched a Faith-Based Community Development Initiative. We will expand our support of religious organizations that are already building shopping centers, offering job training, and providing childcare in their communities. I am proud to announce a State commitment of $5 million for this initiative. We have already found two business partners, and we'll look for more.[56]

The New Jersey Legislature quickly approved Whitman's initiative and allocated $5 million to the new Office of Faith-Based Initiatives, establishing a program that would work in conjunction with the private and nonprofit sector. The types of programs that would receive grants would be those for nonprofit healthcare services, transitional housing programs, food pantries, after-school safe haven programs, tutoring services, homeowner education programs, soup kitchens, drug rehabilitation programs, midnight basketball programs, homes for mothers with AIDS and their children, and community centers for the elderly. Isaiah House in East Orange, New Jersey, received state funding to lease minivans to transport teenagers—of whom Isaiah House has physical custody—to sports and cultural events. In Cherry Hill, New Jersey, the Jewish Community Center also received a grant for minivans to transport the elderly to shopping centers.[57]

In accordance with state and federal constitutions, the New Jersey Office of Faith-Based Initiatives does not fund houses of worship. A program must be an incorporated entity, a 501(c)(3) nonprofit group, to qualify for funding. Faith-based organizations are defined as those that are created by a community of faith and have a relationship with it. They must also have a separate 501(c)(3) nonprofit status and make a critical impact on neighborhood stability. Additionally they must provide services and programs to low- to moderate-income families. These groups are not allowed to proselytize or receive grants for construction. All recipients must follow civil rights laws in personnel practices with a wary eye against nepotism.

In addition to grant allocation, the office runs training conferences to help small churches with accounting, grant-writing, and training for board membership (the board of directors of the social service program must be separate from the board for the mosque or church or synagogue). The need for such technical assistance is so great that the office has developed the New Jersey Faith-Based Training Institute to provide training sessions more frequently (about four times a year). This institute is in partnerships with the Center for Non-Profit Corporations, Kean University–Gateway Institute for Regional Development, the University of Medicine and Dentistry of New Jersey, and Rowan University. Learning how to incorporate as a nonprofit entity, select board members, run board meetings—all of this is essential for small faith communities who provide neighborhood social services. Acquiring these skills builds capacity and strengthens their ability to apply for and implement grants from other sources.

It seems evident from the above that the New Jersey Office of Faith-Based Initiatives has, from the start, avoided some of the major criticisms leveled against the Bush administration's initiative. It insists there be no proselytization or sectarian teaching, and it mandates nondiscriminatory hiring in accordance with civil rights laws. It has built into its requirements onsite monitoring with both announced and unannounced visits. It has also been asked by the New Jersey Department of Human Services to assist people transitioning from welfare rolls to work.

Since its inception, the New Jersey faith-based initiative has allocated a total of $17.5 million to 142 groups. In addition, the annual conferences and training workshops conducted by the office should enable some of these faith-based groups to apply for the federal funding made available under President Bush's initiative.

PROFILES OF SOME FUNDING RECIPIENTS

The New Jersey Office of Faith-Based Initiatives announced its first round of grants in December 1998. A total of $3.6 million was distributed among thirty-seven faith-based organizations from across the state, funding a wide range of neighborhood revitalization and social service programs. The groups receiving funding were diverse and included Christian, Jewish, Muslim, and several interfaith organizations. The United Jewish Federation–MetroWest received a $150,000 grant to expand statewide programs that help senior citizens and others in need through services such as home-delivered meals and preventative health care. WARIS, a Muslim organization based in Irvington, New Jersey, received $150,000 to assist people making the transition from welfare to work by offering training in workplace literacy, computer skills, and job placement services. In Perth Amboy, Cathedral CDC Vision 2000 was awarded a $140,000 grant to expand its trackless trolley providing transportation to and from the city's downtown business district, to provide support services for the homeless, and to provide training for people coming off welfare.[58]

It is possible to get a better sense of the New Jersey Faith-Based Initiative through a more detailed description of three grant recipients, Isaiah House, New Community, and Shiloh Baptist Community Development Corporation.

Isaiah House, an interfaith group in East Orange, a largely black suburb of Newark, was one of the first recipients of a grant under the New Jersey policy. Isaiah House received $120,000 to expand programs to help people overcome substance abuse and find jobs. Groups accepted for funding in the first round of grants received funding at approximately the same level for a term of three years. In October 2001, Isaiah House received another grant of $75,000 for employment counseling and training for the hard to employ.

As a nonprofit agency for children and families, Isaiah House is community based and supported. The people who depend on Isaiah House are homeless, and many have HIV or AIDS. Since 1988, this organization has been the only shelter in the area that provides temporary lodging, food, social, and financial services for more than a hundred families a year. In addition to being an emergency shelter, Isaiah House provides a residence for teenage girls, a food pantry, prenatal outreach, childcare, and HIV services. Many clients are mothers with AIDS (who may soon die) and their children. Part of its initial grant from the Office of Faith-Based Initiatives was used to lease minivans for transportation to various clinical and educational service programs.[59]

New Community in Newark is the largest community development corporation in the United States, as well as New Jersey's largest nonprofit housing corporation. Founded in 1968 by the Rev. William J. Linder and a group of Newark residents, New Community was a direct response to the tragic Newark riots of July 1967. In the intervening thirty-four years, it has been a major contributor to urban revitalization in Newark, especially in the Central Ward, which was devastated by the 1967 disorders.

New Community owns and manages 3,000 units of affordable housing and employs 2,300 people (93 percent of whom are minorities). It operates eight different Babyland childcare centers, community-based health care programs, social services, job training, and education programs. In 1990, it persuaded Pathmark, a major supermarket chain in New Jersey, to move to Newark, thereby providing the first supermarket in Newark's Central Ward in twenty-five years. The shopping center created by Pathmark Supermarket's relocation has also attracted other franchises such as Dunkin' Donuts, Nathan's, a copy center, and a pharmacy. New Community also runs a job training and continuing education facility, a large welfare-to-work program, and community-based charter schools.

New Community's mission is "To help residents of inner cities improve the quality of their lives to reflect individual God-given dignity and personal achievement." In accordance with this mission, New Community focused on affordable and decent housing, opening its first housing development in 1975. They then sought to use the new housing to spur neighborhood revitalization and build a community. To promote interest and pride, they developed a process for community participation, actively involving residents in the design and management of new housing.

In 2000, the New Jersey Office of Faith-Based Initiatives awarded New Community Corporation a $75,000 grant for welfare-to-work services. New Community is a community development corporation with net assets of $3 million. Even so prosperous an enterprise as this, however, needs grants and funding from outside sources to carry on its many activities.[60]

Shiloh Baptist Community Development Corporation (CDC) is an affiliate of Shiloh Baptist Church in Port Norris and Vineland, New Jersey. These localities are in South Jersey in Cumberland and Salem counties. Shiloh Baptist CDC was one of the first recipients of grants from the Office of Faith-Based Initiatives, using funding of $218,250 over three years to provide job training and supportive services to juvenile high school dropouts and criminal offenders. Shiloh has established a Juvenile Readiness Center to provide people between the ages of sixteen and twenty-one with job training, computer training, and support toward the completion of their GEDs (high school equivalency education).

Shiloh also received a separate grant to help former welfare recipients locate a variety of supportive services available to help them make a successful transition into the work world. In July 2000, it was awarded a $75,000 grant for welfare to work services, and in June 2002, it received a second grant of $59,215 to continue this work.[61]

Of these three grant recipients, Isaiah House is an interfaith organization, Shiloh is an organization affiliated with a Baptist church, and New Community is a community development corporation led by a Catholic priest. These are three examples of the types of faith-based organizations funded by the New Jersey Office of Faith-Based Initiatives.

WHAT MAKES IT ALL WORK?

What is attractive about the New Jersey faith-based initiative? And what makes it work? There seem to be a number of interrelated factors. First, the programs are noncontroversial. Who can quarrel with government funding that provides minivans to the Jewish Community Center in Cherry Hill, New Jersey, to transport the elderly to shopping centers? Is it so awful that public funds supply minivans to Isaiah House in East Orange, New Jersey, a home for mothers with AIDS and their children? Perhaps the theoretical strictures about church-state separation take on less urgency when the practical operation of these programs is considered. The plain fact is that small, nonprofit organizations are desperate for funding to enable them to meet the needs of the poor and the dispossessed. Thus, other religious/private programs, like the Amachi Project in Philadelphia, are the kinds of practical services that government might be able to assist and that would seem to have the best chance of success at the national level.

Second, programs that make a difference are the ones that have the best chance of receiving government resources. It could be argued that, to the extent that assistance to faith-based neighborhood organizations helps build "social capital," this is all to the good. One recipient of a New Jersey faith-based grant emphasizes the positive, beneficial effect of the program. In particular she points to a lasting capacity improvement for these small nonprofits and church-related groups. "The net beneficial effect is not so much the grants themselves (these are important, to be sure, but they come and go) but the building of capacity to network and acquire the skills to manage such programs and to attract future funding. This is why the New Jersey Faith-Based Training Institute is so important."[62]

Third, programs that are innovative are needed in public/ private partnerships. Finding housing, feeding the poor, training for jobs, and taking care of those who cannot take care of themselves will always be the primary responsibilities of public and private social providers. However, encouraging the beneficiaries to take pride in themselves, to accept responsibility for their futures, and to empower them to take care of their families in new and different ways is what both state and federal and collaborative programs can do. Timothy Matovina, for example, has detailed the faith-based community organizations of Latino-Catholics, and points out that they are an outgrowth of a religious movement for social justice in America. He claims that "these organizations link 3,500 congregations plus 500 other institutions like public schools and labor union locals," thus bringing together between 1.5 and 2.5 million members in major urban areas and secondary cities across the nation.[63]

His point is that local groups, often in parishes, have given new meaning to religious activism by incorporating a larger commitment to family, church, and neighborhood. They have begun to engage in politics by playing critical roles after elections—planning the priorities of their communities and working for infrastructure improvements in their neighborhoods.

Fourth, faith-based programs work because they emphasize the personalism of projects and social services. It is important to realize that any government program must be based on that fact that an impersonal federal bureaucracy must work with neighborhoods and communities where people know and trust one another. As one New Jersey state official remarked, "This program works because these faith-based organizations are neighbors of the people they serve. They encourage self-sufficiency and self-improvement while giving people the support they need to improve their lives."[64]

Fifth, faith-based programs need committed individuals with the political will to make them happen. When Mayor Goldmsith left Indianapolis, hundreds of links to articles and speeches mentioning the Front Porch Alliance, as well as a description of its project, were removed from the city's website. The new mayor, Bart Peterson, inherited a program "too popular for him to discontinue but too closely associated with his predecessor to adopt as his own."[65] As a result, the project was moved out of the mayor's office, assigned a liaison, and had the number of its community workers cut. While the Front Porch Alliance has not been disbanded in Indianapolis, the new mayor has his own agenda. The same is true in New Jersey. The new governor, James McGreevy, has taken office during a time of fiscal difficulty. The Office of Community and Faith-Based Services has now been moved from the Office of Community Affairs to the Office of the Secretary of State. Its budget has been cut down to $3 million for the coming fiscal year, and its very existence might be challenged by the fact that a significant amount of money has been given to faith-based groups without any accountability or evaluation of the programs that have been put in place. Seed money, in short, yielded a small, and in some cases, a nonexistent financial crop, jeopardizing the continued nurturing of faith-based organizations that had originally applied for public funds. Financial exigencies could possibly bring further cuts or radical change in the way that the New Jersey faith-based initiative is funded and operates in the future. It is the kind of program that an embattled governor, who has no real ownership of the initiative, like New Jersey's McGreevy, will be able to cut with few political ramifications. On the other hand, insiders report that the McGreevy administration has plans to emulate the Bush initiative and apply for federal funds for the faith-based program to compensate for cutbacks in the state budget.

Sixth, faith-based programs need money to survive. As past studies have shown, faith-based groups, particularly African American churches, carry a large burden of the help that inner-city minorities receive. They cannot continue to do this job alone. Thus, the Compassion Capital Fund of the president's faith-based initiative was— and still is—a critical component to the success of public/private charitable programs. Matching funds to model initiatives, programs that teach grant writing, seed-money for innovative projects to small agencies—these must be in place in order to start and nurture efforts at making changes in the lives of those in need. Currently, the Bush administration has not provided any new funds for the faith-based initiative, although it has directed each of the cabinet agencies that have faith-based offices to make information available, on an equal basis, to secular and religious nonprofits who want to compete for government funds.

Seventh, public/private partnerships need dedicated collaborators. The faith-based initiative also needs corporate and foundation partners. One example is that of the Robert Wood Johnson (RWJ) Foundation. Recently, the philanthropic organization committed itself to provide $100 million for a "Faith in Action" initiative. It was designed to create 2,000 interfaith, volunteer, caregiving sites across America to help people with long-term health needs.[66] To this end, RWJ provides $35,000 in seed money to organizations that have 501(c)(3) status to help community-based agencies to provide long-term care to all those in need regardless of age, gender, race, religion, or sexual orientation. Reports of financial progress are required. This is a program designed to get faith-based organizations up and running. It is also the kind of a program that could serve as a conduit to screen programs for future federal assistance. These kinds of triangular projects between foundations and faith-based and federal organizations are models of what could be done with appropriate funding and accountability on a variety of levels and in a myriad of areas.

There has been little said about the New Jersey faith-based initiative and office that is negative. In this, the New Jersey case is rather unlike the controversial federal initiative of the Bush administration. But, it is still possible to conclude that the *objectives* of both are good. They seek to help those in need in a collaborative public/private way. They offer help at the local level and attempt to bring about financial and personal change. They pursue innovative ways to empower individuals and to help in capacity building. They provide personal help, often under emergency conditions. And they strengthen families and communities while recognizing that government, religious agencies, and individuals have a responsibility for the common good.

NOTES

1. Citation from "God and the Governor," *Charisma Magazine Interview*, 29 August 2000. <www.beliefnet.com>

2. "God and the Governor."

3. Interview of Steven Waldman, editor-in-chief of Beliefnet.com, with George W. Bush, October 2000. <www.beliefnet.com>

4. Texas Department of Community Services, "Philosophy," 24 January 2003 (last updated). <www.dhs.state.tx.us/about/mission>

5. Marvin Olasky, *Compassionate Conservatism* (New York: The Free Press, 2000), 8.

6. Steven Waldman, "Town Meeting," Columbia, South Carolina, 12 February 2000.

7. Olasky, *Compassionate Conservatism*, 9.

8. He is also a senior fellow at the Acton Institute and editor of *World*, a Christian weekly news magazine.

9. Olasky, *Compassionate Conservatism*, 4.

10. Marvin Olasky, *The Tragedy of American Compassion* (Washington, D.C.: Regnery, 1992), xv.

11. Olasky, *The Tragedy of American Compassion*, 113.

12. Olasky, *The Tragedy of American Compassion*, xii.

13. Myron Magnet, *The Dream and the Nightmare: The Sixties' Legacy to the Underclass* (New York: William Morrow and Company, 1993), 19.

14. Magnet, *The Dream and the Nightmare*, 38.

15. Dave McNeely, "The Book That Helped Shape Bush's Message," *Austin American-Statesman*, 27 January 1999, A11.

16. McNeely, "The Book That Helped Shape Bush's Message."

17. Myron Magnet, "What is Compassionate Conservatism?" *Wall Street Journal*, 5 February 1999, A14.

18. Magnet, *The Dream and the Nightmare*, 226–27.

19. Magnet, "What Is Compassionate Conservatism?" A14.

20. Alison Mitchell, "Bush Draws Campaign Theme from More Than 'the Heart,'" *New York Times*, 12 June 2000, A1.

21. Stephen Goldsmith, *The Twenty-First Century City: Resurrecting Urban America* (Washington, D.C.: Regnery, 1997), 7.

22. Goldsmith, *The Twenty-First Century City*, 7.

23. Goldsmith, *The Twenty-First Century City*, 9–10.

24. Goldsmith, *The Twenty-First Century City*, 181.

25. Goldsmith, *The Twenty-First Century City*, 181.

26. Goldsmith, *The Twenty-First Century City*, 184–89.

27. Crime Prevention Association of Michigan, *Program, Practice and Policy Brief*, Issue 9, April 2000. <www.preventcrime.net>

28. Crime Prevention Association of Michigan, *Program, Practice and Policy Brief.*

29. Terry M. Neal, "Midwestern Mayor Shapes Bush's Message," *Washington Post*, 5 June 100, A3.

30. Neal, "Midwestern Mayor Shapes Bush's Message," A3.

31. Neal, "Midwestern Mayor Shapes Bush's Message," A3.

32. John J. DiIulio Jr., "The Lord's Work: The Church and Civil Society," in *Community Works, the Revival of Civil Society in America*, ed. E. J. Dionne Jr. (Washington, D.C.: Brookings Institution, 1998), 51.

33. John DiIulio Jr., "Not By Faith Alone: Religion, Crime, and Substance Abuse," in *Sacred Places, Civic Purposes*, ed. E. J. Dionne and Ming Hsu Chen (Washington, D.C.: Brookings Institution, 2001), 83.

34. DiIulio, "The Lord's Work," 54.

35. John DiIulio Jr., "The Political Theory of Compassionate Conservatism," *Weekly Standard*, 23 August 1999, 10.

36. DiIulio, "The Political Theory of Compassionate Conservatism," 10.

37. For a fuller discussion of "proxy-government" see John DiIulio Jr., "Government-by-Proxy: A Faithful Overview" (unpublished paper). In it (page 2), he argues that all federal departments outsource many responsibilities resulting in the fact that there are six government-by-proxy employees for every one federal civil servant.

38. DiIulio, "The Political Theory," 10

39. See profiles of some of these individuals and an in-depth look at the kind of work they do in Jo Renee Formicola and Hubert Morken, eds. *Religious Leaders and Faith-Based Politics. Ten Profiles* (Lanham, Md.: Rowman & Littlefield, 2001).

40. Marvin Olasky, "In From the Cold," *World*, 10 February 2001, 20.

41. George W. Bush, "On the Creation of a White House Office for Faith-Based and Community Groups," *New York Times*, 30 January 2001, A18.

42. Bush, "On the Creation of a White House Office for Faith-Based and Community Groups," A18.

43. Bush, "On the Creation of a White House Office for Faith-Based and Community Groups," A18.

44. Bush, "On the Creation of a White House Office for Faith-Based and Community Groups," A18.

45. Speech of John DiIulio Jr. to the National Organization of Evangelicals on 7 March 2001 in Dallas, Texas. Herein referred to as the NAE speech.

46. John DiIulio Jr., "What Is Compassionate Conservatism?" *Weekly Standard*, 7 August, 2000, 33.

47. George W. Bush, "The Duty of Hope," Speech of Republican Presidential Candidate George W. Bush, Indianapolis, Indiana, 22 July 1999.

48. NAE Speech.

49. NAE Speech.

50. NAE Speech.

51. *"Ready, Willing and Able—Citizens Working for Change: A Survey for the Pew Partnerships for Change* (Philadelphia: The Pew Charitable Trust, 2001, Tables 42 and 43) as quoted by John DiIulio, in NAE Speech.

52. Ram A. Cnaan, "Keeping Faith in the City: How 401 Religious Congregations Service Their Neediest Neighbors," *Center for Research on Religion and Civil Society, CRRUCS Report* (2000–1), University of Pennsylvania, as quoted by John DiIulio in NAE speech.

53. New Jersey is a very small state in area. It ranks 46th among the states with a total area of 8,224 square miles. According to the 2000 census, the population per square mile of land is 1,134.2 persons. See U.S. Census Bureau, *Statistical Abstract of the United States: 2001*, 121st edition (Washington, D.C., 2001), 26–27. See also League of Women Voters of New Jersey, *New Jersey: Spotlight on Government* (Montclair, N.J.: League of Women Voters of New Jersey, 1969).

54. Debra L. Dodson and Laura D. Burnbauer, *Election 1989: The Abortion Issue in New Jersey and Virginia* (New Brunswick, N.J.: Eagleton Institute of Politics, Rutgers University, 1990), 7.

55. An indication of the state's diversity is the fact that *U.S. News & World Report* has named Rutgers University's campus in Newark the most diverse university in the nation for the last four consecutive years.

56. Barrie A. Peterson, "Working with the New Jersey Office of Faith-Based and Community Development Initiatives: A Case Study." Paper presented at the Annual Meeting of the Northeastern Political Science Association, Philadelphia, 18 November 2001, 2.

57. Presentation by El-Rhonda Williams Alston, Esq., Director, New Jersey Office of Faith-Based Initiatives, to Rutgers University class on Ethical Issues in Public Policy and Administration, 12 March 2002.

58. New Jersey Department of Consumer Affairs, *Annual Report 1998*. See www.state.nj.us/dca/98annual/aisle2.pdf.

59. See www.isaiahhouse.org. This description is also based on information provided by El-Rhonda Williams Alston, Executive Director of the New Jersey Office of Faith-Based Initiatives.

60. See www.newcommunity.org. Information about the New Community Corporation distributed by Monsignor William J. Linder at the Annual Meeting of the American Society for Public Administration held at Rutgers University in Newark, New Jersey, March 2001.

61. "State Awards Shiloh Baptist CDC $59,215 Faith-Based Grant." News Release, New Jersey Department of Community Affairs, 18 June 2002. Also, "Gov. Whitman Announces New Recipients of Faith-Based Community Development Grants." News release, New Jersey Department of Community Affairs, 27 July 2000. See www.state.nj.us/dca/news.

62. Confidential phone interview. Herein known as Confidential Interview "A," 2 August 2002.

63. Timothy Matovina, "Latino Catholics and American Public Life," in *Can Charitable Choice Work?* ed. Andrew Walsh (Hartford: Trinity College, 2001), 58.

64. Jane Kenney, Department of Consumer Affairs Commissioner. "Acting Governor Announces $2.5 Million for Faith-Based Groups," News release, 30 October 2001.

65. Linda Lutton, "Indy Builds a Front Porch, Gov. Bush Likes the View: City Hall Change Makes a Shaky Porch," *Youth Today*, May 2000, 33.

66. Dr. Burton v. Reifler, "Faith in Action," letter from the director of the program. <www.FIAVolunteers.org>

2

The Bad in the Faith-Based Initiative

Paul Weber

Chapter 1 has shown the idealism and good intentions of most of those involved in the faith-based initiative, including President Bush. One has to be impressed that so many conservatives were determined to do better than previous administrations in bringing relief to people in need. But as the idea of compassionate conservatism matured, and as the Bush administration struggled to put public/private partnerships on the policy agenda, real problems and seemingly insurmountable divisions appeared. Perhaps this chapter, following a chapter on "the good," ought to be titled, "But Don't Hold Your Breath." It analyzes a number of constitutional and legal problems that plague faith-based initiatives. It takes a hard look at whether it is wise policy to change, in a fundamental way, a longstanding tradition in America—separation of church and state. Finally, it questions whether or not the financial and philosophical assumptions and expectations of faith-based initiatives are realistic. In short, it takes a kind of Murphy's Law look to see what will likely go wrong.

The authors have long been students of American law, American history, and indeed of human nature. So, while they can see promising results, they can also see the dangers and uncertainties in the faith-based initiative. These are considerable. There is serious danger of undoing decades of progress in constitutional law—coming to a consensus on the meaning of the Establishment Clause, the range and limits of free speech, and ending employment discrimination. There is a danger of undermining one of the great arrangements America has modeled for the world: separation of church and state. There is the danger to religious institutions themselves as expectations for saving taxpayers money, providing effective social services, and ending fraud prove to be illusory. That realization will trigger resentments and antagonism against religion.[1] And, finally, there are questions about the philosophical assumptions of the faith-based initiative. Will the rhetoric of compassionate conservatism belie the reality of government abdicating to religious and other voluntary organizations its responsibilities for those in need? The Bush administration has exhibited a consistent pattern of paying more attention to cutting taxes than to funding social services, a pattern that continues in the proposed 2004 budget.[2] This author is fearful that faith-based initiatives, despite the good intentions of many of their proponents, are a significant step toward undoing the safety net established in the New Deal. That would be bad!

For the sake of clarity this chapter has been divided into four parts: Constitutional and Legal Problems; Rejecting the Lessons of History?; Financial Pitfalls and Illusions; and Philosophical Problems and Differences.

CONSTITUTIONAL AND LEGAL PROBLEMS

The purpose of his faith-based initiative, President Bush reports, is to "level the playing field" between religious and nonreligious social service providers.[3] Religious social service providers have a long and successful history of applying for and receiving government funding. The new approach, however, is designed to broaden the pool of potential providers by removing barriers to participation by religious organizations that have traditionally not participated. The barriers to participation of faith-based groups are essentially the four basic parameters within which they must function, namely (1) refrain from direct or indirect proselytizing; (2) provide service to their clients without respect to religious affiliation; (3) keep religious and government grant funds separate, with the latter spent only according to government mandated procedures and subject to audit; and (4) compliance with other generally applicable laws against discrimination in hiring or service based on race, religion, color, age, gender, or national origin.[4]

The use of a playing field analogy is most apt. Playing fields are used for competitive contests resulting in winners and losers. Faith-based initiatives will lead to competition between religious groups hoping to obtain government funding, between mainstream and "marginal" groups, and between groups with competing views of what the constitution requires and allows. There is one major difference between sports teams competing, even on a level playing field, and religious groups seeking government funds—the former play games and the latter provide services. For sports teams, losses are temporary and have little significance in the larger scheme of things. Battles between faith groups can have long-term social consequences. Constitutional disputes can be equally unsettling and divisive. This section focuses on constitutional and legal questions, specifically the Establishment Clause questions, free exercise clause issues, free speech issues, and employment discrimination dangers.

The Establishment Clause Challenge

To put the first question bluntly: Do faith-based initiatives violate the Establishment Clause? The answer is a cloudy "it depends." The Establishment Clause reads, "Congress shall make no law respecting an establishment of religion. . . ." There are two probable areas for conflict: preferring some religious groups to others, and coercing religious exposure or participation on needy but uninterested clients.[5] It is important to look at each in turn.

1. *Unequal religious preferences.* When most people think of funding religious groups, they think of Baptists, Catholics, Methodists, and Presbyterians—the large, familiar, traditional religions in the United States. Support drops off sharply when there is a possibility of funding nonmainstream religious groups such as the Scientologists, the Nation of Islam, the Unification Church, Hare Krishna, Wicca, and the like.[6]

According to a Pew survey, 69 percent of American voters supported funding charitable religious organizations as a general principle, but only 62 percent supported funding Catholic Churches, 52 percent supported evangelical Christian Churches, 51 percent supported Mormon Churches, and 38 percent supported funding Muslim Mosques and Buddhist Temples.[7] And this survey was taken prior to September 11! More than half opposed funding the Nation of Islam or the Church of Scientology. Indeed, President Bush has said that he does not "see how we can allow public dollars to fund programs where spite and hate is the core of the message."[8] The president was referring to the Nation of Islam, an organization widely perceived as being anti-Semitic. At the very least, there will be political pressure to discriminate against groups that are more controversial.

Obviously, any legislatively mandated discrimination against unpopular religious groups would be unconstitutional on its face, but will there be more subtle discrimination? Two hypothetical situations illustrate the problem. Envision a group such as the Freedom from Religion Foundation (an atheist group) applying for grants to fund an alcohol and drug counseling center and being denied. Or imagine there is an application from the Nation of Islam, which has a long record of community service. If the Freedom from Religion Foundation or the Nation of Islam's grant applications were turned down, would it be because of the quality of their applications or their identities? The truth almost does not matter. Any number of lawyers would be happy to sue to find out.

2. *Coercing religious exposure or participation.* As was pointed out in chapter 1, under the original plan, secular alternatives are to be provided for client recipients who are not interested in religiously provided social services.[9] Like the now-discredited "separate but equal" doctrine, this sounds acceptable in theory, but utterly unrealistic. At the very least, this requirement will require a duplication of services. Duplication may not be an issue in densely populated urban areas where there are often more people in need of social services than can be

accommodated by a single provider, but in rural, sparsely populated areas of the country alternative services may well be in distant towns.

As Elbert Lin and his collaborators point out, there are three problems with the secular alternative approach.[10] First, people who wish to have nonreligious services have to make a specific request. That is not likely when the clients are poor, hungry, homeless, handicapped, or mentally distressed. Second, alternative services will most likely be at some distance. At the very least, this will be inconvenient. More likely, especially in rural areas, it will be impossible. Poor clients often do not have the transportation available to exercise such options. Third, religion here is treated as a general category. The alternatives are religious or secular services. One can easily envision a scenario in which a Muslim in need will request a Muslim provider rather than a Christian, Jewish, or secular one. Certainly, in areas of the country, many Protestants in need would find it repugnant to utilize Catholic services. Jews may be particularly reluctant to avail themselves of services offered by Protestant groups. The following example shows why. "Teen Challenge, a Christian group devoted to treating alcoholism, is seeking federal funding, but is unwilling or unable to 'disassociate their religion-teaching mission from the provision of the social services for which they are receiving government funds.' Alarmed observers noted that Teen Challenge based their assessment of Jewish patients' success on their willingness to convert to Christianity—Jewish beneficiaries were labeled either 'uncompleted' or 'completed' Jews based on whether they had fully converted."[11]

What makes these matters problematic is that most Americans (including the authors) believe that religion has the power to change lives, whether to turn a person away from a career in crime or to overcome alcohol and drug abuse problems. But does using religion to solve social problems at taxpayer expense violate the Establishment Clause?

In the absence of legal challenges to specific laws and actual practices of organizations receiving and expending federal funds, it is too early to state whether and how faith-based initiatives might violate the Establishment Clause. The best one can do is look at Supreme Court precedents in past cases, look for principles and analogies, then make predictions. While this is a step up from reading entrails and consulting soothsayers, it still leads even the experts to conflicting conclusions.[12] That, of course, is one of the faults of faith-based initiatives: these will be highly divisive and will open a new arena for legal challenges. Nonetheless, relevant precedents can show how the courts might decide the issue of preferring some religious social service providers to others and the problem of coercion.

Certainly, the most relevant precedent will be *Bowen v. Kendrick*,[13] a 1988 case that tested the constitutionality of the Adolescent Family Life Act. It is precisely the kind of social service legislation that likely will be tested under the faith-based initiatives. The Family Life Act provided grants to public and nonprofit organizations for programs to limit or discourage premarital adolescent sexual relations and pregnancy. Kendrick alleged that some organizations with ties to religious denominations received grant money in violation of the Establishment Clause. The Supreme Court held that preventing adolescent pregnancies is a valid secular purpose of the legislation. Thus, it allowed religious organizations, along with a wide variety of other groups, to receive grants without regard to whether or not any of the groups is religious or secular. This participation as one among many does not improperly advance religion or cause excessive entanglement. The Supreme Court applied a neutrality rule and found the Adolescent Family Life Act constitutional at face value. However, it did remand the case to determine whether specific grants violated the Establishment Clause by funding "specifically religious activities in an otherwise substantially secular setting."[14] The implication, of course, is that funding specifically religious activities, even those designed to achieve secular ends, would be unconstitutional. *Bowen* supports neutrality—that is, treating religious social service providers on the same basis as nonreligious providers. Under the Bowen rule, it would violate the Establishment Clause if religious organizations are preferred over secular groups (a kind of religious affirmative action President Bush sometimes seems to prefer), or if some religious groups are preferred over others in reception of grants. The Supreme Court would also rule an initiative unconstitutional if there is evidence of providers coercing clients.

A second line of cases, those dealing with aid to sectarian schools, has provided much of the development of Establishment Clause jurisprudence. Since aid to schools is very similar in some respects to aid for social services, the school aid cases also provide some insight into how the courts may decide faith-based initiative cases. Contrary to much of the rhetoric of both the proponents and opponents of faith-based initiatives, the Supreme Court has only rarely taken a strict separation stance in relation to religion. As will be shown more fully in the next section, the court has focused on government neutrality. The basic principle of neutrality was articulated as a three-pronged test in *Kurtzman v. Lemon*:[15] namely, that aid must have a secular purpose, have effects that neither promote nor hinder religion, and not cause excessive entanglement. In a subsequent case, *Agostini v. Felton*, the Supreme Court modified its "Lemon test."[16] It left the secular purpose prong intact, but in determining whether or not a government program advances religion, poses three questions: (1) Does the program result in government indoctrination? (2) Does the program define its recipients with respect to religion? (3) Does the program create excessive entanglements? This more sophisticated set of rules is sometimes referred to as part of "the new neutrality." If the government program does any of these three it is considered to be advancing religion and will be held unconstitutional. Finally, the court considerably relaxed *Lemon*'s "excessive entanglement" prong by throwing out the need for pervasive monitoring of government-funded activities, even activities in sectarian settings. Such rules may seem like nitpicking to the nonexpert, but the court has been struggling to find ways for governments to support services offered by religious organizations while not discriminating for or against them. No mean task

Specifically, the Supreme Court let it be known that aid given by governments to eligible recipients through some process such as issuing vouchers (checks that can only be "cashed" at approved schools), and then "cashed" at the sectarian schools chosen by the recipients, does not advance religion. Nor do these private choices cause entanglement. Thus, argued the court, vouchers do not violate the Establishment Clause. This part of the new neutrality view of the Establishment Clause was expanded in a subsequent case, *Mitchell v. Helms.*[17] In *Mitchell* the court upheld a program that provided substantial loans of public school educational materials to private schools. The majority, a plurality of four plus Justice O'Connor, who wrote a concurring opinion, ruled that if aid is offered to a broad range of recipients without concern for their religious affiliation, it maintains neutrality and there is no taint of government indoctrination of religious beliefs. If recipients had been defined by religion, this would have created a financial incentive to choose a sectarian over a public education and would thus be "endorsement." This court would have held to be unconstitutional. Interestingly, the plurality would have approved a plan that allowed direct funding to go to religious institutions on a per-recipient basis (i.e., depending simply on the number of students enrolled). Justice O'Connor disagreed.

Justice O'Connor has consistently been the fifth vote among the nine justices. As the critical swing vote, she has been called the most powerful woman in America. What she writes is taken seriously by other justices. In fact, her opinions on religious topics tend to set precedents for the court. She had written the *Agostini* opinion and concurred in *Mitchell* to emphasize a second element of the new neutrality, i.e., that any aid going from government to sectarian institutions must be the result of "true individual choice" of aid recipients. Aid must go first to participants and be submitted by them to secular or sectarian providers as participants might choose. This requirement will certainly have a major impact if the court requires that it be integral to faith-based initiatives. Constitutionality would depend on how the social services delivery plan is structured.

The Supreme Court's 2002 decision in *Zelman v. Simmons-Harris* further solidifies the new neutrality.[18] The majority supported the Cleveland school district's use of educational vouchers to allow pupils in failing public schools to choose to attend private religious or nonreligious schools, attend public schools in neighboring districts, or receive tutorial assistance if they remained in the public schools. A 5–4 majority decided the case and Justice Rehnquist wrote the majority opinion. However, once again, Justice O'Connor's concurring opinion provides the strongest evidence yet as to what a likely standard will be in case a faith-based initiative challenge comes before the court:

> Courts are instructed to consider two factors: first, whether the program administers aid in a neutral fashion, without differentiation based on the religious status of beneficiaries or providers of services; second, and more importantly, whether beneficiaries of indirect aid have a genuine choice among religious and nonreligious organizations when determining the organization to which they will direct that aid. If the answer to either query is "no," the program should be struck down under the Establishment Clause.[19]

So, will faith-based initiatives pass Establishment Clause muster? Possibly, but they will require careful structuring of aid programs to ensure that some religious groups are not chosen over others, and that religious groups are not chosen over nonreligious groups in such a way as to constitute endorsement or preference. Also they must be structured and run so that there is no coercion or enticement through the use of financial incentives. Aid recipients must have a genuine choice in selecting between religious and nonreligious social service providers. This is what Justice O'Connor would require, and she casts the deciding vote on the current court.

The Freedom of Speech Challenge

At first glance, it might not seem that faith-based initiatives would raise free speech issues, but indeed they do. As one commentator has observed, ". . . groups barred from government funding due explicitly to their belief that proselytizing is necessary might bring allegations of free speech violations. . . . The exclusion of funding to some religious groups because their service programs involve proselytizing implies the Free Speech Clause.[20] President Bush and the first director of the Office of Faith-Based Initiatives both promised that proselytizers would not be funded, but making that distinction will not be easy.

Perhaps it is free speech rather than establishment that will be more troubling for faith-based initiatives. Paying tax dollars to religious organizations to provide social services leads to one set of problems. But what if *religion itself* is the social service? This is not a hypothetical question. We know that for some people and some problems religion "works." There are countless stories of prisoners who turned their lives around when they "found Jesus Christ," or were inspired by the Prophet Mohammed. One might go so far as to say that *evangelization as social service* was at the core of early Methodism, a religion that began in the slums of London. Methodism succeeded because its religious message led people out of alcoholism, poverty, and related problems. Professor David Kuo asserts that "Overwhelming evidence suggest that faith is not only important, it may be *the* deciding factor in determining whether an at-risk child, a welfare mother, or a convicted criminal is able to turn his or her life around."[21]

Evangelization is speech, religious to be sure, but speech nonetheless, and therefore protected by the Free Speech Clause of the First Amendment. The question then becomes, if religious speech (evangelization) works as well as, or better than, other approaches to problems such as alcoholism, teen promiscuity, convict recidivism, and the like, why can it not be funded along with the other approaches? The answer that comes most immediately to mind is that direct funding of religious speech violates the Establishment Clause. Protecting the right to speech is one thing; funding it is quite a different matter. But does this distinction not rest on a violation of the Free Speech Clause because in funding it discriminates against one viewpoint—that religion saves (occasionally seen on billboards as "Jesus Saves")?

This is a complex issue and Supreme Court precedents do not provide a clear answer. In fact, the decisions in *Rust v. Sullivan* and *Rosenberger v. Rector and Visitors of the University of Virginia* point in two directions. If the court follows its decision in *Rust v. Sullivan*[22] it will allow governments to discriminate between social service providers based on the message they deliver—for example, fund providers that teach sexual abstinence and not those that teach how to use condoms. In *Rust* the court ruled that "the government can, without violating the Constitution, selectively fund a program to encourage certain activities it believes to be in the public interest, without at the same time funding an alternative program which seeks to deal with the problem in another way."[23] The reasoning is that a government-funded program can turn agencies that voluntarily accept the grants knowing the conditions attached to the grants, into "public functionaries" that convey the government's message.[24] Therefore, if the court follows the *Rust* precedent, it will uphold discrimination against religious speech. Indeed, it may need to do so in order to avoid the endorsement message, as required by Justice O'Connor in her *Mitchell v. Helms* concurrence.[25] O'Connor's point was that government action cannot even appear to endorse one religion over others.

If, on the other hand, the Supreme Court follows its ruling in *Rosenberger v. Rector and Visitors of the University of Virginia*[26] it may decide that faith-based grants create a kind of limited public forum. The phrase is meant to convey the idea of government supporting an area, something like a small park, where all sorts of speakers can participate and speak their minds. In limited public forums, viewpoint discrimination is not constitutionally permissible. In *Rosenberger* the court confronted a situation at the University of Virginia where the Student Activities Fund paid for publication of all student newspapers and newsletters except for religious ones. The court held that since the fund established a limited public forum (limited in that funding was available only to student organizations), student religious speech had to be funded along with the rest. *Rosenberger* followed the precedent in *Lamb's Chapel v. Center Moriches Union Free School District.*[27] There the court ruled that "to permit school property to be used for the presentation of all views about family issues and childrearing except those dealing with the subject matter from a religious standpoint" is viewpoint discriminatory.[28] A critical question, then, is: Do faith-based initiatives create a limited public forum? Our answer is, probably not. In both *Lamb's Chapel* and *Rosenberger* all who wanted to participate were given the resources to do so— payment for publication in one case, and facilities to meet in the other. With faith-based initiatives many groups are eligible to apply for funding but only a very few will be awarded grants. Choices must be made.

The free speech issue presents a cruel dilemma. Government can either fund some religious social service providers, but not those for whom religion itself is the social service, thus leaving the playing field still not level; or it can fund religious speech and provide a message of endorsement, thus violating the Establishment Clause.

The Employment Discrimination Challenge

One of the most notable American achievements during the second half of the twentieth century was the near elimination of legal employment discrimination. Three remarkable pieces of legislation attempted to make equality of opportunity a reality. Title VII of the Civil Rights Act of 1964,[29] the Age Discrimination in Employment Act of 1967,[30] and the Americans with Disabilities Act of 1990[31] together prohibit discrimination in hiring or termination on the basis of race, color, national origin, religion, sex, age, and disability.

However, there are two exemptions to these broad laws. The first, written into Title VII by Congress, exempts religious employers from the ban on religious discrimination. Originally this exemption applied only to persons in clerical or religious ministry positions (basically priests, ministers, rabbis, and nuns) but was expanded by Congress in 1972 to include all employees. It basically means that Methodists can hire only Methodists, Baptists only Baptists, Jews only Jews, and so forth.

The second exemption, usually referred to as the ministerial exemption, is a judicially created right of churches to be autonomous in making internal decisions "in matters of discipline, faith, internal organization, or ecclesiastical rule, custom, or law."[32] This exemption, which protects religious organizations from judicial interference, can be traced back to the 1871 *Watson v. Jones* case.[33] The ministerial exemption has two objectives: to protect the free exercise rights of religious groups to make decisions based on their own beliefs and governing structures and to take judges out of the business of making decisions about theological matters.

While both exemptions make sense within the context of internal church governance,[34] taken together they present a serious challenge in the context of faith-based initiatives. They open the door for religious groups—and no one else—to discriminate against people on any basis they want with impunity and still be beyond the reach of the law. Yet the ministerial exemption to employment discrimination may be the more troubling of the two because it is created by the judiciary and therefore is not so easily changed as the exemption created by Congress. As one commentator has pointed out, "the scope of the ministerial exception to Title VII is both broader and narrower than the statutory exemption. It is broader because it shields religious employers from race, color, national origin, sex, age, and disability challenges; it is narrower because it applies only to ministerial positions, whereas the Title VII exemption applies to *all* employees of religious organizations."[35] Since there are numerous religious groups that consider all who administer their programs to be "ministers," one can see trouble coming.

A key factor to consider in Charitable Choice is the fact of funding by federal, state, and local governments of faith-based initiatives. How much does that change the Title VII and ministerial exemptions that allow employment discrimination? While President Bush has promised that religious organizations receiving federal funds would be prohibited from employment discrimination, the reality is far less clear in light of Supreme Court precedents and Congressional intent. The Supreme Court has upheld the Title VII exemption in *Corporation of Presiding Bishop v. Amos.*[36] This case involved the Church of Jesus Christ of Latter Day Saints that was allowed to fire two employees who held what might be reasonably termed secular jobs. One was a personnel employee at a church-owned clothing factory and the other a building engineer at a church-owned gym. These individuals were terminated because they did not meet the "worthiness requirements" for full membership in the Mormon Church. The court essentially ruled that if Congress wanted to protect the free exercise rights of the church, but not those of the two employees, it could do so since it was the church, rather than the government, which made the employees choose between their jobs and their religious practices.[37] In other words, government cannot discriminate, but if churches do so, it is acceptable. What is not known yet is the impact of government funding. How would the court rule if that clothing factory or gym happened to be funded by some government agencies? *Amos* does not address this issue, but it is of critical importance to faith-based initiatives.

The Supreme Court also rejected an equal protection challenge in this case because the right to discriminate under Title VII
is available to all religions. It is "rationally related to the legitimate
purpose of alleviating significant governmental interference with
the ability of religious organizations to define and carry out their
religious missions."[38] The net result is not a level playing field, but
a privileged position for religious groups to discriminate in their
hiring, a privilege not available to other groups. This is not neutrality; it is accommodation (a difference that will be discussed at
length in the next section). It is possible that courts will reject this
implication if presented with appropriate cases, as they surely will,
but the unanimous decision in *Amos* does not bode well for those
who think discrimination ought to be strictly limited to clergy positions.

Congressional intent is also unclear in the text and the expressed
intent of Charitable Choice legislation about how far discrimination
can go. Subsection (e) of the Charitable Choice Act states that "A religious organization's exemption provided under [Title VII] . . .
regarding employment practices shall not be affected by its participation in, or receipt of funds from programs described in subsection
(c)(4) [Charitable Choice programs]." But the next sentence reads,
"Nothing in this section alters the duty of a religious organization to
comply with the nondiscrimination provisions of Title VII . . . in the
use of funds from [Charitable Choice] programs."[39] It is not surprising that subsection (e) has led to differing interpretations. As a writer
reports in *The Harvard Civil Rights–Civil Liberties Review*:

> At the markup, for example, Representative Weiner asserted that
> because "we're extending Federal dollars for this nongovernment
> program operating under a religious umbrella . . . for those pur-
> poses, you can't discriminate based on religion." Similarly, Repre-
> sentative Watts interpreted the second sentence as limiting the
> Title VII exemption to recipients' activities not related to chari-
> table choice, whereas "in the use of Federal funds we will not tol-
> erate discrimination." In contrast, Chairman Sensenbrenner
> stated that the Charitable Choice Act enables religious recipients
> to engage in religious employment discrimination in both their
> independent and federally funded activities.

The Judiciary Committee adopted Chairman Sensenbrenner's interpretation in its report to the House floor. The report indicates that subsection (e) of the Charitable Choice Act permits religious recipients to engage in employment discrimination based on religion, but not on any other legislatively proscribed basis. Therefore, as it appears now, the Charitable Choice Act combines with Title VII to permit religious employers to engage in religious discrimination with regard to any employment decision, irrespective of both the religious character of the activity and the activity's source of funding.[40]

It would be bitter irony, indeed, if legislation touted as creating a level playing field provided a wedge to reintroduce discrimination. It would be doubly ironic if such an injustice swept in under the cloak of religion. At the very least, the nation can expect numerous lawsuits to sort out the limits and parameters of employment discrimination by religious organizations receiving federal funds.

REJECTING THE LESSONS OF HISTORY?

Is separation of church and state still important? The idea of transferring tax revenue to religious organizations is not new. Nor is the idea of utilizing the outreach abilities of religious organizations to address social problems a fresh one. In fact, American history provides both precedents and lessons we would be wise to learn. But before recounting that history, the first questions to be asked are: Is separation of church and state all that important? Is separation an eighteenth-century idea that is no longer needed, and a doctrine that creates a barrier to an effective partnership between government and religion as they strive to solve social problems?

This book argues that separation of church and state, properly understood, is as important now as it has ever been in human history. Religions and governments are two of the most powerful human institutions to have ever been created. They trigger motivations deeply rooted in the human psyche. What else can motivate large numbers of people to deliberately sacrifice their very lives as in suicide bombings and terrorist attacks on innocent civilians? Because each is powerful in a different way, each is tempted to use the other to help accomplish its goals.

One difficulty is that religion and governments have different goals (except in theocracies), and utilize different means, but command the loyalty and affection of the same people. Although stated in different ways, the goals of governments are oriented to this world—security, order, protecting social and cultural identity, and promoting economic prosperity. The goals of religion, generally speaking, are to honor God, seek truth, secure eternal salvation for its members, sustain and pass on the faith (for some religions through evangelization), and to promote a particular moral code, often denoted as seeking justice. Likewise, the means used are different. Governments use their perceived legitimacy to entice voluntary compliance with laws—and physical coercion when necessary—to force involuntary compliance. Democratic governments function largely through negotiation and compromise. For the most part, religions no longer have armies and compromises do not come easily to believers. [James O'Sullivan, a career diplomat and subsequent professor at the University of Louisville, was wont to say, "Those who speak directly to God are seldom prone to compromise."] As Kevin Boyle and Juliet Sheen have pointed out in a report on religious freedom, "The inclination of religions to view themselves as the sole guardians of truth can tempt them to intolerance and to fight against whatever [each] defines as deviant, either within [their] own faith or at the boundaries."[41] Among far too many extremists violence is an acceptable, indeed a required means of following God's will.[42] Yet compromises are the heart of democracy. The next chapter on "the ugly" will illustrate this problem among the various constituencies in the Bush administration.

Governments are tempted to use religions to support their own legitimacy and, often with the best of intentions, to utilize the moral authority and outreach of religions to solve social problems. Religions are such valuable props that governments are often willing to support them with privileged positions, financial inducements, and—far too often—the use of force. Lacking armies, religions are tempted to use governments for their own protection and to promote their missions. As history has shown, sometimes religions accept the violence of governments as means to religious ends.

Such mutual support breaks down when governments coerce religious belief or practice, particularly in nations such as the United States that have a plurality of religions. Because each is so powerful in its own way, the collusion of government and religion can be oppressive and violent to those who do not agree with their agendas. As Barrett Rubin has noted, the melding of religion and politics can become lethal when religious organizations "sacrelize" conflicts of identity, power, territory, and assets.[43] Likewise, the clashes between religious believers, with the support of government power on one or both sides, can be extraordinarily violent. Yet religion and government cannot ignore each other because they command the loyalty and affection of the same citizens. Therefore the historical attempt to develop a workable separation has been long and arduous. It has largely been worked out in the United States. This is a story well worth celebrating.[44]

In order to address some of the major issues raised in the discussion of faith-based initiatives this next section is divided into four parts, roughly following an historical development: Taxing for Religion: The Battle in Virginia; Our First Amendment: What Did the Founders Intend?; Developing the Idea of Separation; and Undermining the Idea of Separation.

Taxing for Religion: The Battle in Virginia

At the end of the Revolutionary War, most of the states found themselves with numerous social problems. Crime rates were unacceptably high, many veterans were unemployed, some actually taking up banditry, an alarming number of farmers were over their heads in debt, and there was great uncertainty, including occasional violence, over the ownership of land that had been abandoned by Loyalists. In Virginia, matters were made worse by the wholesale departure of Anglican ministers for England and Canada. A majority of ministers had opposed the Revolution. Now many felt alienated, unwelcome, and in fear for their own economic survival since the newly independent state of Virginia had suspended payment of their salaries in 1776. They had families to feed. No wonder they fled.

A number of eminent leaders, including George Washington, John Marshall, and Patrick Henry, saw an urgent need to reestablish a more stable social order. There were no public schools, of course. Private tutors could educate the landed elites but there were very few venues by which to teach and instill moral principles in those who needed it most. Realistically, there was only one choice. The churches were the only institutions in regular contact with the very poor and those in need. Washington, Marshall, and Henry fervently believed they needed the help of religious leaders. Therefore, in 1784 Patrick Henry sponsored a bill in the Virginia House of Burgess entitled "A Bill Establishing a Provision for Teachers of the Christian Religion." The language of the bill is instructive:

> WHEREAS the general diffusion of Christian knowledge hath a natural tendency to correct the morals of men, restrain their vices, and preserve the peace of society, which cannot be effected without a competent provision for learned teachers, who may be thereby enabled to devote their time and attention to their duty of instructing such citizens, as from their circumstances and want of education, cannot otherwise attain such knowledge; and it is judged that such provision may be made by the Legislature, without counteracting the liberal principle heretofore adopted and intended to be preserved by abolishing all distinctions of preeminence amongst the different societies or communities of Christians;

> Be it therefore enacted by the General Assembly, That for the support of Christian teachers, _____per centum on the amount, or _____in the pound on the amount, or _____in the pound on the sum payable for tax on the property within this Commonwealth, is hereby assessed, and shall be paid by every person chargeable with the said tax at the time the same shall be due; . . .

> And be it enacted, That for every sum so paid, the Sheriff or Collector shall give a receipt, expressing therein to what society of Christians the person from whom he may receive the same shall direct the money to be paid, keeping a distinct account thereof in his books. . . .

And be it further enacted, That the money to be raised by virtue of this act, shall be by the Vestries, Elders, or Directors of each religious society, appropriated to a provision for a Minister or Teacher of the Gospel of their denomination, or the providing places of divine worship, and to none other use whatsoever, except in the denominations of Quakers and Menonists, who may receive what is collected from their members, and place it in their general fund, to be disposed of in a manner which they shall think best calculated to promote their particular mode of worship. . . . [45]

Henry's Bill was intended to be radically progressive and fair—that is, every taxpayer was to be treated equally, and each taxpayer could determine where his contribution was to go. If the taxpayer made no specific designation the money was to go to the state's general fund, no questions asked. Yet it was this bill that sparked the writing of one of America's political classics, James Madison's *Memorial and Remonstrance*.[46] It also led to the Virginia legislature's enactment of another American political classic, Thomas Jefferson's *Bill for Establishing Religious Liberty*.[47]

It is valuable to reflect on these documents, and the history of the idea of separation of church and state, because there are remarkable parallels between the issues confronting the United States at the beginning of the twenty-first century and those confronting the Founding Fathers at the end of the eighteenth century. Henry, Washington, Marshall, and like-minded leaders sincerely believed that unemployment, indolence, substance abuse, homelessness, and weakened family structure resulted in large part from a lack of moral education of the general populace. In light of these problems, it is instructive to review Madison and Jefferson's arguments against the bill to support teachers of the Christian religion.

Madison had several objections to the tax bill, fifteen to be precise, but for purposes of this study they can be summarized in four points. First, he argued that raising tax-funded money and giving it to religions is a dangerous abuse of power because religion is not a part of the social contract that establishes the legitimacy of government, and thus not a fit subject for legislation. One may argue, of course, that the modern context is different, that faith-based initiatives do not attempt to establish Christianity to the exclusion of other religions. This misses the point of Madison's objection. Faith-based initiatives decidedly do give preference to faith-based organizations over secular ones. This is no secret. The argument is that this is an effort to "level the playing field," but the field has been level for some time. Religious groups have long been able to apply for and receive funding on an equal basis with secular organizations *in order to provide secular services*.[48] What was required of religious organizations before the new faith-based initiatives was that they apply for funding on an equal footing with other organizations and refrain from imposing religious constraints on the people whom they employ or proselytizing their clients. It is these limitations that are at issue, not whether religious organizations may have access to government funding on a "purchase of services" basis. Without the limitations, governments would be using tax dollars for religious purposes, precisely what Patrick Henry was proposing and Madison opposing.

Second, Madison argues that religion does not need the support of government; that it has flourished best in periods when it did not have the support of human laws, even "in spite of every opposition from them." Indeed, aid is a "contradiction to the Christian Religion itself, for every page of it disavows a dependence on the powers of this world." Further, he argues that state aid will weaken the appeal of religion both among its adherents and its opponents. This is because this aid will "weaken in those who profess this Religion a pious confidence in its innate excellence and the patronage of its Author; and to foster in those who still reject it, a suspicion that its friends are too conscious of its fallacies to trust it to its own merits." Madison goes on to argue that religious establishments (that is, religions supported by governments), even the watered down, generalized support proposed by Henry, have the inevitable tendency to corrupt religion. What have been the fruits of establishment? Madison minces no words: "More or less in all places, pride and indolence in the Clergy, ignorance and servility in the laity, in both, superstition, bigotry and persecution." Hardly what religions hope to accomplish with government funding.

Third, Madison argued the government does not need to utilize religion to perform its proper duties. In fact, he argues, too close an alliance of government and religion works to undermine the legitimacy of both: "In some instances it can be seen to erect a spiritual tyranny on the ruins of the Civil authority; in many instances they have been seen upholding the thrones of political tyranny; in no instance have they been seen the guardians of the liberties of the people. Rulers who wished to subvert the public liberty, may have found an established Clergy convenient auxiliaries." Madison may well have been thinking of the Anglican clergy before the Revolution, most of whom supported the status quo under British rule. The point most relevant in the current situation is that clergy receiving government funding will be far less inclined to question government policies, even when they find those policies harmful or even immoral. Government-funded churches will rarely be prophetic churches.

Finally, according to Madison, providing tax funds for religious organizations will "destroy that moderation and harmony which the forbearance of our laws to intermeddle with Religion has produced among its several sects." Madison's general argument in the *Memorial and Remonstrance* is for equality, and providing tax funds to some groups and not others will destroy trust and cooperation among the various sects.[49] It is not unreasonable to expect increased competition among churches competing for funds under the new faith-based initiatives. Is there a lesson here for religious organizations in the twenty-first century? Unless there is a major infusion of money, religions will be competing with one another for scarce public funding. Not a recipe for cooperation.

The *Memorial and Remonstrance* provided a powerful instrument for turning public sentiment against the assessment bill. But taking no chances, Madison and Jefferson worked to promote Patrick Henry for governor of Virginia, thus taking him out of a leadership role in the Virginia legislature and undermining his ability to guide the assessment bill. The net result was that the assessment bill was defeated by a vote of 74 to 20.[50] Madison then took the opportunity to call up *A Bill for Establishing Religious Freedom* that Jefferson had submitted in 1779. It had been tabled back then because it seemed too radical. In the aftermath of their victory against the assessment bill, Madison and Jefferson saw an ideal time to reconsider the *Bill for Establishing Religious Freedom*. In the euphoria of the moment it passed. For our purposes the most important words of that document are Jefferson's opposition to using taxes to support religious education:

> . . . to compel a man to furnish contributions of money for the propagation of opinions which he disbelieves and abhors, is sinful and tyrannical; that even the forcing him to support this or that teacher of his own religious persuasion, is depriving him of the comfortable liberty of giving his contributions to the particular pastor whose morals he would make his pattern, and whose powers he feels most persuasive to righteousness; and is withdrawing from the ministry those temporary rewards, which proceeding from an approbation of their personal conduct, are an additional incitement to earnest and unremitting labours for the instruction of mankind . . . [51]

So complete was the victory won by Madison and Jefferson that taxation to support religious activities did not become a major issue again until the twentieth century. However, the idea of separation that was only implicit in the *Memorial* and the *Bill for Establishing Religious Freedom* became explicit. Indeed, it became the basis for understanding the relationship between church and state in the United States. However, as we will see below, the term "separation" did not appear in the religion clauses of the First Amendment, but in a later letter President Thomas Jefferson wrote in response to a petition from the Danbury, Connecticut Baptist Association:

> Believing with you that religion is a matter which lies solely between man and his God, that he owes account to none other for his faith or his worship, that the legislative powers of government reach actions only, and not opinions, —I contemplate with sovereign reverence that act of the whole American people which declared that their legislature should "make no law respecting an establishment of religion, or prohibiting the free exercise thereof," *thus building a wall of separation between church and State.* Adhering to this expression of the supreme will of the nation on behalf of the rights of conscience, I shall see with sincere satisfaction the progress of those sentiments which tend to restore to man all his natural rights, convinced he has no natural right in opposition to his social duties. [52]

Many Americans have not agreed with Jefferson, either in his own day or currently. However, he did imbed the idea of separation of church and state forever in the American psyche. It is also an idea that has served us well and that has spread across the world. But is "separation" only a rhetorical flourish, or is it part of fundamental American law?

Our First Amendment: What Did the Founders Intend?

Although "separation of church and state" later became the defining paradigm for understanding the relationship between religions and government in the United States, these were not the explicit words of the First Amendment. The religion clauses of the First Amendment were a careful compromise drafted in the first Congress and ratified on December 1, 1791. That amendment reads in relevant part, "Congress shall make no law respecting an establishment of religion or prohibiting the free exercise thereof. . . ." "Separation" became the paradigm in part because "a wall of separation" is an easily grasped image, an early example of symbolic politics, and in part because "separation" is a generic term capable of sustaining a variety of meanings acceptable to different groups. Therein lies the problem. What indeed does the First Amendment mean? One may begin by asking, what did those who wrote the amendment intend to be the law of the land?

At one level the Founders' intent is not difficult to establish if one follows the path from the earliest proposals to the enacted amendment. James Madison had initially opposed any Bill of Rights as part of the Constitution. He argued that what was being proposed in the new constitution was a central government with explicit, delegated, but clearly limited powers. Opponents in various state ratifying conventions were unconvinced, and ultimately Madison was forced to agree to introduce a Bill of Rights in exchange for a favorable vote on the constitution itself. True to his word, on June 8, 1789, during the first session of the new Congress, Madison introduced a proposed Bill of Rights. It included the phrase "The civil rights of none shall be abridged on account of religious belief or worship, nor shall any national religion be established, nor shall the full and equal rights of conscience be in any manner, or on any pretext, infringed." Significantly, and often overlooked, Madison also proposed another phrase, "No State shall violate the equal rights of conscience, or the freedom of the press, or the trial by jury in criminal cases."[53] A committee of the House took up his proposal and returned it to the full House of Representatives. It deleted the word "national" so that it now read, ". . . nor shall any religion be established. . . ." After a day of debate and amendments, some accepted, some not, the amendment was changed. Now it read, "Congress shall make no laws establishing religion, or prohibiting the free exercise thereof, nor shall the rights of conscience be infringed." This version was sent to the Senate for its approval.

The Senate's debates were not recorded, but the *Senate Journal* notes several motions made on September 3, 1789, to change the amendment so that it would only ban establishment of one religious society or "any particular denomination of religion in preference to another." These attempts were unsuccessful and the matter was tabled until later in the month when the Senate voted to amend the House's version so that the amendment now read: "Congress shall make no law establishing articles of faith or a mode of worship, or prohibiting the free exercise of religion." What this did, of course, was simply prohibit Congress from establishing or preferring one denomination over others. Congress could, under this version, support or provide aid to all religions on an equal basis (i.e., the Patrick Henry proposal).

This version of the amendment was unacceptable to the House of Representatives, and a joint conference committee, chaired by James Madison, attempted to resolve the differences on this and other amendments. On September 24, 1789, the House accepted a number of other Senate revisions on the condition that the Senate accept a compromise working of the religion clauses, namely "Congress shall make no law respecting an establishment of religion, or prohibiting the free exercise thereof." This is what stuck.

What can be drawn from this legislative history? Primarily two things. First, the Senate failed in its attempt to limit the Establishment Clause, as it has come to be called, to prohibiting support of a single religion. The idea that Congress can support all religions on an equal basis was soundly defeated. Congress can make no law, period. Religion is simply beyond the purview of Congress; it does not fall within the delegated powers of Congress. It is simply outside of this social contract. Second, Madison also failed in his attempt to limit the states. His amendment proposing that "no State shall violate the equal rights of conscience" was defeated. States were free to make whatever laws affecting religion they thought proper. As a result, they continued both restrictions on religious expression and established state religions.[54] So what is the significance of this for faith-based initiatives? At the very least, it means that Congress cannot make any law that specifically refers to religion as such, to say nothing of preferring religions or religious groups that provide social services. It is important to see how the First Amendment and the idea of separation fit together.

Developing the Idea of Separation

The phrase "separation of church and state" appears nowhere in the Constitution. Jefferson applied this meaning to the First Amendment phrases in a piece of private correspondence, the Danbury letter quoted above, but it had no legal standing. The phrase became embedded in law in Chief Justice Morrison Waite's 1879 opinion for the Supreme Court in *Reynolds v. United States*.[55] The key point in the case was the phrase from the *Bill to Establish Religious Liberty*, "It is time enough for the rightful purposes of civil government for its officers to interfere when principles break out into overt acts against peace and good order." Waite used this to deny the Mormons the right to practice polygamy as an expression of religious faith, but then quoted the phrase "thus building a wall of separation" from the letter to the Danbury Baptists. He added, "Coming as this does from an acknowledged leader of the advocates of the measure, it may be accepted almost as an authoritative declaration of the scope and effect of the amendment thus secured."[56] Thus did separation become part of constitutional law.[57]

The separation principle now established rested dormant for sixty-one years. In 1940 the Supreme Court decided *Cantwell v. Connecticut*,[58] a free exercise clause case, and set a very important precedent—that is, it applied the free exercise clause to the states. As Justice Roberts wrote for the court, "The Fourteenth Amendment has rendered the legislatures of the states as incompetent as Congress to enact laws denying the free exercise of religion."[59] Seven years later the Supreme Court again addressed the religion clauses in the landmark case, *Everson v. Board of Education of Ewing Township*.[60] This time the court applied the nonestablishment clause to the states as well as providing a clear statement of the meaning and extent of the First Amendment nonestablishment clause in what is now called separationist terms:

> The "establishment of religion" clause of the First Amendment means at least this: Neither a state nor the Federal Government can set up a church. Neither can pass laws which aid one religion, aid all religions, or prefer one religion over another. Neither can force nor influence a person to go to or remain away from church against his will or force him to profess a belief or disbelief in any religion. No person can be punished for entertaining or professing religious beliefs or disbeliefs, for church attendance or nonattendance. No tax in any amount, large or small, can be levied to support any religious activities or institutions, whatever they may be called, or whatever form they may adopt to teach or practice religion. Neither a state nor the Federal Government can, openly or secretly, participate in the affairs of any religious organizations or groups and vice versa. In the words of Jefferson, the clause against establishment of religion by law was intended to erect "a wall of separation between Church and State."[61]

Together, *Cantwell* and *Everson* handed a belated victory to Madison by decreeing that states are now bound by the religion clauses of the First Amendment. But they also went beyond where he dared to go. They prohibited not only state infringement on "the equal rights of conscience" but state establishment as well. *Everson* also enshrined the separationist principle in constitutional law, but not without ambiguity. For while using "strict separationist" language to announce the meaning of the nonestablishment clause, Justice Black's holding for the court that payment for busing does not violate that clause is certainly an accommodation of religion. This ambiguity was not lost on the dissenters,[62] and set the stage for decades of dispute over the meaning and reach of the religion clauses.

Five years after *Everson* was decided, the court handed down a decision in *Zorach v. Clausen*[63] in which Justice Douglas, writing for the majority, penned what can be considered a classic "accommodationist," or as it is now sometimes called, a "nonpreferentialist" interpretation of the religion clauses:

> We are a religious people whose institutions presuppose a Supreme Being. We guarantee the freedom to worship as one chooses. We make room for as wide a variety of beliefs and creeds as the spiritual needs of man deem necessary. We sponsor an attitude on the part of government that shows no partiality to any one group and that lets each flourish according to the zeal of its adherents and the appeal of its dogma. When the Government encourages religious instruction and cooperates with religious authorities by adjusting the schedule of public events to sectarian needs, it follows the best of our traditions. For it then respects the religious nature of our people and accommodates the public service to their spiritual needs.[64]

The *Zorach* decision no more settled the dispute over the meaning of the religion clauses than had *Everson*. Justice Douglas's statement of an accommodationist interpretation of the religion clauses seemed dangerously overbroad and unlimited in its support for religion. Nevertheless, Douglas made a valid point. Historical evidence makes it clear that neither the Founders nor the First Amendment were hostile to religion.[65] The Supreme Court began groping its way toward a middle ground through a series of cases that culminated in *Lemon v. Kurtzman*.[66]

In 1971 the Supreme Court issued its decision in the *Lemon* case and most importantly, devised a principle of law or legal standard, now called the "Lemon test," that spelled out when and to what extent aid to religion may be considered constitutional:

> First, the statute must have a secular legislative purpose; second, its principal or primary effect must be one that neither advances nor inhibits religion; finally, the statute must not foster "an excessive government entanglement with religion."[67]

Undermining the Idea of Separation

Despite several expressions of dissatisfaction by various members of the Court, the Lemon test has remained the precedent against which efforts to aid or fund religious activities are measured. Although it has been modified in *Agostini v. Felton* and *Mitchell v. Helms*, as noted above, *Lemon* established a "neutralist" interpretation of the religion clauses. This, however, has never set well with either the strict separationists or the accommodationists/nonpreferentialists. This has not been simply on the Supreme Court, but among members of several administrations as well. During the 1980s, Attorney General Edwin Meese III argued that

> The First Amendment forbade the establishment of a particular religion or a particular church. It also precluded the federal government from favoring one church, or one church group over another. That's what the first Amendment did; but it did not go further. It did not, for example, preclude federal aid to religious groups so long as that assistance furthered a public purpose and so long as it did not discriminate in favor of one religious group against another.[68]

The Meese argument, of course, flies in the face of the legislative record of the First Congress. It supports a version of the First Amendment rejected on September 3, 1789. Why would Meese and his supporters take such a position? Professor Walter Berns, a scholar who agreed with Meese, provides one answer: "[L]iberal democracy must preserve what it cannot itself generate (i.e., religion), and it must do this without jeopardizing the private character of religion."[69] Leonard Levy, one of the most respected opponents of this position states the case even more strongly, but with a negative slant:

> Nonpreferentialism, unfortunately, is but a pose for those who think that religion needs to be patronized and promoted by government. When they speak of nonpreferential aid, they speak euphemistically as if they are not partisan. In fact they really are preferentialists. . . . Nonpreferentialists prefer government sponsorship and subsidy of religion rather than allow it to compete on its merits against irreligion and indifference. They prefer government

nurture of religion because they mistakenly dread government neutrality as too risky, and so they condemn it as hostility. They prefer what they call, again euphemistically, accommodation.[70]

What is going on here, and what does it have to do with faith-based initiatives? First, the long-term battle between strict separationists, accommodationists, and neutralists over how to interpret the First Amendment religion clauses continues to rage. It has been the general consensus of the academic and legal communities since the early 1970s that the neutralist interpretation comes closest to correctly following the intent of the Founders. Separationists and accommodationists have vigorously opposed this interpretation. It is now under attack primarily from the conservative Republican accommodationists who control the Bush Administration and their apologists. One line of attack has been to blur the differences between the neutralist and accommodationist/nonpreferentialist positions, claiming they are one and the same and that faith-based initiatives simply rely on a neutralist interpretation of the religion clauses.[71] The authors reject this interpretation. Neutralist and accommodationist/ nonpreferential positions are substantially different from each other, and faith-based initiatives rely on the latter interpretation, not the former.

The second line of attack has been to undermine the very idea of separation as a value of the Founders. In a recent book, *Separation of Church and State*,[72] Professor Philip Hamburg makes several provocative arguments, including evidence that (a) Jefferson and Madison were not in the mainstream of thought about religion among the Founders, and that (b) the idea of separation was not a central concern of the Founders. They were more concerned about not allowing one religion to dominate, protecting freedom of conscience, and asserting the rights of the states to make their own arrangements between government and religion. Further, Hamburg argues that (c) the idea of separation became a major concern in the nineteenth century when Protestants asserted it as a form of anti-Catholicism. They were intent on preventing governments from funding Catholic schools and social services. Hamburg has written an excellent book with many useful insights, but it has one serious flaw. While he acknowledges that there are several meanings to the term separation, his argument is really that the Founders rejected "strict" or "absolute" separation. In this, he is technically correct. What they did not reject, indeed, what best expresses their intent, is equal separation, or as it is more commonly called, neutrality.[73] Insofar as he misses this point and thereby undermines the idea of equal separation, Professor Hamburg does us a major disservice.

Two arguments summarize this section. First, proponents advertise faith-based initiatives as a way to level the playing field between religions and between religious and secular social service providers. They argue that we need to return to the more favorable view of religion held by the majority of the Founders. I disagree. Faith-based initiatives do precisely what Patrick Henry proposed and both James Madison and Thomas Jefferson so adamantly opposed—*provide aid to religious organizations so that religion may support government policies, most notably aid to the poor and needy.* Madison's objections are as valid today as when they were published in the *Memorial and Remonstrance.* Is it wise, then, to accept the approach of Patrick Henry and turn our backs on Madison and Jefferson?

Second, a great gift the United States has given to the world through its short history has been the idea that church and state can and should be separate; that each will thrive much better with that arrangement. The concept of separation has developed over time into the constitutional principle of neutrality. This principle is different from strict separation and different from accommodation. As the twenty-first century begins, the United States, and indeed much of the democratic world, are locked in battle with people claiming to represent Islam—the one major religion that consciously and adamantly rejects the idea of separation of church and state. This version of Islam seeks to impose the one true faith. Now is not a time to forget, reject or distort an idea that has made it possible for the United States to become such a strong, diverse nation, the idea of the separation of church and state.

FINANCIAL PITFALLS AND ILLUSIONS

In the above sections faith-based initiatives were criticized for their constitutional, statutory, and historical shortcomings, confusions, and dangers. Indeed several lawsuits have been filed, alleging violation of the First Amendment's Establishment Clause, Free Exercise Clause and nondiscrimination statutes, and more can be expected.[74]

This section, in contrast, looks at an aspect that has not received adequate attention, but which has the potential to be the source of both judicial challenges and public disenchantment with religion—financial pitfalls and illusions. There are three popular myths about faith-based initiatives. First, it is assumed that this initiative will result in less fraud than occurred under the AFDC and other social service programs. Second, some are claiming that utilizing faith-based organizations will be more cost-effective than utilizing traditional contracting agencies such as Catholic Charities, Lutheran Social Services, World Vision, and Jewish Social Services or governmental agencies. Third, it is being touted that utilizing faith-based organizations will increase the quantity and quality of social services delivered to those in need.

It is difficult to critique a concept or policy in the abstract, especially one that has not been adequately tested under real world conditions. Such is the problem of analyzing the financial implications faith-based initiatives. Although President Bush has issued several executive orders and encouraged several agencies to pursue faith-based initiatives, actual new funding has not been significant. As a result, for the most part this is an untested policy. Experience tells us that implementation is rarely as good as advocates project or as bad as critics fear. Therefore, in this section three areas of potential financial risk are explored, areas that have not received sufficient attention: fraud, administrative overhead, and resource shifting. The focus here is on the money and the analysis begins by drawing a portrait of a little-known crime, religious affinity fraud. It then moves to the need for intermediary organizations to assist service providers, which might be called faith-based bureaucracies, and concludes with the likelihood of revenue shifting within religious organizations.

Religious Affinity Fraud

In August 2001, the North American Securities Administrators Association issued a press release warning that "investment frauds taking advantage of victims' religious or spiritual beliefs are rising dramatically."[75] Joseph Borg, director of the Alabama Securities Commission, provides an appropriate definition: "Affinity fraud in general is when someone in an organization takes advantage of fellow members. Affinity fraud occurs in all types of organizations, but is most common in religious groups."[76] The extent of religious affinity fraud is simply not known; securities administrators have identified a number of high-profile cases in which the perpetrators have been caught. They believe there are numerous small operators who are not reported either due to victim embarrassment or a refusal to believe a fellow religionist could have actually engaged in fraud. As a result, many scam artists are not caught. The number of known cases, however, provides a sorry picture of what can happen when religion and money mix without adequate oversight. Three frauds that were discovered—Greater Ministries International Church, the Baptist Foundation of Arizona, and the IRM Corporation—resulted in losses to investors estimated at nearly $1.5 billion. In fact, however, these are the numbers from only three scams. From 1998 through 2000 securities regulators in twenty-seven states have taken actions against hundreds of companies and individuals that used religious or spiritual beliefs to gain the trust of investors—nearly 90,000 nationwide—before swindling many of them out of their life savings.[77]

This was not unique. In the six years between 1993 and 1999 Greater Ministries International Church, based in Tampa, Florida, raised $578 million by promising investors that they could double their money through investment in foreign currency markets, cargo ships, and gold, silver, and diamond mines in the Caribbean and in Africa. Greater Ministry promoters utilized scripture in their appeals, especially Luke 6:38: "Give, and it shall be given unto you; good measure, pressed down, and shaken together, and running over, shall men give into your bosom." Some 20,000 investors, both in the United States and abroad, were persuaded to send money, some mortgaging their homes, borrowing on their credit cards and cashing in their retirement funds. Church founder and Minister Gerald Payne essentially ran a Ponzi scheme—using money from new investors to pay old investors rather than actually investing in ships, mines, or whatever else they promised. Reverend Payne and his colleagues are now in prison, but only after his investors lost out.

The Baptist Foundation of Arizona apparently began as a legitimate investment firm, managing church building funds and retirement accounts. Most of the funds were put into the Arizona real estate market, but when property values fell in the late 1980s fund managers refused to report their losses. Instead they set up a maze of more than a hundred shell corporations to raise funds, apparently in the hope that real estate values would have an upturn before they needed to pay on the investments. The Baptist Foundation "fielded an aggressive sales force and set up offices at some churches."[78] It used new money to pay earlier investors, eventually raising more than $590 million from over 13,000 individuals and churches nationwide. Eight top officials were indicted on thirty-two counts of fraud.[79]

Michigan securities regulators shut down the IRM Corporation in May 1999, but not before the company raised approximately $400 million from investors in five states through the sale of bogus promissory notes and limited partnerships in California real estate. Regulators estimate there were some 2,400 victims in Michigan alone, recruited through church-based organizations or religious television and radio programs such as the "Back to God Hour." IRM had some 120 affiliates to make its transactions more difficult to trace.

On a smaller scale, a Tennessee organization, Capital Plus Worldwide Financial Services, was shut down by state regulators after more than 100 investors recruited from African American churches were defrauded of some $3.2 million. Investors were sold on the investments by promises that the money was to be used "to rebuild wartorn African countries while returning between 96 and 120 percent annually from joint venture partnerships and nonexistent 'bank debentures' issued by European banks."[80]

In the state of Washington a company called Island Mortgage Company/Northwestern Investment Company raised more than $26 million from the Society of Friends (Quakers) for premiums for nonexistent health insurance. Before it was shut down, the company also raised more than $14 million selling bogus promissory notes.

In Indiana elderly victims were bilked out of $1.4 million by three scam artists whose modus operandi was to kneel and pray with their marks.

Deborah Bortner, director of securities for the state of Washington and past president of the North American Securities Administrators Association, sums up the problem with this insight: "I've been a securities regulator for twenty years, and I've seen more money stolen in the name of God than in any other way."

In one sense, of course, it is unfair to the faith-based initiative to discuss it in the same article as religious affinity fraud. It should be clear that these were not mainline churches or ministers, but imposters and scam artists. Nor was government funding involved. Rather it was the savings of private investors that were stolen. But are there lessons to be learned for faith-based initiatives? With frauds uncovered in twenty-seven states it seems clear that wherever there are religious people there is the opportunity and temptation to misuse religion and religious affiliation for fraudulent purposes. It is also clear that religion itself is no protection against human greed.

In fact, there are several similarities that should raise warning flags for faith-based initiatives. First, there will be federal funding available in significant amounts to those who can craft innovative and appealing proposals. Second, there will be new, inexperienced social service entrepreneurs, including pastors, and other church service workers, comparable to amateur investors, who will arguably be more susceptible to fraudulent schemes than traditional service providers. This is because they do not have the experience, or in many cases the training, to utilize funds effectively. Third, many front-line service providers tend to be poorly paid. Therefore, even if they are scrupulously honest, as no doubt the vast majority will be, they will not have the discretionary resources to pursue the training needed to become effective government service providers. The temptation may be greater since they will not be "investing" their own money but government funds. If President Bush's vision is implemented as he apparently intends, there will be thousands of such providers spread across the nation, concentrated in areas of poverty, high unemployment, crime, and other problems. Finally, there is a rather undefined and unlimited range of services to be funded, including job training and placement, marriage and family counseling, food and shelter provision, healthcare, daycare, after-school programs, drug and alcohol treatment centers, and gang reduction initiatives. This will provide ample opportunity for imaginative but untried programs and, sadly, criminal activities. They will open the door to false promises, fraudulent schemes, and cooked books. One may speak sincerely of outcome-based evaluation of programs, but anyone who has worked in these areas realizes that successes and failures are not so easily separated.

In brief, past experience with religious affinity fraud raises several warning flags for faith-based initiatives. Will what was once called "welfare fraud" simply be replaced by faith-based fraud? Or will human nature change? Don't bet the farm on it.

Faith-Based Bureaucracies

It is fair to say that in *popular* understanding, faith-based initiatives are seen as a way to take government funding and services directly to people who need it. It is expected that they will go primarily the poor, the trapped, and the vulnerable in society—and to the groups, faith-based organizations, that can provide that aid honestly, effectively, and with a minimum of bureaucratic red tape. In brief, faith-based organizations are perceived as being a less bureaucratic and more cost-effective way of providing services. As two authors who have followed the development of Charitable Choice closely observe, "The attraction of charitable choice for the Right was its promise to cut public spending while maintaining a spirit of care, whereas the Left saw it as a way to circumvent bureaucratic administration of publicly funded services."[81] People more knowledgeable about social service delivery realize that the process does not—indeed cannot—work that simply. Getting large numbers of new, faith-based providers up and running will be particularly challenging.

Building programs, establishing boards of directors, writing grants, keeping records, and preparing timely reports for funding agencies all require knowledge and expertise normally outside the scope of training of most pastors and other potential providers of faith-based initiatives. These activities also require resources such as staff, office space, computers, phones, and faxes. Who will help "front-line" faith-based organizations new to the process do the things that need to be done to be effective service providers? The answer is professional, often faith-based, facilitators. Some see this as adding a layer of bureaucracy. They are correct.

In a recent executive summary entitled "Empowering Compassion: The Strategic Role of Intermediary Organizations in Building Capacity among and Enhancing the Impact of Community Transformers," Amy L. Sherman, director of the Hudson Institute's Faith in Communities initiative, reports on a study of twenty-two intermediaries that is relevant to this book. In the background section Sherman writes,

> Hudson's 'Faith in Communities' initiative has been investigating the role of faith-based organizations (FBOs) in the provision of social services from several angles over the last few years. Three conclusions have emerged. First, to strengthen and expand their contributions, many FBOs need technical assistance and other capacity-building aids. Second, for fruitful government-faith collaboration to flourish, grassroots ministries often need administrative help from trusted organizations that can mediate their interface with the public sector. And third, not nearly enough is currently known, by policymakers, the faith community, and philanthropists, about intermediary organizations that can fulfill these vital functions.[82]

Administrative officials are quite cognizant of the need for such intermediary organizations as the following examples illustrate. In April 2002, the Department of Labor solicited grant applications from intermediary groups as well as small faith-based nonprofits to increase collaboration between One Stop Centers and the faith community. Five million dollars was specifically earmarked for intermediary groups. The 2002 Charity, Aid, Recovery, and Empowerment Act (CARE), which has subsequently failed to pass the Senate, specifically allowed the government to contract with intermediate grantors. On June 7, 2002, the *Federal Register* gave notice of a $30 million Compassion Capital Fund to be administered by a division of the Department of Health and Human Services.[83] Of the total amount, close to

$25 million was earmarked for intermediary organizations to provide for technical assistance and to make sub-awards. As the Hudson Institute's Army Sherman summarizes, "Clearly, federal policymakers active in the social service arena are giving serious attention to the unique and important role of intermediary organizations—particularly faith-based intermediaries."[84]

Intermediaries are by definition organizations that help other organizations with technical support, training, advocacy, community development, program development, and various kinds of mentoring. There are a wide variety of such organizations, including those that function as financial pass-through agencies, those that combine their own direct, grassroots programs with assistance to other programs, those that are faith-based in various degrees (and of various faiths), and some that are strictly secular. Intermediaries can be large or small, national, regional and local in scope. Some are well established and have functioned successfully for years; others are quite new and inexperienced. As faith-based organizations are created and expand, intermediary organizations can be expected to expand as well.

Intermediary organizations perform a wide variety of both quantifiable and nonquantifiable "value-added" services. Among the top ten findings reported in the Hudson executive summary are: (1) "that intermediary organizations have assisted grassroots FBOs in obtaining millions of dollars of funding they most likely otherwise would not have secured. Intermediaries have connected frontline groups to new sources of volunteers and in-kind donations. Intermediaries have provided grassroots leaders with relevant, accessible training and technical assistance they otherwise would not have gained. And intermediaries have increased the public exposure of grassroots groups' work, winning them public recognition, endorsements, and media coverage." (2) "Frequently, frontline ministry staff reported that the most important help they had received from an intermediary was coaching, advice, or 'moral support.' Though unable to put a dollar figure on this form of aid, many related anecdotes specifying how an intermediary leader's advice or intervention solved a key problem, led to a 'visioning breakthrough,' saved the grassroots group from making a critical error, or decisively influenced the design of a program or service." And (3) "The charismatic personalities and zeal of the individual leaders of the intermediary organizations are key factors in the level of impact the intermediaries are making. In sports terminology, some of the intermediaries examined lack a 'bench' beyond the founder or current leader. This person was highly successful in building the network of personal relationships and credibility that made the intermediary such a valuable repository of information and connections. In the absence of this individual, it is unclear whether the intermediary as an institution would have 'staying power' and continued influence."[85]

The Hudson Institute study draws some powerful conclusions. It is clear that intermediaries, including faith-based intermediaries, will be crucial for the success of faith-based organizations. This is especially true for those that are new to social services, are unfamiliar with government contracting, and whose officers and ministers are not trained in this type of service delivery. Intermediaries will be invaluable for service providers in many of the small, inner-city, and isolated rural poverty areas—precisely the type of front-line deliverers faith-based initiatives are designed to reach and utilize. Second, with such a broad, relatively undefined mission and wide range of providers to service, the potential for waste and fraud is large. This is particularly true when so many of the services provided, however valuable, are not quantifiable (e.g., workshops, mentoring, encouraging, visioning, and community building). Third, there is no reason to think that faith-based intermediaries will be less expensive or more cost-effective than current intermediaries. These groups are by definition staffed by people with expertise, which means they will tend to be moderately well paid. How much will intermediary organizations cost? Government grants to existing organizations such as universities allow indirect costs, often called "overhead" or facilities and administration costs, to be written in at 45 percent and, in some cases, at an even higher rate.[85] This may be a higher rate than will be allowed social service intermediaries, but it would not be an unreasonable amount granted the work and expertise needed.

In brief, for the reasons noted, funding of faith-based organizations will require extensive use of intermediary organizations. While these can assist the organizations in being effective, they are themselves expensive, and their costs must be covered either by government grants or private donations. There may be many values to utilizing faith-based organizations to deliver social services. Cost-savings is not one of them.

Resource Shifting

Resource shifting has been the most difficult portion of this argument to develop. In part this is because it covers new ground and in part it is because no previous studies were found that address the issue directly. This may be because it is unclear how one could measure the effect. It may be an untraceable reality.

An April 11, 2002, a State Department Fact Sheet included the following announcement: "President Bush called on the Senate to pass the CARE Act—bipartisan legislation that reflects key parts of his Armies of Compassion agenda to strengthen America's charitable groups—and for Congress to send him a final bill to sign by Memorial Day. The President was joined by representatives from local and national charitable and faith-based groups, *many of which are struggling to cope with recent declines in giving and increases in demand for the services they provide.*" (Emphasis added)

The Fact Sheet continues: "As millions of Americans prepare to file their tax returns, the President noted that the legislation will help an estimated 84 million taxpayers to receive a deduction for charitable giving—providing billions of dollars of support for charitable groups in America."[86]

The question posed in this section is whether there may well operate a law of unintended consequences. A hypothetical situation provides an apt illustration. St. Mark's, a struggling inner-city church that has provided social services in its neighborhood for years, applies for and receives funding for these services through the faith-based initiatives. The value of the services rendered, a soup kitchen, a job-hunting service, and drug counseling, is estimated at $100,000 a year. News comes that St. Mark's will now receive $100,000 in government funding for these services. The pastor gives thanks to the government and praises the Lord. Now he can be paid for the drug counseling and job-hunting services he provides, thereby bringing his salary slightly above poverty level. Now he can also shift some of the funds that had been designated for the soup kitchen to modest salary boosts for the religious education teacher and choir director as well as much needed repairs to the sanctuary. Such a shifting of funds would be entirely legal. In a period of very tight budgets, as noted by President Bush, it would also be a rational decision. In other words, there is no assurance that provision of government funding would increase either the quantity or the quality of social services offered by St. Mark's.

Likewise, a non-itemizing taxpayer could also now deduct $400 for charitable giving, but what assurance would a parishioner have that this will go to a social service agency? Why wouldn't a member of St. Mark's put the money into the collection box or in a sanctuary repair fund rather than the soup kitchen fund, since one benefits the church and the other does not? Indeed, the pastor might feel quite justified in asking people to do so, since the social services offered by St. Mark's are now funded in large measure by the government. Again, this would be both legal and rational. If the government will pay for it, why should the parishioner? In brief, due to the probability of resource shifting it is unclear that Charitable Choice will lead always to greater quantity or quality of services to the poor.

In summary, the purpose of this section has been to explore financial aspects of faith-based initiatives that have not been adequately explored elsewhere. From a prudent financial perspective Charitable Choice looks good until one takes a closer look. In addition to potential constitutional and statutory problems, there are three potential areas in which results will likely be disappointing to Charitable Choice advocates. (1) The potential for fraud expands as the number and variety of programs and program recipients expands beyond the well-established, traditional faith-based government contractors. This will be even more likely if normal procedures for certifying eligibility and compliance are abbreviated or "expedited" for the purpose of including more providers.[87] Religious affiliation or affinity is no insurance against fraud. (2) The need to obtain assistance from intermediary groups with expertise in grant writing, program development, community building, advocacy, etc., means that the cost-savings many advocates had hoped for will not occur. We would add that, to his credit, President Bush has not promoted cost-savings as a rationale for the Charitable Choice Initiative, but many supporters have understood this to be one of the benefits. (3) There is no assurance that there will be a proportional expansion in the scope or effectiveness of social services through the use of faith-based organizations. Many faith-based providers will take the legal and rational route of shifting funds from provision of social services to other pressing needs within their religious communities.

PHILOSOPHICAL PROBLEMS AND DIFFERENCES

A successful retired entrepreneur, Lee Thomas, teaches an ethics course at Bellarmine University in Louisville, Kentucky. He likes to sum up his semester's work with one phrase: "If it smells bad, don't do it." While recognizing the hopes and aspirations of those who proposed faith-based initiatives as a way to better serve those in need, reasonable, reflective observers also see the dangers and limitations inherent in this approach to social service delivery. To be blunt, faith-based initiatives *as currently structured* flunk the bad smell test. It is now time to examine the final reason this conclusion is valid.

As serious as the constitutional, legal, historical, and fiscal problems with faith-based initiatives are the philosophical assumptions upon which they stand. The faith-based initiatives approach social problems and services from the perspective of "compassionate conservatism." That philosophy itself needs examination. While there are differences among them, most conservatives agree on several points: (1) that the poor themselves are to blame for the deprivation they face and must be motivated to take responsibility for their self-improvement; (2) that poverty results from the immoral behavior of the poor; and (3) that in order to fight social problems effectively, the federal government should devolve resources to state and local governments as well as private organizations."[88] What's wrong with this picture? Each of the three points distorts reality. Many, if not most of those needing social services are not to blame for their deprivations. Poverty often does not result from immoral behavior but from a free market system. Business cycles, normal obsolescence, and the need for retooling cause periodic massive layoffs. Corporate corruption that leads to bankruptcy and routine shifting of jobs to foreign nations as a result of globalization are at least partially responsible for the problems faced by the poor. As Elizabeth Bounds notes,

> Moral rhetoric about the poor is always careful to shift public attention away from critical analysis of the political economy, which has been radically restructured in the past quarter-century as capitalism becomes a global system. Public attention continues to be maintained now, as in the past, on the regulation of individual behavior, especially female sexual behavior, cast as "personal responsibility."[89]

This is not an argument against the capitalist, free market system. It is a vibrant, productive, self-renewing economic system. Rather, it is imperative to recognize that there are systematic as well as personal causes of poverty. Since that is the case, the nation needs systematic as well as personal solutions to poverty.

Second, President Bush's focus in proposing the faith-based solutions has been on the personal or familial failures of those who need assistance. His "Rallying the Armies of Compassion" speech illustrates this. The president lists eight problems the nation must address: (1) As many as 15 million young people are at risk of not reaching productive adulthood—falling prey to crime, drugs, and other problems; (2) About 1.5 million children have a father or mother in prison; (3) Over half a million children are in foster care, more than one fifth of whom are awaiting adoption; (4) In 1997, more than one million babies were born to unwed mothers, many of them barely past their own teen years; (5) More than one out of six American families with children live on an annual income of $17,000 or less; (6) Millions of Americans are enslaved to drugs or alcohol; (7) Hundreds of thousands of our precious citizens live on the streets; and (8) Despite the many successes of welfare reform, too many families remain dependent on welfare and many of those who have left the rolls can barely make ends meet.[90] Note that the emphasis here is largely on personal and family failures. That is consistent with conservative mythology about the poor. However, an accounting of those who actually need and use social services is much broader and deeper. It includes citizens who are blind or deaf or suffer other physical handicaps. It encompasses those who are mentally ill or retarded, those who have lost employment due to companies closing or moving and need to be retrained, and the elderly, many of whom are poor because their employers mishandled their pensions or because of sickness. In brief, the assumption that people who need social services are in need because of their own or their family's moral failures is a grotesque distortion of the real problems faced by real people.[91] If the assumptions are wrong, what about the proposed solutions?

The third conservative assumption noted above is that the optimal solution is devolving federal programs to states and localities and private organizations. While state, local, and private social service organizations can use all the help they can get, there are problems with this solution. First, it rests on the twofold assumption that federal programs have been wasteful and ineffective, and that state, local, and religious programs will be more effective and less wasteful. As President Bush stated this proposition: "Traditional social programs are often too bureaucratic, inflexible, and impersonal to meet the acute and complex needs of the poor." [92] Certainly there is always room for improving efficiency in the delivery of social services. However, substantial proportions of federal social services are already delivered through state, local, and private organizations (the latter through grants and fee for service contracts). Second, there is simply no evidence to show that religious organizations engaged in social services deliver those services more effectively than secular organizations.[93]

As Thomas Ross points out in a thoughtful article, "The [faith-based] initiative's unstated but fundamental contention is that faith-based programs ought to command government funding because they influence the *religious* beliefs of clients. Accordingly, the initiative assumes that fighting poverty effectively entails changing the moral beliefs of the poor and that government-sponsored service agencies have failed precisely because they have not done so."[94] In addition to the constitutional problems noted above, the effectiveness of the proposed solution is itself based on faith. There is simply no empirical evidence to support it.

Many experts believe the biggest problem facing organizations that deliver social services is inadequate funding—not moral failure, inefficiency, or lack of commitment. Many of the problems of those needing social services are such things as lack of affordable housing, an inadequate minimum wage, and understaffed agencies. Conservatives will immediately dismiss these as liberal assertions, but they are accurate statements about real issues. What do faith-based initiatives do to address them? The answer is very little. At this point in time there is no substantial new money allocated to faith-based initiatives. Rather, money is reallocated from existing programs. With the budget deficit ballooning, there is likely to be even less money for the foreseeable future. Despite President Bush's assertion that budgets were being increased to work on social problems, the reality is quite different.[95]

The argument in this section is that the conservative philosophical underpinnings of faith-based initiatives are wrong. The proposed causes of the problems of those who need social services are in large part distorted. Moral shortcomings are only a small part of the problems. The proposed solutions are equally misplaced. It is no wonder that Thomas Ross entitled his article about faith-based initiatives, "Anti-Poverty or Anti-Poor?" What is bad on the philosophical level is that faith-based initiatives could do more harm than good for those in need. They absolve large institutions of their responsibilities for causing the problems, and they are a giant step toward withdrawing government from its responsibilities to care for its citizens in need.

This chapter has taken a hard look at the real and potential problems engendered by faith-based initiatives. These problems range from violations of the constitution, specifically the Establishment and Freedom of Speech Clauses, to expanding and condoning employment discrimination in government-funded programs. They include undermining the historical principle of separation of church and state that has taken decades to develop and that has functioned so successfully in American history. Problems also include unrealistic expectations of religious organizations and the potential that welfare fraud will simply become faith-based fraud. Finally, this chapter argues that misdiagnosing the causes of social problems leads to prescribing unworkable solutions. Does this lead to the conclusion that faith-based initiatives are worthless or worse? Not necessarily. They can be modified to better serve both the providers and the recipients of social services. Why this has been and will continue to be so difficult is the topic of the next chapter.

NOTES

1. Among the predominantly Christian industrialized countries, the United States is remarkable in both the low level of anticlericalism and the high level of trust in religious leaders. That could change if religious organizations are seen as too closely related with government programs.

2. "Ross Wiener, an education trust analyst at the Education Trust, a nonprofit organization that has backed [the Bush Administration's] No Child Left Behind law, compared the education budget to the president's latest proposed tax cut, totaling $647 billion over ten years. 'If money indicates priorities, the president believes No Child Left Behind is one sixty-seventh as important as cutting taxes,' Mr. Wiener said." Diana Jean Schemo, *New York Times*, 5 February 2003, A22.

3. President George W. Bush, "Rallying the Armies of Compassion," White House Office of Faith-Based and Community Initiatives. <www.whitehouse.gov/news/reports/faithbased.html>, 3.

4. Steve Monsma, *When Sacred and Secular Mix* (Lanham, Md.: Rowman & Littlefield, 1996); Paul Weber and Dennis Gilbert, *Private Churches and Public Money* (Westport, Ct.: Greenwood Press, 1982).

5. Although we have organized the material differently, we are indebted for much of this analysis to Elbert Lin, Jon D. Michaels, Rajesh Nayak, Katherine Tank Newberger, Nikhil Shanbhag, and Jake Sullivan, "Faith in the Courts? The Legal and Political Future of Federally Funded Faith-Based Initiatives," *Yale Law and Policy Review* 20 (2002): 183.

6. The Pew Forum on Religion and Public Life, "Faith-Based Funding Backed, but Church-State Doubts Abound," pt. I. <http://pewforum.org/events/0410/re-0rt/1.php3> (10 April 2001)

7. The Pew Forum on Religion and Public Life, "Faith-Based Funding Backed."

8. Laurie Goodstein, "Bush's Call to Church Groups Get Untraditional Replies," *New York Times*, 20 February 2001, A1.

9. Lin et al., "Faith in the Courts?" 183.

10. Lin et al., "Faith in the Courts?" 183.

11. Lin et al., "Faith in the Courts?" 195. Taken from testimony of Richard T. Foltin, Legislative Director and Counsel for the American Jewish Committee Office of Government and International Affairs before the Senate Committee on the Judiciary, 197th Congress (2001). See also Karen Branch-Brioso, "Faith-Based Drug Rehabilitation Program Offers Only One Treatment: Jesus Christ," *St. Louis Post-Dispatch*, 11 February 2001, A1.

12. For example, see Carl H. Esbeck, "Charitable Choice and the Critics," *New York University Annual Survey of American Law* 57 (2000): 17, arguing that charitable choice does not violate the Establishment Clause; Steven K. Green, "Charitable Choice and Neutrality Theory," *New York University Annual Survey of American Law* 57 (2000): 33, arguing that charitable choice does violate the Establishment Clause; Carmen M. Guerricagoitia, "Innovation Does Not Cure Constitutional Violation: Charitable Choice and the Establishment Clause," *Georgetown Journal on Poverty Law and Policy* 8 (2001): 447, arguing that charitable choice violates the Establishment Clause; and Lewis D. Solomon and Matthew J. Vlissides Jr., "Faith-Based Charities and the Quest to Solve America's Social Ills: A Legal and Policy Analysis, *Cornell Journal of Law & Public Policy* 10 (2001): 265, arguing that charitable choice does not violate the Establishment Clause. These are just a sampling of the many articles arguing each side of this case.

13. 487 U.S. 589 (1988).

14. Bowen, 487 U.S. 593–98.

15. *Lemon v. Kurtzman*, 403 U.S. 602 (1971).

16. *Agostini v. Felton*, 521 U.S. 203 (1997).

17. *Mitchell v. Helms*, 530 U.S. 793 (2000).

18. *Zelman v. Simmons-Harris*, 536 U.S. 639 (2002).

19. *Zelman v. Simmons-Harris*, 536 U.S. 639 (2002), 667. (J. O'Connor, concurring)

20. Lin et al. "Faith in the Courts?" 196.

21. David Kuo, "Poverty 101: Liberals and Conservatives Can Learn from One Another," *Brookings Review* (Fall 1997), 37. Emphasis added.

22. 500 U.S. 173 (1991). This case upheld a government program that funded family planning projects of private social service providers while prohibiting grantees from discussing abortion.

23. 500 U.S. 173, 193.

24. See Robert C. Post, "Subsidized Speech," *Yale Law Journal* 106 (1996): 156.

25. 530 U.S. 793, 843 (2000).

26. 515 U.S. 819 (1995).

27. 508 U.S. 384 (1993).

28. 508 U.S. 384, 393.

29. 42 U.S.C. * * 2000e to 2000e-17 (1994).

30. 29 U.S.C. * * 621–23 (1994).

31. 42 U.S.C. * * 12101–12112 (1994).

32. *Serbian Orthodox Diocese v. Milivojevich*, 426 U.S. 696, 713 (1976).

33. 80 U.S. 679 (1871).

34. For example the Title VII exemption allows Roman Catholics to employ only single straight and gay men but exclude women or married men from the priesthood without fear of lawsuits. It allows Methodists to employ only Methodist ministers, Baptists to employ Baptist ministers, etc. The ministerial exemption has gotten the courts out of lawsuits such as those to determine which faction in a church dispute is most faithful to the scriptures (and therefore entitled to the church property).

35. Laura B. Mutterperl, "Employment at (God's) Will: The Constitutionality of Antidiscrimination Exemptions in Charitable Choice Legislation," *Harvard Civil Rights–Civil Liberties Review* 37 (2002): 412.

36. 483 U.S. 327 (1987).

37. 483 U.S. 327, 337.

38. 483 U.S. 327, 339.

39. H.R. 7 * * 201 at 1991(e).

40. Mutterperl, "Employment at (God's) Will," 419–20.

41. Kevin Boyle and Juliet Sheen, eds., *Freedom of Religion and Belief: A World Report* (New York: Routledge, 1997), xv.

42. See Mark Juergensmeyer, *Terror in the Mind of God: The Global Rise of Religious Violence* (Berkeley, Calif.: The University of California Press, 2000).

43. Barnett Rubin, Presentation to the Program of Pew Fellows in Religion, Columbia University Center for the Study of Human Rights, 15 October 1997. Cited in Carrie Gustafson and Peter Juviler, eds., *Religion and Human Rights* (New York: M.E. Sharpe, 1999), 7.

44. For more extensive discussion of religious freedom, see Paul Weber, "Freedom of Religion" in Robert Wuthnow, ed., *The Encyclopedia of Politics and Religion* (Washington, D.C.: Congressional Quarterly Press, 1998), 270–75. For a discussion of separation of church and state, see Paul Weber, "Separation of Church and State: A Potent, Dynamic Idea in Political Theory," and Lamin Sanneh, "Separation of Church and State: A Principle Advancing the Struggle for Human Rights," in Wuthnow, 684–91.

45. Reprinted in Thomas Buckley, S.J., *Church and State in Revolutionary Virginia* (Charlottesville, Va.: University of Virginia Press, 1977), 188–89.

46. William T. Hutchison and William M.E. Rachal, eds., *The Papers of James Madison* (Chicago: University of Chicago Press, 1962) vol. 8, 298–304.

47. Julian P. Boyd, ed., *The Papers of Thomas Jefferson* (Princeton: Princeton University Press, 1950), vol. 2, 545–46.

48. To give an example using 1994 figures, Lutheran Social Ministries had an income of $2.41 billion, of which 54 percent came from government sources; Catholic Charities had an income of $1.93 billion, of which 62 percent came from government sources; Jewish Federations had an income of $1.82 billion, of which 45 percent came from government sources; the Salvation Army had an income of $1.35 billion, of which 15 percent came from government sources. Cf. Milt Freudenheim, "Charities Say Government Cuts Would Jeopardize Their Ability to Help Poor," *New York Times*, 5 February 1996, B8.

49. Paul Weber, "James Madison and Religious Equality: The Perfect Separation," *Review of Politics* 44 (1982): 163ff.

50. As Thomas Buckley points out, so astutely and relentlessly had Madison and Jefferson built their case against assessment that "the opposition had not yielded; it had collapsed." Buckley, *Church and State in Revolutionary Virginia*, 159.

51. Boyd, *The Papers of Thomas Jefferson*, 545.

52. Andrew A. Lipscomb and Albert E. Bergh, eds., *Writings of Thomas Jefferson*, vol. 16 (1903–1904), 281–82. Emphasis added. Jefferson was not the first person to use the term "wall of separation." Roger Williams used the phrase in 1644 arguing that the garden of the church must be protected by a wall of separation from "the wilderness of the world." Quoted in Leonard Levy, *The Establishment Clause: Religion and the First Amendment* (New York: Macmillan, 1986), 184, for an extraordinarily well researched and insightful understanding of Jefferson's letter, see Daniel Dreisbach, *Thomas Jefferson and the Wall of Separation between Church and State* (New York: New York University Press, 2002).

53. For a more complete version of this argument, see *The Debates and Proceedings in the Congress of the United States*, vol. 1 (Washington, D.C.: Gales and Seaton, 1834–1856), 451–52.

54. As David O'Brien has pointed out, "Massachusetts, for one, denied Jews the right to hold public office until 1828 and did not remove its final vestiges of establishment until 1833. See David O'Brien, *Constitutional Law and Politics: Civil Rights and Civil Liberties*, 5th ed., vol. 2 (New York: W. W. Norton and Co., 2003), 668.

55. 98 U.S. 145 (1879). In this case the Supreme Court upheld the right of Congress to prohibit polygamy in what was then the Utah territory. Reynolds had challenged that right on freedom of religion grounds.

56. 98 U.S. 145, 163–64.

57. See Robert M. Healey, "Thomas Jefferson's 'Wall': Absolute or Serpentine?" *Journal of Church and State* 30 (Autumn 1988): 441.

58. 310 U.S. 296 (1940). This case involved two Jehovah's Witnesses who had been arrested for distributing religious literature and playing an anti-Catholic phonograph record in a Catholic neighborhood.

59. 310 U.S. 296, 303.

60. 330 U.S. 1 (1947). In this case the Township was reimbursing parents of students who attended Catholic schools for their bus transportation to and from school. The court held that such reimbursements do not violate the nonestablishment clause of the First Amendment.

61. 330 U.S. 1, 15–16.

62. 330 U.S. 1, 19. Justice Jackson pointedly remarked that Black's opinion reminded him of Byron's Julia, who, saying "I will ne'er consent," consented.

63. 343 U.S. 306 (1952). In this case the Supreme Court upheld the constitutionality of a released time program in which public school students could attend religious instruction classes during a period of the school day as long as the instructions were held off public school grounds.

64. 343 U.S. 306, 306. In recent years this position has begun to be called "nonpreferentialism."

65. In support of this position see Chester Antieau, et al., *Freedom from Federal Establishment: Formation and History of the First Amendment Religion Clauses* (Milwaukee: Bruce Publishing Co., 1964); Robert Cord, *Separation of Church and State: Historical Fact and Current Fiction* (New York: Lambeth Press, 1982); Michael Malbin, *Religion and Politics: The Intentions of the Authors of the First Amendment* (Washington, D.C.: American Enterprise Institute, 1978).

66. 403 U.S. 602 (1971). This case considered the constitutionality of various types of aid to religious schools in Pennsylvania and Rhode Island.

67. 403 U.S. 602, 612–13.

68. Edwin Meese III, "Address before the Christian Legal Society," given in San Diego, 29 September 1985. I am indebted to David O'Brien, *Constitutional Law and Politics: Civil Rights and Civil Liberties,* 5th ed., vol. 2 (2003): 668ff for this quotation and the two that follow.

69. Walter Berns, *The First Amendment and the Future of American Democracy* (New York: Basic Books, 1976), 12.

70. Leonard Levy, *The Establishment Clause: Religion and the First Amendment* (New York: Macmillan, 1986), 93–94.

71. E.g., George Muckleroy, "Double Entendre: How the Two Interpretations of the Establishment Clause Will Determine the Future of Charitable Choice," *Texas Tech Law Review* 33 (2002): 1197. Anyone who wonders why conservatives are considered mean, hard-hearted, cynical, and manipulative should read this article.

72. Philip Hamburg, *Separation of Church and State* (Cambridge: Harvard University Press, 2002).

73. Several years ago one of the authors, Paul Weber, edited a book, *Equal Separation: Understanding the Religion Clauses of the First Amendment* (New York: Greenwood Press, 1990) in which this was debated. Indeed, there are at least five identifiable meanings for the concept of separation: (1) structural, (2) trans-valuing (removing religion from the culture, e.g., in the old Soviet constitution), (3) absolute or strict, (4) supportive (now called accommodation or nonpreferentialism), and (5) equal or neutral separation. The book argues that the Founders intended (5), equal separation.

74. See the websites of ADL (Anti-Defamation League) <www.adl.org>, Americans United <www.au.org>, People for the American Way <www.pfaw.org>, and the National Council of Churches <www.ncccusa.org>, among others.

75. See report "Investment Frauds Using Religion on the Rise, State Regulators Warn," 7 August 2001. <www.nasaa.org/nassa/abtnasaa/display_top_story.asp?stid=185>

76. Alabama Securities Commission, "Securities Commission Warning: Fraud on the Rise!" Press release, 7 August 2001. <www.asc.al.us/News/8.71AffinityNASSA.htm>

77. Alabama Securities Commission, "Securities Commission Warning."

78. *Wall Street Journal*, 1 September 1999, C1.

79. It will come as no surprise that the foundation's auditor from 1984 to 1999 was Arthur Andersen.

80. Press release, North American Securities Administrators Association (NASAA) "Investment Frauds Using Religion on the Rise, State Regulators Warn."

81. Ram A. Cnaan and Stephanie C. Bodde, "Charitable Choice and Faith-Based Welfare," *Social Work: Journal of the National Association of Social Workers* 47 (July 2002): 224–38.

82. Hudson Institute, www.hudsonfaithincommunities.org.83.

83. U.S. Department of Health and Human Services, "HHS and the President's Faith-Based and Community Initiative," *HHS Fact Sheet*, 15 March 2001. <www.aoa.gov/pressroom/Pr2001/01fsfaith-based.html>

84. Hudson Institute, 1–2. The facts and figures in this section come primarily from the Hoover Executive Summary.

85. Ibid.

86. For example, if a faculty member at the University of Louisville writes a federal grant to do $100,000 worth of research, the government allows her to add $45,000 to the total for indirect costs. This money goes directly to the university and not to the research itself.

87. The White House, "Fact Sheet: President Calls for Action by Memorial Day to Help America's Charities." <www.whitehouse.gov/news/releases/2002/04/20020411-4.html>

88. For example, President Bush proposes an EZ Pass process to help small, community-based groups get tax deductible status more easily. The State Department press release also states that the administration planned to establish a $150 million Compassion Capital Fund to educate and empower community-based organizations.

89. Thomas W. Ross, "The Faith-Based Initiative: Anti-Poverty or Anti-Poor?" *Georgetown Journal on Poverty Law & Policy* 9 (Winter 2002): 173. The author bases his conclusions on several sources, among them Michael King, "The Last Puritan: Meet Marvin Olasky, Governor Bush's Compassionate Conservative Guru," *The Last Observer*, 14 May 1995, available at www.bushfiles.com/bushfiles/olasky.html, and Vanessa Gallman, "Conservatives Fear GOP Missing Its Chance to Help Poor," *Dallas Morning News*, 28 January 1996, 7A.

90. Elizabeth M. Bounds et al., "Welfare 'Reform': A War against the Poor," *Welfare Policy: Feminist Critiques* (Cleveland: Pilgrim Press, 1999), 1.

91. The White House Office of Faith-Based and Community Initiatives, "Rallying the Armies of Compassion. <www.whitehouse.gov/news/reports/faithbased.html>

92. This is not to deny that there are people in need as a result of their moral failures. Nor is it to deny that sometimes the moral failures are those of employers and government officials, and that those in need are victims. We wish to emphasize that the causes are multiple and include personal, systematic, and natural causes.

93. Bush, "Rallying the Armies of Compassion."

94. Mary Leonard, "The Real Issue Is Trust," *Boston Globe*, 29 April 2001, D1. Susan Anderson, "Don't Take Bush Plan on Faith," *Los Angeles*

Times, 29 April 2001, M2. Mark Chaves, "Congregations' Social Services: Testing the Assumptions Behind the Policies," in *Sacred Places, Civic Purposes,* ed. E. J. Dionne and Ming Hsu Chen (Washington, D.C.: Brookings Institution, 2001). We are grateful to Thomas Ross, "The Faith-Based Initiative," for these citations.

    95. Ross, "The Faith-Based Initiative," 177.

    96. For a detailed analysis of the budgetary realities and implications of faith-based initiatives, see Ross, "The Faith-Based Initiative," 185–89.

3

The Ugly Politics of
the Faith-Based Initiative

Jo Renee Formicola and Mary Segers

*P*resident Bush's faith-based initiative was the charitable opportunity of a lifetime, a chance to help the under-served and to welcome godly people back into the public square. It represented a national effort to mobilize communities of faith together with nonprofit organizations and government agencies to work as partners for the poor. The idea was to create a bipartisan coalition, to overcome the dichotomy between religious and secular concerns, and to bridge the divide between public and private efforts. On paper and in theory, the faith-based policy looked like it could accomplish all these worthy objectives. However, it fell short of its expectations and proved extremely difficult to implement. In retrospect, everyone is asking: What went wrong? How could something so positive end up in legislative limbo?

The answer to that question is complex and involves many factors. Politically, the effects of the Florida election controversy shortened the presidential transition and led to a premature launching of the faith-based initiative. The shift in party allegiance of Vermont Senator James Jeffords led to a major change in party control of the Senate from a Republican to a Democratic majority. The president's faith-based policy was also bedeviled from the start with questions about constitutionality in terms of First Amendment rights to religious freedom and church-state separation. Further, a one-year review of the faith-based initiative by the Pew Forum on Religion and Public Life reported other drawbacks—namely, that policy implementation was hindered by a lack of autonomy for the director of the White House Office of Faith-Based and Community initiatives, by the absence of internal White House coordination, and by inflated expectations.[1] Moreover, because of external events, such as the September 11 attack, the White House dramatically shifted its policy priorities as well. Clearly, terrorism and the need for security trumped all social programs. This chapter explores these factors and shows how, in the end, politics and ideology worked against the president's faith-based initiative.

EXTERNAL EVENTS AND THE
POLITICAL CLIMATE POST-FLORIDA

The 2000 presidential election and the thirty-six-day Florida recount left everyone in the new Bush administration exhausted, frazzled, and with a relatively short period of time to make the transition from the Clinton to the Bush presidency. But, in order to capitalize on an abbreviated honeymoon period, the new administration felt it had to "hit the deck running" with initiatives after George W. Bush was inaugurated as the forty-third president on January 20, 2001. The White House was determined to unveil a new policy every week in order to convey a sense of momentum and to feed Beltway media hungry for information on the new administration. In the first week of the Bush presidency, the White House announced its tax cut and education initiatives. In the second week, the faith-based policy was announced with two executive orders creating both the White House Office of Faith-Based and Community Initiatives and similar agencies in five cabinet departments: Justice, Labor, Housing and Urban Development, Education, and Health and Human Services. However, John DiIulio, who had been appointed the director of the new White House office at the last minute, got off to a slow start and, in fact, had no office, no staff, no stationery—nothing. It took until April to get a staff of six that eventually included Stanley Carlson-Theis, Don Eberly, Don Willett, Michele Tennery, Rev. Mark Scott, and Lisa Trevino Cummins.

The Florida election controversy also left President Bush in an awkward position vis-à-vis minorities; he had lost their votes in the 2000 election generally and particularly in the state of Florida. This fact affected the media and public perception of the new policy. For some, the Bush faith-based initiative seemed less a vehicle to implement the philosophy of "compassionate conservatism" and more of a political strategy to attract African American and Hispanic voters. The Florida recount was also a factor in the thinking of Representative J. C. Watts (R-OK), who was anxious to get the new administration to court African Americans after the 2000 election. He decided to move quickly with House legislation to implement the Bush initiative. Thus Watts put House GOP leaders on a collision course with DiIulio, who favored a cautious, go-slow approach to educate the public to the merits of the president's plan.

The defection of Senator James Jeffords (R-VT) from the Republican Party further complicated matters for the Bush policy. Once control of the Senate passed from the Republicans to the Democrats, the White House could no longer be assured of congressional passage of the president's plan. There was no guarantee that a Democratic Senate would accept a bill approved by the Republican House of Representatives. Different House and Senate bills would have to be worked out in a joint conference committee. This was an unexpected blow to proponents of faith-based initiatives.

The Bush policy was also handicapped from the start by internal conflicts within the administration centering on ideology and political strategy. The *New York Times* characterized the squabbles in the West Wing as ones in which Rove and Bush saw "every debate as a morality tale, with the White House on the virtuous side of every argument. Rove's insistence that every single decision is about right and wrong, and not about votes, can have the effect of making much of what he says seem incredible. It has also proved, so far at least, to be a very effective strategy."[2]

President Bush's proposed policy called for government partnerships with faith-based organizations and promised to protect the religious freedom of recipients of social services from proselytizing. However, presidential adviser Karl Rove realized that this policy was risky for a Republican administration. Rove did not want to alienate two key constituencies of the Republican Party—the libertarians, who were fiscal conservatives and wanted no government involvement in social welfare programs; and the religious right, who were mainly conservative evangelicals and supported government funding of religious proselytizing by faith-based organizations. The failure of Bush's faith-based initiative may be due, then, not only to external events that overtook the initiative, but also to an internal political struggle within the White House. Moderates like DiIulio who favored the initiative clashed with political operatives like Rove who were willing to sacrifice the policy if it meant alienating the Republican Party's base constituencies.

More obviously, the events of September 11 really put domestic policies such as the Bush initiative on the back burner as the new administration struggled to deal with foreign policy and national security issues. Karl Rove contended that the president met on a regular basis with the bipartisan leadership of the House and the Senate before September 11,[3] and that things really did not change much after the attack on the Twin Towers. However, the need for homeland security, and the president's call for legislation to create a new anti-terrorism department within the government, sent many in the Congress scurrying to protect their oversight responsibilities and jurisdictions. The faith-based initiative, to many, simply became a sideshow in a much bigger power circus.

THE UGLY POLITICS OF THE FAITH-BASED INITIATIVE

Ugly things happen in Washington, D.C.—within the White House and the Congress and among the special interest groups who attempt to impact the policy process. Moreover, even the simplest of issues look different and much more complex from a variety of perspectives.

This chapter provides several accounts of what happened to the faith-based initiative during the first two years of the Bush administration. While the versions illustrate the intricacies of policymaking in the nation's capital, they, unfortunately, also attest to the ugliness of politics inside the Beltway.

Several colorful policymakers and lobbyists were instrumental in framing and promoting the Bush faith-based initiative. From Grover Norquist, Karl Rove, and Marvin Olasky; to Stephen Goldsmith, John DiIulio, and Jim Towey—the reader is introduced here to some of the Bush insiders, advisers, and staffers who are or were important in creating and implementing one of the signature policies of the president. In addition, the various accounts given here have very different emphases, depending upon the perspectives of particular political actors. For example, the interest of Congressman J. C. Watts in faith-based policies has been portrayed as a concern born out of religious conviction because he is a minister; and as an issue stimulated by politics due to a desire to attract African Americans to the Republican Party. John DiIulio is characterized as a moderate by some, and uncommitted to clear principles by others. Differing tales about the motivation and interests of political figures mentioned here makes the analysis of policymaking on the Bush faith-based initiative complex and difficult to sort out—but intriguing nonetheless.

A White House Version

John DiIulio was a big fish in the academic pond before he left to swim with the sharks in Washington, D.C. As previously mentioned, he had a Ph.D. from Harvard, had been a member of the faculty at Princeton and later a professor with an endowed chair in political science at the University of Pennsylvania. DiIulio had also distinguished himself as a member of the liberal Brookings Institution and its conservative think-tank counterpart, the Manhattan Institute. He was the author of a number of major publications[4] with members of the scholarly elite. And, when people talked about the faith-based initiative, he was mentioned in the same sentences with the likes of Marvin Olasky, the father of "compassionate conservatism," William Bennett, former secretary of the Department of Education, and James Q. Wilson, a past president of the American Political Science Association.

In the mid-1990s, DiIulio knew some of the Clinton people, and even did some work for Al Gore. But by end of the decade, he began to be courted by Karl Rove, who was Governor George W.

Bush's confidante and eventual political adviser in the White House. Rove had called DiIulio several times to come to Texas to discuss policy issues with the Republican presidential candidate, but DiIulio refused until Stephen Goldsmith, the mayor of Indianapolis and the domestic policy advisor of the Bush campaign, prevailed on him to attend a meeting in April 1999.

DiIulio recalled[5] his first meeting on the faith-based initiative with Bush and his advisors. Appearing impressive and genuine, the Texas governor underscored DiIulio's importance by giving him a bear hug, seating DiIulio next to himself, taking notes on what he said, and turning to him on all controversial matters. The meeting ended with Bush asking DiIulio to "stay in touch," and Rove following up by asking him to screen position papers and to "be the true voice of compassionate conservatism"[6] on the new policy effort.

As the faith-based initiative began to evolve, however, DiIulio felt that it was taking on "libertarian overtones," and he became less convinced that there was really a place for him on the Bush team. This notion came from the ideological leadership of Grover Norquist.

Norquist has been described as everything from a right-wing strategist, to a lobbyist, to a coalition builder, to a formidable go-to guy, and a power broker; in short, he has been referred to as the "managing director of the hard-core right in Washington."[7] He is the Harvard-educated president of Americans for Tax Reform, self described as a "coalition of taxpayer groups, individuals, and businesses opposed to higher taxes at both the federal, state, and local levels."[8] Norquist also serves on the boards of the National Rifle Association and the American Conservative Union, writes the monthly politics column for the *American Enterprise Institute Magazine*, and serves on the National Commission on Restructuring the Internal Revenue Service. He was an economist and speechwriter for the U.S. Chamber of Commerce, on the staff of the 1988, 1992, and 1996 Republican Platform Committees, and former executive director of the National Taxpayers Union and the College Republicans.

Norquist wrote *Rock the House* in 1994, an account of the conservative drive to take over the House of Representatives. He has connections with everybody who is anybody in Republican Washington, D.C., but in reality, he is a libertarian whose "goal is to cut government in half in twenty-five years" so that it can get "down to the size where we can drown it in the bathtub."[9]

Norquist's real influence has come from his ability to bring together all elements of the right wing of the Republican Party; to keep them on message, and to reinforce their priorities. Within the Beltway, Wednesdays are put aside for the Norquist "meeting," which can bring together as many as one hundred of the party faithful, often a standing-room-only affair at his office. The weekly event has been described as "impeccably egalitarian" and filled with eclectic groups of people sitting around a table "littered with bagels and reams of flyers" and literature from conservative think-tanks.[10] Briefings from White House and Congressional staffers provide the substance of the gathering, but often, political candidates come seeking money as well. It is at this salon, of sorts, and often later at Norquist's house, that he reports bits of information from the White House to a variety of right-wing lobbyists, media gurus, and political wannabes, all of whom are tied together by Norquist's signature concern and issue: tax reform.

One writer summed up his appeal:

> Taxation, defined broadly to encompass government redistribution of wealth, is the central political question of the moment. A tax cut . . . predetermines how government will (or will not) respond to a vast array of other issues—entitlements, defense policy, environmental regulation, health care, education, welfare—you name it.[11]

Beyond tax reform, Norquist was quietly working behind the scenes to bring American Muslims into the Republican Party for the 2000 election, and to give credibility to their concerns and causes. The founder of the Islamic Institute, Norquist works as an advocate for conservative issues that would appeal to Muslims, acts as an "interlocutor" with the White House, and claims to have delivered the Muslim vote for Bush in 2000.[12] Khaled Suffuri, a former deputy director for the American Muslim Council, is one of his partners in the Islamic Institute who "began regularly appearing at the White House . . . to discuss the faith-based initiative and concerns about law enforcement persecution of Muslims after 9-11."[13] Norquist also worked with Rabbi Daniel Lapin to bring conservative Jews into the party as well; Lapin later appeared prominently with Bush when he unveiled the Faith-Based Initiative in January 2001.

The faith-based initiative then, was peripheral to Norquist's larger agenda: a public policy that could conceivably use the charitable community to overhaul an already stretched social welfare policy that, according to him, was in need of change. But, the tax implications of the faith-based initiative were uppermost in his mind. Even during its inception, Norquist understood the faith-based initiative as a case of having to spend money to get money. Later, the Office of Management and Budget (OMB), charged with monitoring federal spending, categorized the costs in the faith-based initiative in four areas. First, incentives for charitable giving; second, spending for equal treatment of nongovernment organizations (NGOs) in the federal grant process; third, money for EZ Pass recognition of 501[c](3) status; and fourth, finances for new programs. OMB estimated that the tax incentive part of the initiative could cost between $11 to 13 billion, of which the charitable giving tax incentives would account for $8 to 10 billion of the total cost, whereas new programs for compassion capital funds and group homes for unwed mothers would only amount to $154 million.[14] Norquist's help would be critical, then, in getting the fiscal conservatives to support the tax implications of the faith-based effort.

Norquist had been George W. Bush's "unofficial liaison to so-called movement conservatives"[15] since 1998. Immediately after Bush was reelected as Texas governor and began thinking about the White House, Norquist traveled to Austin at the behest of Karl Rove, whom Norquist had known for two decades. Norquist came away convinced that Bush was not an authentic conservative, but that he was the right's best hope because of his views on tax cuts, school choice, tort and pension reform, and paycheck protection." [16] When he returned to Washington, he started spreading the word that the "right ought to line up behind Bush," and he personally mobilized conservatives "against McCain in the early primaries, especially in South Carolina—and in the process, cemented his ties to Bush and Rove."[17]

From the very beginning, DiIulio saw the potential for fragmentation within the Republican Party over the question of financing the faith-based initiative—a battle that could be fought out in terms of tax-credits, vouchers, and grants. He did not want to end up "an all-purpose consigliere," or be part of an "exercise in futility," so, during most of the campaign, he did little more than edit some speeches for Bush. Then, in June 2000, the presidential candidate came to Philadelphia for a political rally on DiIulio's home turf. Because of the time that had intervened between the Austin and Philadelphia meetings, DiIulio was genuinely surprised when Bush invited him to come to Carpenter's Hall, where the event was to take place. And it became even more intriguing when Bush asked DiIulio to stay afterward and walk with him as he shook hands with voters. Then, in the final coup de grace, DiIulio was whisked into the candidate's limousine and asked by Bush pointedly, What was the one big idea in the faith-based initiative that could make it work?

DiIulio was impressed by Bush's sincerity, but could see that he was also being cross-pressured by the libertarians (a.k.a., Norquist et al.) and by conservative demands from the religious right (a.k.a., the National Association of Evangelicals) that could compromise the potential for a bipartisan effort for the public good. He felt that Bush's heart was really set on the faith-based initiative, and that he wanted to advance a new public discussion of how to mobilize communities of faith with secular nonprofits for the under-served. DiIulio also believed that Bush "intuitively got Catholic social teachings," and that he was a man of faith. However, DiIulio still did not see a place where he personally could make a political contribution.

DiIulio stayed in the background for the next several months and watched the policy evolution of the faith-based initiative throughout the campaign and the election debacle. But, after all was said and done, it was clear that the new administration would have to try hard to score some quick points with several new legislative efforts during its fragile 100-day honeymoon period—or fall flat on its face. Taxes and education would take priority, and both would be unveiled during the first two weeks after the Inauguration. But what would the administration do then to keep its momentum going?

The transition team led by Karl Rove decided that the faith-based initiative would be the signature policy effort that would best identify and advance the principles of the new administration. But the first choice to carry the initiative forward was Stephen Goldsmith, not John DiIulio.

Goldsmith, as previously mentioned, had served two terms as mayor of Indianapolis and had become legendary outside the city for giving new meaning to the term "efficiency." His commitment to saving urban America through asset sales, outsourcing, franchising, charging user fees, and implementing vouchers had made him the model for fiscal innovators. Many of his ideas came from his involvement with the right-wing Manhattan Institute and Reason Foundation. During his tenure as mayor, he wrote *The Twenty-First Century City: Resurrecting Urban America*, a book that the Manhattan Institute embraced, purchasing 5,000 copies of the 8,000 run.[18]

Goldsmith then quickly became the darling of the conservative intelligentsia. Lauded by Newt Gingrich who called him "the most innovative and creative leader in the country," Goldsmith was named public official of the year by *Governing* magazine and one of the "Rising Republicans" in 1996 by *Time* magazine. [19] DiIulio, also taken with Goldsmith's thinking, described him as a true academic, a person who could throw out ideas like "confetti into a room, with one idea leading to four others."[20] The *National Review* labeled Goldsmith as "bright, even brilliant" and "one of today's most impressive politicians."[21]

The Indianapolis mayor had also founded the Front Porch Alliance to "match religious and neighborhood groups with city resources to meet local needs."[22] To many, it appeared as though Goldsmith had given form and brought success to his social and charitable ideas. His commitment to the poor and to conservative goals made him a star in Republican political circles, an official who soon caught the eye of the Bush campaign team. Goldsmith was tapped by George W. Bush to serve as his domestic policy advisor during the 2000 presidential campaign and, because of his personal belief in public/private partnerships, was immediately considered for a White House post to head the Bush faith–based initiative after the election.

Goldsmith, however, had been gone for a time during the latter part of the campaign due to a family illness, and by the time he had gotten back had lost some of his "insider" status that had been useful for attracting public intellectuals."[23] Nonetheless, he was with the campaign in Florida during the recount fiasco, and was still considered a viable contender for the position of faith-based director up to several days before the appointment was to be announced. On January 25, DiIulio got a call to come to the White House for a meeting to discuss the position, at which point he realized the Goldsmith appointment was already on "the cutting room floor."[24] Two members of the transition team, Don Eberly and Don Willett, felt that Goldsmith was out of the loop with the staff but were still giving the former mayor verbal assurances that if he wanted the job it would be his.[25] Seeking a high priority for the policy and cabinet status for himself, Goldsmith's demands soon sparked a debate between two members of the Bush transition team—Karl Rove and John Bridgeland.

Rove, who was Bush's chief strategist during the campaign, rose from president of the college republicans,[26] thanks to his friend Lee Atwater, to political consultant to the elder Bush in his bid for the presidency in 1980. In 1981 he founded his own consulting business and succeeded in helping U.S. senators Phil Gramm (R-TX) and Kay Bailey Hutchinson (R-TX) win elections. In November 1993, he began advising George W. Bush for his Texas gubernatorial bid. And when the governor decided to run for president sometime after the 1996 election, Rove sold his consulting firm and signed on for the duration.

Rove, then, had been with the president for a long time, had earned his trust, and, in the transition phase, was one of the critical players, if not the king-maker, as far as political appointments were concerned. Strategically, Rove was motivated by the need to enlarge the base of the Republican Party and transform its religious rhetoric. He believed that moving the government to the center through educational reform, tax breaks, and the faith-based initiative was the way to do it. Rove wanted people to say "We accept government, but we need to find a way for mediating structures."[27] Thus, compassionate conservatism became the ideological linchpin in an attempt to pull together disparate policy ideas for a major change in the way that the Bush government was going to do business in the future.

In order to make this happen, Rove had brought Stephen Goldsmith to Florida to play a part on the Bush transition team. Because of the former mayor's background and the evolution of the Bush agenda, it appeared as though Goldsmith would be the logical person to be appointed to the position of Special Assistant to the President, with the charge of promoting the faith-based initiative. In Rove's view, the job would essentially consist of implementing the Charitable Choice provision as it already existed in the Welfare Reform Act of 1996.

Rove saw the faith-based initiative as part of a larger, centrist agenda. Therefore, he did not want the program to be held hostage by the ideological forces on the right, that is, by those libertarians and certain religious groups who wanted to see Charitable Choice extended rather than simply implemented. He was concerned that they would compromise the president's initiative, a policy that in his mind already had bipartisan support in the guise of welfare reform. Rove wanted to see a better implementation of Charitable Choice, a sort of Charitable Choice II, something he considered a centrist slam-dunk.

John Bridgeland, on the other hand, had different ideas. A Harvard graduate with a J.D. from the University of Virginia, and former chief of staff to Congressman Rob Portman, he was also the founder of Civic Solutions, a company that worked with nonprofits, foundations, faith-based institutions, and corporations on public policy issues. Dubbed a "conservative idealist" and "drawn to public service" by John F. Kennedy and the Rev. Martin Luther King Jr.,[28] Bridgeland had morphed from a policy director for the Bush presidential campaign to become the co-director of the policy team during the Bush transition. Most "passionate when talking about public service,"[29] Bridgeland believed that the faith-based initiative was an important public policy for the Bush administration to pursue, not just because it could bring support to the administration, but because it was worthwhile in itself. He saw it as a way to help the under-served in society. A "ground-smoother" rather than someone who enjoyed confrontations, Bridgeland was described by insiders as someone who would "lead you down the path he wants you to go—without you realizing you're on the journey."[30] Thus, Bridgeland wanted the leader of the faith-based initiative to be a person who could play a critical part in taking the policy of Charitable Choice farther than it existed, possibly to a legislative package or a federal agency. He envisioned the creation of state liaisons and saw the faith-based initiative as a way to address the larger issue of volunteerism in America.

With the inauguration only days away, and no consensus within the White House on how to deal with the scope of the faith-based initiative, the president wanted to appoint Steven Goldsmith as the first director of the White House Faith-Based Initiative. Events moved quickly after that. By January 30, Goldsmith had already begun to build public support for the Bush effort. Taking on critics of the initiative, Goldsmith wrote in *The Wall Street Journal* that their opposition was focused only on the relationship between church and state. Such criticism, according to him, reflected a basic "misunderstanding of the principles" that would "guide the partnerships between government and the faith-based organizations that the president envisioned."[31] He proceeded to spell them out in the article. Faith action would not be an excuse for government inaction. Government dollars must not subsidize religion or evangelizing. Those in need should have the freedom to choose from a variety of successful providers. Faith-based programs could not simply be a panacea. Increased charitable giving and smarter use of the tax laws were better ways to help faith-based groups than government support.

Had Goldsmith attempted to make more of the faith-based initiative than Rove had intended? Had he crossed some kind of a policy line in public? Had the potential director polarized the left and the right? Had he moved from the center and alienated the base? Had Goldsmith somehow hinted that he would do more than just implement the existing Charitable Choice legislation? Was there more going on than such public comments in the West Wing? Was Goldsmith giving the staff pause and leading it to quickly reexamine the wisdom of his appointment? It is hard to say, but within days Rove called DiIulio for advice on how to deal with the evolving Goldsmith dilemma.

DiIulio immediately contacted Goldsmith. The two men had been friends for a while, moving in the same intellectual circles, and holding many of the same views on the role of public/private partnerships for social and charitable programs. After several hours of discussion, the two decided that Goldsmith should remove himself from the White House turbulence. Then DiIulio and Bridgeland worked out a compromise. Goldsmith would head up the Corporation for National and Community Service (CNCS), the agency that included AmeriCorps, the Senior Corps, and the Peace Corps. It was envisioned that the CNCS would ultimately become the action arm of the "armies of compassion" and implement other social and charitable programs. Together they agreed: Goldsmith would lead the CNCS, and DiIulio, under certain conditions, would take a position in the Bush administration as Assistant to the President and Director of the White House Office on Faith-Based and Community Initiatives. DiIulio thought that he and Goldsmith would work together to make a difference, DiIulio in the White House carving out the policy, and Goldsmith at the CNCS making it happen.

Neat? Gentlemanly? Civil? As it turned out, none of the above. DiIulio's demands were personal, professional, and ideological. First, he announced that he would only stay for six months—a fatal error. He basically announced that he was a lame duck before the shooting season even began. Second, he insisted that no legislation be considered for at least six months, claiming that a performance audit was necessary to gather information on the status of Charitable Choice. It was his original intention to follow the Rove formula and better implement the existing faith-based funding opportunities in the Welfare Reform Act. Like Rove, he also simply wanted to create a Charitable Choice II unless his study unequivocally showed that some legislation might, indeed, be necessary. This was his second mistake. For, what is the Washington endgame, if not legislation? How does a Congressman/woman look good without bills, pork barreling, and something to show the voters at home what he/she is accomplishing? Simply studying the matter for six months to a legislator was akin to sending it to a dead letter file, with the stamp of "Dead On Arrival" in their minds. Third, DiIulio insisted that the faith-based initiative, as a better implementation of Charitable Choice, be developed in the ideological center and stay there. This was his third miscalculation, and his last. For DiIulio's insistence on currying favor with neither the left nor the right put him in a position of being without supporters in either camp. He had no coalition of his own. The libertarians, under Norquist, had an agenda; and the evangelicals, he would soon learn, wanted none of DiIulio's emphasis on grant-making and performance audits. This was a sad realization, for in Washington—and especially in the White House—every political initiative needs allies from the bottom to the top of the power structure to make something happen.

DiIulio, who described himself as the "colorful cheerleader in chief," partly out of naïveté, partly out of arrogance, but always out of principle, thought he could move the faith-based initiative forward by himself. With his charge from the president to be a "forceful advocate" for the policy, and the chief executive's personal guarantee that DiIulio was always "free to get on my dance card," DiIulio believed that he could advance the faith-based cause through the policy labyrinth. So, the professor entered the world of political operatives, thinking he could use his bipartisan and personal contacts, especially as Karl Rove and his staff focused on other issues. But the West Wing operatives had not forgotten Goldsmith's demands for agenda priority and high office, memories that marred DiIulio's credibility by association. Just as important, everyone knew the faith-based director would only be around for six months. Thus, while DiIulio confidently set out to do what he thought he needed to do in the time he and Rove had allotted to the faith-based effort, the policy clock was running out to a full stop.

DiIulio did, in fact, have many former students from his Harvard days who worked on the Hill, and he bragged that he had a variety of information sources from a diverse number of legislative offices. He prided himself on his contacts. He gained the support of Hillary Clinton (D–NY) and Joseph Lieberman (D–CT), Democrats that he had brought around to his way of thinking. But he did not have the support of House Republicans, who wanted to move fast on legislation that would give a partisan advantage to the new president. A meeting with the staffers from Speaker Dennis Hastert's (R–IL) office immediately after the inauguration signaled the rush. Kiki Kless, the policy adviser to Hastert along with legislative assistants in Rep. J. C. Watts's (R-OK) office, namely Jack Horner and others, had already prepared, and were circulating a draft of the faith-based initiative as H.R. 2—the second bill that would be introduced by the House in the new legislative session!

According to DiIulio, the speaker's office had anticipated an attack from the right: a push for an expansion of Charitable Choice. They believed it would come in the guise of a demand for vouchers, as a way to fund religious social services with public money. Therefore, DiIulio believed that Rep. J. C. Watts, a minister, had already been enlisted to co-sponsor a new bill that would take the conservatives' concerns into consideration. The White House, he thought, had co-opted Tony Hall (D-IL) to give it a broader appeal. But still— DiIulio was stunned by their quick moves. He claimed: "They jammed me."[32]

Within a month of his appointment, then, DiIulio was in the thick of the political fray. On February 26, at a three-hour question and answer meeting with the leaders of the Jewish Council for Public Affairs, he claimed that evangelical programs like Teen Challenge, a drug treatment program based on the need for religious change, would not get public money. In a perfect sound bite, he said it was because "Bible-thumping doesn't cut it"[33] in the delivery of social services. The remark immediately antagonized the entire religious right, and DiIulio was forced to back away from his statement.

At the same time, the faith-based initiative began to take on a life of its own in the House—without DiIulio. It emerged as a fait accompli in the form of H.R. 7, the Community Solutions Act. It was introduced on March 29, only three months into the president's term, and the day before it was to go to the floor to be voted on, a faxed copy of the bill was sent to DiIulio. He claimed he had no input and that he had no help from the Office of Congressional Liaison. As a result, he was rendered irrelevant.

During that same month, March 2001, Senators Rick Santorum (R-PA) and Joseph Lieberman (D-CT) also introduced S. 592, the Senate version of H.R. 7. A piece of legislation[34] that would have advanced the faith-based initiative, it provided tax incentives and charitable deductions for food donations, as well as a means to streamline the rules to obtain 501(c)(3) status for religious, charitable organizations. The bill also provided a $100 million Compassion Capital fund—that is, monies to train individuals on how to gain access to social service dollars. It would have used the CNCS (Goldsmith's organization) to train faith-based volunteers, and would have allotted $67 million for a national mentoring programs for the children of prison inmates.

DiIulio was called to testify before the House Government Reform Committee around the same time—but with no preparation, none of the usual processes, and no lawyer. Grilled by the members, he made a poor showing, but decided to stick to his own agenda and continue to advance a Charitable Choice II version of the president's faith-based initiative. DiIulio chose to respond to conservative legislative demands by providing public education, which was in line with his "no legislation needed" approach. He decided he would hold conferences at the White House, do outreach, and give as many speeches as possible. But in the process, he managed to continue to antagonize many by his direct manner and attitude.

In fact, DiIulio soon made a fatal error. He spoke to the National Association of Evangelicals (NAE) at its annual meeting in March 2001, in an effort to mend fences and to get the organization to line up behind the president's faith-based initiative. His address was more of a lecture, and taken as an accusation that the evangelicals were polarizing national views on both the House and Senate legislation. DiIulio told the leadership that "predominately white, ex-urban evangelical and national para-church leaders should be careful not to presume to speak for any persons other than themselves and their own churches."[35] He called on the NAE to "get affiliated church leaders to get real—about helping the poor, the sick, the imprisoned, and others."[36] And, if they could not or would not work within the president's initiative, he reminded them that they could simply opt out altogether.

His remarks were interpreted by National Public Radio as displaying the "unattractive side" of compassionate conservatism and of lending itself to lecturing about morality.[37] But it is safe to say that the NAE was more than offended by DiIulio's remarks. It had begun to question the faith-based initiative earlier, and now began to oppose it in every way possible: on the issue of funding, vouchers, the hiring exemption, and grant making. Thus, DiIulio had cut off a major group of conservative supporters who originally had the potential to champion the faith-based initiative. Now the evangelicals were gone. The libertarians were gone. And the left had opposed the initiative from the start.

In April, a religious summit consisting of more than 400 influential members of the clergy, supported by Congressman J. C. Watts, took place in Washington, D.C. DiIulio, who was scheduled to speak, claimed that he was not informed that he was expected to do so, and up until the day before was not even sure if he was going to attend. He did appear, reluctantly, but continued to feel that he had been all but locked out of the legislative process that was in progress to advance H.R. 7. It looked as though there was going to be faith-based legislation to be considered with or without his performance audit or input.

It also began to become apparent that the president was starting to lose faith in some of those around him who had been charged to turn his charitable vision into a legislative reality. After attending a Rose Garden ceremony in early May, Michael S. Joyce, the conservative head of the Bradley Foundation and a school choice supporter, got a phone call from Karl Rove. He told Joyce that the president wanted him "to undertake a private initiative to help get [the] legislation through."[38] Insisting on independence from the White House, Joyce opened a new office called Americans for Community and Faith-Centered Enterprises, hired a number of consultants and lobbyists, and worked to convince centrists, corporate leaders, social conservatives, and members of Congress to get behind Bush's proposal. Joyce summed up the need to build bridges by saying that DiIulio was basically the wrong person to "battle with the good old boys. . . ."[39] Then, he took on the libertarians and accused them of "fanaticism" and of viewing government as "oozing and putrefying" and of "consuming everything in its path."[40] The politics began to get even uglier.

In fact, the Catholics and a few minority religious groups were the only supporters left who still could be counted as Bush political allies. Thus, DiIulio tried to build on their initial support to further the faith-based initiative. The Catholic Bishops had originally seen the president's effort as a potential means to gain new funds for their many charitable services in the United States. But its "proxy-network," that is, Catholic Charities and Catholic Hospitals USA, which functioned largely with government contracts, was wary that competition might compromise their missions and programs.[41] To assure them that this was not the case, DiIulio enlisted the president's aid. In May, the faith-based initiative was the basis of the president's commencement address at Notre Dame. Injecting his bipartisan approach, DiIulio got Bush's speechwriters to allude to Lyndon Johnson's Great Society and Dorothy Day's social justice values as he called for social and charitable service from the graduates. Both the speech and the initiative received kudos in the media.

DiIulio also turned to his other source of political support: Hispanic ministers. In May 2001, he invited the national leadership of the Hispanic faith-based organizations to a meeting at the White House. The president made remarks, thanked the clergy for their charitable efforts, and agreed that the government should "set money out there to encourage faith-based initiatives."[42]

DiIulio and the president hoped that some inroads were being made. But it was clear that DiIulio was sensing the loss of momentum for the faith-based initiative. He decided to broaden his outreach and prevailed upon the president to make the faith-based issue the centerpiece of his remarks to the National Conference of Mayors in June. Some reports said that the president was trying to revive the legislation and get it back on track by adding stricter requirements on the use of public funds that were earmarked in H.R. 7.[43] Stressing the benefits of the initiative to black congregations, of which approximately 70 percent have community outreach programs,[44] Bush hoped to win both minority and local mayoral support for his signature charitable plan.

Reports that White House officials had mishandled the initiative and complaints that the bill as introduced in the House was unacceptable to Democrats and that it had no chance in the Senate began to filter into the press. In fact, the White House reportedly tried to work with House aides to "add language spelling out protections" right before the meeting of the president with the mayors.[45] Although Bush successfully solicited and got the municipal leaders' support for the faith-based initiative, it was slowly slipping into legislative oblivion.

In July, the Salvation Army, one of the largest providers of social services in the United States and a recipient of government funds, called the White House to request support for a hiring exemption with regard to homosexuals. Although Karl Rove claimed to have done nothing to give such assurances to members of the Salvation Army, the entire incident began to dissipate the goodwill that had existed since the Notre Dame speech.

By the end of the summer, both Karl Rove and John Bridgeland were losing patience with the politics surrounding the faith-based initiative. They just wanted to get the Senate to vote on S. 592 and pass it. DiIulio at the time was concerned about the "beliefs and tenets" aspects of the legislation, that is, the requirement that those who were to be hired by faith-based organizations had to be members of the denominations that were hiring them. Such an exemption in hiring practice smacked of discrimination to many centrists and liberals who considered the bill to be a violation of civil rights. But the White House staff, at that point, seemed willing to concede the matter and let the exemption stand. This way it could appease the right and get the legislation on the books. Rove and Bridgeland were willing to allow the courts to fight out the legalities of the bill; now they simply wanted to point to a legislative win on the faith-based issue.

Lieberman and Santorum, who were still committed to the president's policy, felt that S. 592 could not pass, so they introduced a different bill, S.1300, in August 2001. They believed that their new charitable incentive package[46] had a better chance of passage than their original bill, but by the end of the session, both agreed that the faith-based initiative was in trouble and dropped their sponsorship of S. 1300 as well. Publicly, Lieberman declared that there were too many church-state issues that had not been resolved, and Santorum claimed that the legislation was a "hot-button issue." Lieberman eventually decided that he would do further study and write his own bill.

DiIulio delivered his performance audit of the five government departments that were providing faith-based assistance at the end of the summer as well, and promptly resigned as he had promised. Citing health and family responsibilities, DiIulio returned to the University of Pennsylvania to the Fox School of Political Leadership. Marvin Olasky and the evangelicals called it "a merciful resignation."[47] Rove denied any inferences that he had forced out DiIulio. But had politics reared its ugly head? DiIulio had clashed with the political operatives and lost. They wanted a bill, something tangible that could be counted for their reelection bids in the future. He wanted a study—for policy implications down the line. They wanted an early Republican win. He wanted a bipartisan victory for later. They wanted to keep and expand the political base. He just wanted to advance the faith-based effort as proposed by Bush's Executive Orders and the existing Charitable Choice provision that already existed. His tenure ended after six months—with DiIuio's major regret: that he did not follow up when the president told him that he was always on his dance card and could come in and talk to him about the initiative whenever he needed to do it.

Another White House Version

DiIulio's departure left a leadership void in the White House with regard to the faith-based initiative. Now, who would take over the job of trying to revive the program that was in legislative limbo? On February 1, 2002, James Towey, an attorney who served as legal counsel to Mother Teresa for twelve years and had headed up Florida's health and services agency, was named the new director of the Office of Faith-Based and Community Initiatives. A soft-spoken man who had worked for Democratic Governor Lawton Chiles and Republican Governor Jeb Bush, Towey is more of a pragmatist than his predecessor. He is intent on creating a meaningful public-private relationship between the Bush administration and social providers in the United States while being cognizant of the pitfalls and criticisms of the program. "The focus," he says, "should be on the quality of the service provider. The question shouldn't be, 'Does your organization believe in God or not?' The question should be, 'Does your program work?' Are people's lives being turned around? Is there accountability? Is the group maintaining separation of its public funds from its private funds?"[48] Towey has been forging ahead without any legislation on the books and no new public money to fund those religious agencies that are seeking to compete for a piece of the welfare pie. His backing comes only from President Bush's executive orders, i.e., administrative policies that established the faith-based initiative and set up special agencies in a variety of cabinet offices.

Perhaps most indicative of the changed status of the faith-based initiative is Towey's new title: "director" rather than assistant to the president. He now also answers to John Bridgeland, who during the first year of the Bush administration had served as head of the Office of Policy Development and soon thereafter as director of the Domestic Policy Council.

Bridgeland had gained considerable internal influence within a year and had found the bureaucratic key to bypass the legislative roadblock that had all but scuttled the faith-based initiative. He proposed a reorganization of all federal and state voluntary services, one that would stress the charitable mission of black and Hispanic churches, help them to qualify for federal grants, and in turn, attract unpaid workers to their organizations.[49]

> Even before Bush took office, nearly 6,000 of the total 40,000 AmeriCorps positions were in faith-based organizations . . . Approximately 45,000 Senior Corps volunteers provided 10 million hours of service to faith-based organizations, such as the Salvation Army and Lutheran Social Services. Dozens of service-learning grants went to faith-based organizations and universities.[50]

On January 29, 2002, in his State of the Union Address, the president took Bridgeland's advice on how to implement the faith-based initiative without formal legislation. Bush simply reshuffled the bureaucratic deck and announced the establishment of the USA Freedom Corps. A "comprehensive, integrated citizen service initiative, it was intended to engage more citizens in service at home and abroad."[51] The new organization would be led by John Bridgeland and would subsume the Corporation for National and Community Service headed by Stephen Goldsmith, with its attendant divisions, AmeriCorps, the Senior Corps, and the Peace Corps. While the expanded citizen corps would now fall under Bridgeland's purview, *so would* the Office of Faith-Based and Community Initiatives, repackaged now as a voluntary, minority, social, and charitable effort.

Was this a bureaucratic coup for the Bush administration? The reorganization of all volunteer services under one office in the White House now had the potential to centralize the administration of all social and charitable programs, both secular and religious. Further, there are now offices in every state, which have the potential to reach to the local level and answer to state governors. With the ability to get the federal government closer to the grassroots, there is now also the possibility of providing diverse services by both public and private groups, as well the opportunity to influence, penetrate, and coordinate layers of government bureaucracy in social and charitable work.

One year into the Bush administration, then, Rove and Bridgeland had determined to take the faith-based initiative down a pragmatic, rather than an ideological, path. DiIulio had predicted that such an effort would simply become a "political to-do" list of government obligations.

But, right after the State of the Union address, the president announced an agreement with Senators Lieberman and Santorum that resulted in their introduction of a revised bill to the upper house that provided federal money to religious charities and other nonprofit organizations. The new bill, S. 1924, was known as the Charity Aid, Recovery, and Empowerment Act. It proposed new tax breaks to encourage charitable giving and included extra money for a social services grant program. The bill eliminated the right of religious groups to favor members of their own faith in hiring. And— it was killed in November 2002 right before the Senate adjourned for its holiday recess.

A HOUSE VERSION

Immediately after the election of 2000, Speaker of the House Dennis Hastert began to formulate a legislative agenda that would accommodate the president's priority agenda items. He, rather than the president, prevailed upon Rep. J. C. Watts to co-sponsor a bill with him on the faith-based initiative. It was going to be treated as a leadership bill, that is, as a presidential priority sponsored by the Speaker of the House and the House Republican Conference Chairman. The choice of Watts also reflected the fact that he was a minister who had continually expressed a sense of interest in faith, values, and compassion. Contrary to the press and political pundits, Watts was not used to bringing the African American clergy on board to bolster the Republican Party or to enlarge its base.

In the late fall, a draft of a faith-based bill was being put together by Kiki Kless in the speaker's office, Jack Horner in Representative Watts's office, and others. Starting by essentially cutting and pasting old bills that had been written and discarded, the group began circulating a draft to outside groups before the president had even come to town. It was their intention to get input from religious organizations, to build a coalition and eventually get the special-interest groups to write letters to their representatives in order to get them to co-sponsor a viable faith-based bill.

The earliest legislation was designed around creative deductions and a simple extension of the Charitable Choice provision of the Welfare Reform Act. It was sent to a variety of groups, including the Islamic Institute, the Jewish Congress, Catholic Charities, and various foundations. It circulated for several months, during the time period that is sometimes referred to as the "dead zone"— the time between Congress coming back after the holidays and really getting down to business. January is usually taken up with committee assignments and shuttling back and forth to congressional districts. February is budget time, and by March, representatives are looking for something to vote on in order to look good at home. The timing was right for H.R. 7. On March 29, the bill was introduced in the House with the blessing of the president, the speaker, and J. C. Watts; and then it was sent to the Ways and Means Committee and the Judiciary Committee for hearings.

According to sources in Watts's office,[52] DiIulio was kept informed at every step in the process, but he did not attempt to have any input into the bill. In fact, those who were shepherding the bill claimed they were never really clear about what the White House exactly wanted in the bill. They claimed that Carl Esbeck, counselor to John Ashcroft in the Department of Justice, and Don Eberly, one of DiIulio's staffers, were their point men. More importantly, they claimed that either Esbeck or Eberly did not inform DiIulio about meetings or that DiIulio simply did not take the responsibility to find out what was going on. Perhaps it was due in part to the fact that DiIulio really did not want to see a new bill, that he was studying the existing law and was simply trying to create the context for Charitable Choice II as he reported.

In any event, Jack Horner, who was the legislative director working on the bill for Representative J. C. Watts, claimed that DiIulio was invited to every meeting but, when it came to the moment of going over the bill line by line, Esbeck was called by the House framers, rather than DiIulio. It was he who pointed out policy differences on the phone. Horner maintained that DiIulio was simply "asleep at the wheel."[53] In fact, he says that when H.R. 7 went to committee, it was tightened and the language was changed, but that DiIulio did nothing about it. At that point, the hiring controversy was not addressed in the bill. Instead, the bill reaffirmed the past religious exemption as it existed in Title VII of the 1964 Civil Rights Act. That is, it allowed religious groups to discriminate in hiring, but it demanded that religious groups serve all their clients without exception. Thus, while the bill allowed a hiring exemption, it provided for civil rights protections for beneficiaries, as well. It was written ambiguously so that the law would remain the same but allow for possible changes, as the context of the new law became apparent in the legislative process.

On April 25, about a month after the bill was introduced in the House, J. C. Watts's office sponsored a religious summit. Watts would give the keynote address. DiIulio was also scheduled to speak. Claiming that he had been informed only the day before the event, and believing that he was being upstaged, DiIulio only grudgingly agreed to attend. In fact, Watts's people contended that the meeting had been set up the previous October (2000), invitations had been sent out, and DiIulio informed from the time of his appointment. Horner claims that either DiIulio was guilty of acting without due diligence, his staff was keeping information from him, or DiIulio was so busy on the road that he just did not know what was going on.[54] The Faith-Based Director, the day before, had wanted the meeting canceled, but because it had originally been scheduled as an outreach event, Watts's office refused. In any case, H.R. 7 had been introduced between the original planning and the actual summit, resulting in the fact that the meeting became a de facto rallying point for the bill. It was going to pass without, or in spite of, DiIulio's involvement.

In July the bill passed in the House. Considering the length of time it takes to usually pass a bill, H.R. 7 was a quick, as well as a significant, win for the president, Hastert, and Watts. Horner claimed that no coalitions were formed around the passage of the bill. Instead, he said it was simple: Republicans stood behind it; Democrats opposed it. But in the end, after the Salvation Army problems about hiring favoritism, certain representatives such as Mary Bono, Mark Foley, and Nancy Johnson had second thoughts. The bill, however, was worked out on the floor by a colloquy—that is, a dialogue with the bill's manager in which the concerned parties ask how the bill is to be read (understood) in certain sections. The manager—in this case Watts—explained its intent and content, so that the bill would pass and the problems about hiring could be worked out in conference.

A Senate Version

Senator Rick Santorum had been committed to public-private partnerships in a variety of forms for a number of years.[55] A devoted pro-life Catholic, Santorum came to the Senate in 1994 after serving two terms in the House. He was a member of the Renewal Alliance in the Senate[56] and had been chosen as the chair of National Bible Week for 2002. He was interested in seeing a bill in the Senate that would expand on H.R. 7 and wanted to use the basic framework of the original Charitable Choice provision of the Welfare Reform Act. In short, he wanted to increase resources and funding, and even go so far as "voucherizing" a potential Senate bill in order to minimize the constitutional debate on the church-state quandary. Santorum wanted to widen the range of service delivery, and he felt a comfort level working on this issue.

Santorum had worked with Joseph Lieberman on the Subcommittee on Air-Land Forces of the Senate Armed Services Committee and both had a mutual acquaintance, John DiIulio. Santorum and DiIulio knew each other from Pennsylvania policy circles, and Lieberman and DiIulio knew each other from the latter's work on the Gore campaign. So, it was a natural that Santorum and Lieberman would come together to be the point men in the Senate on the faith-based bill. They had common ground on a variety of issues; the idea of two former opponents in the 2000 election now coming together looked good; and both could work with DiIulio in the White House to advance the faith-based initiative.

Both set out to work on the issue, but strategic questions began to nibble away at the bill. The House was moving fast on H.R. 7, but the actual first Senate bill, S. 592, was taking a long time to get though the process of negotiation. The provision on hiring would not go away and could not be reconciled. Finally, the Lieberman people decided at the end of the summer of 2001 to write their own bill in order to deal with church-state concerns that they felt the White House had not addressed. Santorum communicated his worries but ultimately could not get over the hiring question, either, and so dropped his support for S. 592 at that time.

In August 2001, Santorum decided to try to move the faith-based initiative forward again in the Senate. With Lieberman, he introduced S. 1300, the Foundational and Corporate Charitable Giving Incentives Act of 2001, and attempted to advance it as a "resource package." Particularly after September 11, the anthrax scare, and other distractions, he tried to show that a redistribution of social resources was occurring and that the faith-based initiative could fill the void where those funds and volunteers efforts were being diverted. By that time, however, coalitions in the Senate had developed around two themes. Those Democrats who supported the notion of public/private partnerships were looking to advance some sort of a faith-based bill that would increase social services spending, while Republicans and the White House were pushing for increased deductions to aid in charitable work.

What resulted from this stalemate was the introduction of the Charity Aid, Recovery and Empowerment Act (CARE Act), S. 1924, in 2002. Among other things it allowed donors to transfer funds from IRAs to a charity with favorable tax consequences; raised the cap on corporate charitable contributions, created a charitable deduction for non-itemizers on their tax forms, and enhanced deductions for contributions of food and scientific and computer equipment. It was estimated that the cost of the Santorum-Lieberman bill would be about $10 billion over the next ten years.[57] Because it had taken so long to negotiate the bill, it became the proverbial five-legged horse built by a committee.

The logistics, rather than the substance, seemed to kill the bill in the end. Sources close to Senator Santorum have maintained that the bill died for three main reasons. First, the long time frame for the debate and passage of the bill in the House resulted in a loss of interest for members of the Senate. What started out to be a sure thing became so enmeshed with church-state and civil rights matters that many members who originally favored the bill began to have second thoughts about it. In fact, within the extended debate and passage process, the Senate power structure changed radically. When Senator Jeffords left the Republican majority, he forced the need for collaboration between the Democrats and Republicans, a move that did not happen easily or within the life of the impending bill.

Second, there was a leadership problem among the Democrats. Senator Tom Daschle (D-SD) had been on board for the CARE Act, giving it his support in a speech in South Dakota shortly before it was to come up for a vote on the Senate floor. Then on the day that it was to be voted on, Daschle gave each amendment one hour for discussion. Senator Richard Durbin (D-IL) brought up four amendments and Senator Jack Reed (D-RI) brought up one. Senator Clinton was unclear about her stance. Senator Levin wanted to include SEC matters and corporate accounting issues and Senator Sarbanes suddenly also had items he wanted in the bill. Since the end of the session was closing in, the Majority Leader decided that the bill could not take up five hours of the Senators' time because there were more pressing matters before the body. Therefore, it never came up for a vote. Republicans resented the fact that the Democratic Whip, who had counted his members on board, suddenly lost control of their votes. In short, there was no champion for the bill among the Democrats and no political will among the members of their party to see it passed.

Third, latent special interest groups in opposition to the CARE Act became vocal and argued against it at the very end. The issue of hiring and a hiring exemption became a hot-button issue toward the conclusion of the debate. Suddenly the lobbyists weighed in, showing concern and giving cover to members who voted against the bill.

Sadly, for those who worked on the bill, there was little support from the White House in the end. Most of the faith-based infrastructure had turned over after the resignation of DiIulio. David Kuo, who had helped draft the original Charitable Choice provision of the Welfare Reform Act, was appointed a special assistant to the president and replaced Rev. Mark Scott as Deputy Director of the White House Office of Faith-Based Initiatives. Kuo wanted the House to bow to the Senate bill.[58] House staffers were appalled, especially since Kuo had also previously been executive director of American Compass, a nonprofit organization whose purpose it was to reinvigorate the private sector to mobilize for the care of the needy. They were unwilling to throw out all the previous work that had gone into the bill. They resented Kuo's lack of understanding of House and Senate protocol and felt that the House was being asked to play a subservient role in the legislature. The entire faith-based exercise left a disappointed taste in the mouths of those who had worked so hard to develop a meaningful relationship between the White House and the entire Congress on a presidential priority.

An Organized Interest Groups Version

A variety of interest groups worked for and against the faith-based initiative. Those who lined up against it were the usual suspects: Americans United for Separation of Church and State, the American Atheist Association, the American Association of University Women, the American Federation of Teachers, the Service Employees International Union, and the National Education Association. The Coalition against Religious Discrimination, consisting of members of the clergy concerned about the right of the hiring exemption, as well as the American Federation of State, Country, and Municipal Employees, also jumped into the fray. Local unions feared that the faith-based initiative was "going to pit religious, nonprofit, and public agencies against each other and put government in the business of picking and choosing among religions."[59]

The supporters of the faith-based initiative were dwindling but got a shot in the arm from a newly formed Coalition for Compassion in the spring of 2001. It was made up of members of the Eagle Forum, American Values, the American Conservative Union, and individuals such as Marvin Olasky who still wanted to believe that public/private partnerships could happen on Bush's watch. The Coalition attempted to mend the fences that Pat Robertson and Jerry Falwell had originally breached by their criticism of the president's charitable efforts. Other groups were brought together under the umbrella of the Michael Joyce–led Americans for Community and Faith-Centered Enterprise. Within a number of months, Joyce had been able to rally virtually every conservative religious organization and include them on its membership roster.

It also appeared that the special interests who had the possibility of gaining resources and a closer relationship with the government could also be counted on for support for the faith-based initiative, particularly H.R. 7. Among these, the Catholics, particularly the Bishops' organization (USCCB), the Salvation Army, and Lutheran Services were the most supportive. Because they had all been receiving government contracts and acting as proxy networks for the public sector, they were a natural religious alliance with the faith-based initiative. But many other religious groups did not show the same support.

The Christian Right initially supported the president. However, the largest group, the evangelicals, who were a large part of the president's political base, became skeptical after about a year of fits and starts and broken promises about the faith-based initiative. Marvin Olasky, the original true believer, and the one who had done so much to advance compassionate conservatism, became disenchanted with the faith-based initiative after about a year. As editor-in-chief of *World*, a conservative Christian magazine, Olasky began to write about the politics of the faith-based initiative, and in an article entitled "Rolling the Dice"[60] told the story of the fight for the passage

of H.R. 7 from the evangelical point of view. It is summarized below, all the quotes being from his article.

According to Olasky, evangelicals began with the assumption
that equal access to government funding for religious charities meant
equal opportunity for all faith-based groups, even those that were
pervasively faith-based. In their view, substance-abuse programs and
other social services were ineffective without religious grounding.
They therefore objected strongly to any requirement that religious
activities be segmented from social services. As Star Parker, president
of the Coalition on Urban Renewal and Education, a group of 500
independent, inner-city churches and charity organizations, maintained, "You can't gut proselytizing from religious-run programs and
expect them to work. . . . The most successful of these programs are
those that incorporate their religion throughout the curriculum of
the program."

However, Olaksy maintained that "White House officials and
other tacticians close to the president, had a different view." He
claimed that the president was committed to the principles of compassionate conservatism, but that some contended that he "had no
confidence that he could sell those principles to the nation as a
whole over the opposition of liberal secularists." So, they decided on
"a Beltway strategy rather than a populist one." This involved compromise, that is, the willingness of Bush strategists to make concessions to "Congressional secularists" in framing and promoting H.R.
7. These concessions included a ban on religious proselytizing by any
faith-based group receiving government funding, and insistence
upon a provision by government of a secular alternative for recipients (clients) who objected to the religious elements in social service
programs. The overall strategy was to make the initiative acceptable
to "radical secularists" in order to win the votes necessary for Congressional passage.

The first part of their strategy, according to Olasky was to appoint someone as head of the new White House Office of Faith-
Based and Community Initiatives who would show liberals that he
was not in the religious right's corner. He reported that John DiIulio,
who had been an adviser to both Gore and Bush during the campaign, "was perfect for the role," in the words of one executive close

to the White House. According to this view, "it would be fine if conservative Christians became irritated at Mr. DiIulio, because liberal Republicans and Democrats would be far more likely to vote for measures and trust a man criticized by people they distrusted."

According to Olasky, the opposition of conservative evangelicals surprised White House strategists who were intent on making H.R. 7 acceptable to moderate Republicans and liberals. DiIulio was caught in the middle—trying to both allay the fears of the left and placate the forces of the right. Olasky reported that DiIulio agreed in April to drop his position that faith-based programs needed to be devoid of preaching, teaching, or evangelism in order to be eligible for federal grants. However, as the controversy over H.R. 7 intensified, Congressional and White House leaders began to fear an embarrassing legislative defeat unless they agreed to further weakening of the bill. The administration therefore tossed overboard the April agreement and accepted the stipulation that religious activities be segmented from the provision of social services in any faith-based program receiving public funding.

Olasky reported that conservative dismay at the shape of H.R. 7 increased in June when other concessions to the left were considered. A provision for a "secondary opt-out" caused consternation among many leaders of religious right groups. H.R. 7 already protected religious liberty by stating that if a recipient of services from a faith-based group objected to the program on religious grounds, the government would make sure that an alternative was available. But the new clause stated that, if a person comes to a faith-based group and does not like the religious flavor, that group has to provide a secular alternative.

Conservative evangelicals considered this revision to H.R. 7 "a complete loser," one that "would destroy our programs." William Murray of the Religious Freedom Coalition said his group "cannot support the president's Faith-Based Initiative if recipients are allowed to dictate to the provider which parts of the program they will accept. People should be able to choose from a variety of programs, but once a person chooses a Christian program there should not be an 'opt out' provision that allows the recipient to dictate a custom program to the provider." Mr. Murray, the Christian son of the late atheist leader Madalyn Murray O'Hair, concluded, "'Opt out' is just a plain stupid giveaway to Barry Lynn [of Americans United for Separation of Church and State] and the far left."

Conservatives also strenuously opposed an amendment proposed by Representative Mark Foley (R-FL) that would force religious organizations receiving federal dollars to comply with state and local civil rights ordinances. Under Title VII of the 1964 Civil Rights Act, they would otherwise be exempt. Shannon Royce, director of government relations and legislative counsel of the Southern Baptist Convention, immediately called legislators about the "killer amendment" and said, "If that amendment passes we will oppose the bill. We're not going to support a broadly expanded civil rights measure to the benefit of homosexuals."

White House lobbying to keep conservative and evangelical organizations in line was intense, according to Olasky. Essentially, they used three strategies to reassure conservatives. First, they noted that a stealth voucher provision had been inserted into H.R. 7. This meant that faith-based providers did not have to worry about government bureaucrats dictating the style and content of their programs. "If you take a voucher, you don't have to change your program." Second, Speaker Dennis Hastert and other House Republican leaders promised to try to work out a compromise regarding exemption from civil rights ordinances ("the gay amendment") later on. Their assumption was that, if the Democratically controlled Senate passed a faith-based initiative bill, it would most likely incorporate gay concerns. These would then be hammered out in a House-Senate conference committee. Third, White House lobbyists suggested creative ways to circumvent what conservative evangelicals viewed as onerous restrictions in the bill. They argued that the draft language was vague and general and had, in effect, many loopholes. One executive said that "a homeless shelter that had, say, a short sermon after dinner could still have it by offering those who came a choice between writing a paper after dinner or listening to the message." "They'll come to the sermon but it's been voluntary, because you've given them an option," he said. Asked about H.R. 7's mandate to separate the "religious" and "nonreligious" parts of programs, a Team Bush insider said that biblical and secular teaching could be interwoven, "as long as you do it right and keep separate books." White House advisers argued that the language of H.R. 7 allowed many opportunities for religious groups. "For example, say a church sets up a government-funded program, 'Fight Poverty, Inc.,' that teaches biblical principles using secular language. Someone from the church may pass out free Bibles before class, 'and if someone asks a question about a principle, the instructor can go to the Bible,' because he is responding to participant interest. The instructor can also announce that the church will offer personal counseling or individual help after class."

Finally, Olasky maintained, Beltway conservatives pointed to the complexity of policymaking in Washington and the need for compromise in order to get legislation enacted. They argued that Christians and conservatives were used to being in opposition, and needed to develop a realistic understanding of how "the Washington game" is played.

Ultimately, conservatives and evangelicals muted their opposition and accepted what they saw as a weakened H.R. 7. According to Olasky, they went along, although reluctantly, because they supported President Bush's principles, because the president went to Capitol Hill and personally appealed to conservative Republican Congressmen, and because they did not want to be "the fly in the ointment." Faith-based organizations on the religious right did not want to be seen as unsupportive of the president's signature bill.

Olasky's account reveals how complex and tortuous the policymaking path is inside the nation's capital. It also provides a religious right perspective on the Bush administration: that Team Bush players sometimes seemed too centrist for conservatives and evangelicals in the Republican Party. His view seemed to be that, unless interest groups on the religious right kept up the pressure, Bush White House officials and Beltway insiders would "give away the store" to "liberal secularists." Perhaps Olasky summed it up best with a quote from Congressman Tom Tancredo (R-CO), who interpreted the White House's Beltway strategy: "There's a terrible problem with that strategy. It gives liberals far more power than they would otherwise have. . . . Shut off outside discussion, you end up with an ugly product."

THE POLITICS OF THE
FAITH-BASED INITIATIVE IN 2002

For better or for worse, H.R. 7 passed the House in April 2001, but Senate Bill 592 died that summer. The emphasis then shifted to S. 1300, which was dropped. In February 2002, the CARE Act was introduced with the fanfare and optimism of a new baby coming home. But, instead, that bill died too.

One reason that Democrats and Republicans could not agree on faith-based legislation in 2002 was the increasingly partisan nature of the debate over what was originally intended to be bipartisan legislation. During the run-up to the 2002 Congressional (midterm) elections, for example, a controversy erupted over what some considered partisan activity by James Towey and his faith-based colleagues. Throughout the summer and fall, Towey appeared with Republican candidates in several closely contested Congressional districts to discuss publicly funded grants to religious groups. In August 2002, he appeared with Republican Congresswoman Shelley Moore Capito in her West Virginia congressional district and presented a $25,000 check to a computer-training program run from a Baptist church in Kanawha, West Virginia.[61] A week later he visited the Covenant Soup Kitchen in a church basement in Willimantic, Connecticut, in the company of Representative Rob Simmons, the Republican incumbent in Connecticut's second congressional district.[62] In all, Towey appeared with GOP candidates in Arkansas, Kentucky, Illinois, Florida, Connecticut, and West Virginia to publicize the faith-based initiative. Predictably, executive director Barry Lynn of Americans United for Separation of Church and State criticized Towey's appearances, charging that "The faith-based office is conducting seminars in congressional districts that just happen to have very close races coming up." Speaking of the Compassion Capital Fund, Lynn said, "They've created a kind of faith-based slush fund and they're dangling it around the country."[63] To Lynn and other critics, it seemed that the Bush faith-based initiative, originally bipartisan and even nonpartisan, had become a political weapon to be used to win GOP control of the House and Senate in the 2002 midterm elections.

When asked about this charge of partisanship at a conference on faith-based initiatives, at Seton Hall University, in New Jersey, Towey stated that he told every single Democratic and Republican congressional candidate that he would come to their district if invited. He said that Connecticut Congressman Simmons had invited him to visit the soup kitchen in Willimantic, but that not one single Democrat had extended an invitation.[64] He also rejected charges that he was politicizing his office by visiting minority communities, saying that he should visit these communities because they are the neediest. In an effort to underscore nonpartisanship, Towey had cleaned house when he took over the White House Office of Faith-Based and Community Initiatives in February 2002, removing staffers more concerned with politics than the poor.[65]

A second event that alarmed critics of the Bush faith-based initiative was the Bush's administration's announcement, on October 3, of a series of grants to twenty-one religious and community groups, including Operation Blessing, a religious charity created and run by the televangelist Pat Robertson.[66] The $500,000 grant award to Operation Blessing, renewable for the next two years, was part of the first round of grants from the Compassion Capital Fund, which had $30 million to dispense in 2002. What struck critics of the faith-based initiative as ironic is the fact that Robertson had been a trenchant critic of the Bush initiative earlier in 2001. He warned then that the Bush program was a Pandora's box that could make legitimate religious charities dependent on government—"It'll be like a narcotic; they can't then free themselves later on." The impression conveyed by this award of a grant to a Pat Robertson organization was that preference would be given to funding conservative evangelical organizations, part of the Republican Party's base constituency. Even the conservative columnist Cal Thomas was skeptical. He noted that "Robertson was right to warn of a 'Pandora's Box.' But he has now opened that box and is taking the money."[67]

Despite the failure of faith-based legislation proposals in Congress in 2002, President Bush would not give up on his signature program. On December 12, 2002, he announced that he would use his executive powers to clear the way for federal aid to flow to religious charities even if they discriminate in their hiring practices on religious and moral grounds. In a speech to religious and charitable leaders in Philadelphia, Bush said he was issuing an executive order requiring that federal agencies not discriminate against religious organizations in awarding money to community and social service groups for programs to assist the needy. He also signed a separate executive order establishing faith-based offices in the Department of Agriculture and the Agency for International Development, joining similar offices already established in five other large cabinet departments. Finally, he directed FEMA to allow religious nonprofit groups to qualify for aid after disasters like earthquakes and hurricanes in the same way that secular nonprofits can qualify.

By far, the most contentious of these executive orders was the one allowing government contracts to religious organizations that refuse to hire people of different faiths. Democrats said Bush's actions undermined a legal principle dating to 1941 under which groups that receive federal contracts must adhere to nondiscrimination standards.[68] They explained that Bush's policy would allow religious groups not only to hire only people of their own faith, but also potentially to rule out some job seekers on the basis of other factors like sexual orientation that might clash with their religion's tenets. Senator Edward Kennedy (D-MA) argued that "Under the new rule, organizations can accept public funds and then refuse to employ persons because they are Jewish, Catholic, unmarried, gay or lesbian. Rather than use the faith-based initiative to undermine our national commitment to civil rights, the president's executive orders should have made clear that no organization receiving taxpayer money can discriminate in its services or its employment practices."[69]

Opponents of the president's action also criticized Bush for using executive fiat to circumvent Congress on a matter of such great constitutional import. They claimed that the president's unilateral order cutting Congress out of the loop on such a controversial issue was unwise, imprudent, and even undemocratic. Moreover, the president's action seemed unnecessary given the fact that the new 108th Republican-dominated Congress was expected to be more receptive to the president's agenda. Christopher Anders, legislative counsel for the American Civil Liberties Union (ACLU) in Washington, said the president had "accomplished at the stroke of a pen what he couldn't get through Congress in the last two years and what he calculated he couldn't even get from a Republican Congress next year; which is a tremendous rollback to civil rights protections."[70]

Defenders of Bush's policy are not alarmed by the president's unilateral actions bypassing Congress. They note the obvious—that Congress failed to approve faith-based measures in the first two years of the Bush administration. Moreover, Congress has in the past approved charitable choice on four separate occasions (Temporary Assistance to Needy Families, 1996; Welfare-to-Work programs, 1997; Community Services Block Grant, 1998; SAMHSA Drug Treatment, 2000). Thus, they claim, the president is not acting in an authoritarian, undemocratic manner; he is simply implementing a policy already authorized by Congress.

Questions about separation of powers and actions by the three separate branches of government have continued to haunt the Bush faith-based initiative. The president's policy failed to win legislative approval in the first two years of his administration. Moreover, his faith-based initiative is so controversial that it will undoubtedly be challenged in the courts, in the judicial branch. Nevertheless, the president is undeterred. Wielding his executive power, Bush has created special offices in six cabinet departments and two other agencies and has charged those officials to seek out and support faith-based providers of social services. It is here that the Bush policy has met with some success. These centers have been actively reaching out to various constituencies, encouraging them to apply for existing government funding. By going through the executive branch bureaucracy rather than waiting for authorization from Congress, the Bush administration has been able to implement, at least partially, its faith-based initiative quietly and without public controversy. According to the report of the Pew Forum on Religion and Public Life mentioned previously, this silent revolution may have been the most important success of the Bush faith-based initiative.[71]

IT AIN'T OVER TILL IT'S OVER . . .

In December, the faith-based initiative ran into an ugly political mess involving its original director, John DiIulio, and some comments he made to the press. Interviewed in *Esquire* magazine for a piece on the White House policy apparatus, DiIulio told these authors that he believed, at first, that his comments were going to be off the record. Then, he understood that if they were going to be on the record, they would be part of a number of statements made by insiders who were asked to discuss domestic and social welfare policy.[72] In fact, he sent the author, Ron Suskind, a follow-up memo to further explain points that he had made during their conversations. Unfortunately, the article by Suskind[73] turned out to be one in which DiIulio's interpretation of the ground rules were different from those understood by the author. The piece turned out to be an unfavorable portrait of Karl Rove as a political operative, and an indictment of the abilities of his policy staff, called the "Mayberry Machiavellians" by DiIulio in his colorful language. The University of Pennsylvania professor came across as the disenchanted public intellectual and as a fierce opponent of the way that domestic policy was being made in the White House. DiIulio accused the policymakers of reducing issues to their simplest terms and steering them to the far right. More importantly, DiIulio was portrayed as the whistle-blower on what Suskind called the "paucity of serious policy discussion" and a "leakproof command-and-control operation" that was "altering [the] traditional laws of White House physics."[74]

Obviously, the White House was furious with this characterization of its policy-making processes. Ari Fleisher, the president's communications director, rejected DiIulio's comments as "groundless and baseless due to poorly chosen words and examples."[75] And, within a day, DiIulio apologized and withdrew his comments. He was contrite and unwilling to blame anyone for the mess that had emerged from his interview with *Esquire*.[76]

It is critical to point out the ramifications of this fiasco, however. DiIulio resigned from his public appointments—that is, with the Brookings Institution and the Manhattan Institute. He is on leave from his teaching position as the University of Pennsylvania. He met with those to whom he had given interviews for publications on the faith-based initiative in attempts to set the record straight, including these authors. Politics had reared its ugly head and all but finished the public life of John DiIulio.

It also closed some White House doors to those trying to understand the faith-based initiative better. James Towey, who had said that he would be willing to speak to the authors of this book about the future of the faith-based initiative, had a change of heart after the *Esquire* piece. Requesting resumes and writing samples from the authors, Towey nonetheless, decided not to meet with them. He sent a letter that said in part:

> I'm sure that you have followed the recent events regarding the comments of my predecessor, John DiIulio, and his reflections on the Initiative. In light of what took place, and the firestorms surrounding it, I must respectfully decline your offer to be interviewed for your book. In the event my failure to participate means that the "ugly" part of the initiative will be more pronounced, that is a regrettable consequence. I just do not feel it is wise for me to be involved in commenting on a Presidential initiative that I am asked to lead.[77]

In April 2003, another version of the CARE Act, minus the hiring exemption, passed the Senate, but what the faith-based initiative will ultimately look like is anybody's guess. Its political constituency has thinned considerably. J. C. Watts has left Congress. The former legislator and sponsor of H. R. 7 has opened J. C. Watts Companies, a new lobbying and consulting firm. Senator Joseph Lieberman has announced his candidacy for the presidency in 2004, and no doubt has played the critical role in eliminating the employment discrimination language from the CARE Act, thus protecting his future political aspirations. Senator Santorum, who now has a leadership role in the Senate, may now find his power compromised due to his controversial comments about the courts and their interpretations of gay rights.

It had been reported that Goldsmith's CNCS is in financial trouble and might not be able to provide the technical assistance that can make public/private partnerships work. AmeriCorps has frozen its recruitment of volunteers and reassigned some managers after CNCS financial reviews were requested by some Senators to examine the books for "possible mishandling of the program's budget."[78]

The evangelicals have all but bailed out on support for the faith-based initiative. Marvin Olasky reports that he will be teaching an interdisciplinary course on the program in the fall at the University of Texas.

The Catholic Bishops cannot be expected to provide heavy political support for the initiative. Owing to their own clerical sexual abuse problems, the Catholic leadership has been rendered all but irrelevant in policy circles.

Perhaps the future will be with Towey and a possible coalition of black and Hispanic clergy, who are still very much committed to making the initiative work. Government change never comes easy. Religious change is almost impossible. This potential strategic change involving both will take creativity and a political will in the United States that has not been seen often in its long and convoluted policy history.

NOTES

1. Kathryn Dunn Tenpas, "Can an Office Change a Country? The White House Office of Faith-Based and Community Initiatives, A Year Review," prepared for the Pew Forum on Religion and Public Life, February 2002.

2. Matt Bai, "Rove's Way," *The New York Times Magazine*, 20 October 2002, 60.

3. See "A Discussion with Karl Rove," at the American Enterprise Institute in Washington, D.C. 11 December 2001. <www.aci.org/past_event>

4. His books include: E. J. Dionne and John DiIulio, eds., *What's God Got To Do with the American Experiment?* (Washington, D.C.: Brookings Institution, 2000); James Q. Wilson and John DiIulio, *American Government: Institutions and Policies* (New York: Houghton Mifflin, 1998); John DiIulio, William J. Bennett, and John P. Walters, *Body Count: Moral Poverty—and How to Win America's War against Crime and Drugs* (New York: Simon and Schuster, 1996); Donald F. Kettl and John DiIulio, *Fine Print: The Contract with America: Devolution, and the Administrative Realities of American Federalism* (Washington, D.C. : Brookings Institution, 1995); and John DiIulio, *No Escape: The Future of American Corrections* (New York: Basic Books, 1991).

5. Interview with John DiIulio, 29 October 2002. All information in this section was obtained from either that session or a second interview on 16 December 2002. Where specific statements are cited, they will herein be

referred to as either "the first DiIulio interview" or the "second DiIulio interview."

6. The first DiIulio interview.

7. Robert Dreyfuss, "Grover Norquist 'Field Marshal' of the Bush Tax Plan," *Nation*, Issue 19 (14 May 2001): 11.

8. Americans for Tax Reform, staff. <www.atr.org/staff>

9. Dreyfus, "Grover Norquist."

10. "A Tale of Two Legacies: Republicans and Tories," *Economist*, no. 8304 (21 December 2002): 52.

11. Peter Beinart, "What Conservatives Understand about Taxes. Going Stronger," *The New Republic*, 21 May 2001, 18.

12. Franklin Foer, "Grover Norquist's Strange Alliance with Radical Islam, Fevered Pitch," *The New Republic*, 12 November 2001. <www.thenewrepublic.com/111201/foer111201.html>

13. Foer, "Grover Norquist's Strange Alliance."

14. "Faith-Based Initiative: Summary of Compromise Bill," 3 January 2002. <www.ombwatch.org>

15. Dreyfuss, "Grover Norquist," 11.

16. Dreyfuss, "Grover Norquist," 11.

17. Dreyfuss, "Grover Norquist," 11.

18. John J. Miller, "W's Whiz Kid," *National Review*, 13 September 1999.

19. Terry M. Neal, "Midwestern Mayor Shapes Bush's Message," *Washington Post*, 5 June 1999, A6.

20. The first DiIulio interview.

21. Neal, "Midwestern Mayor Shapes Bush's Message," A6.

22. Corporation for National and Community Service, "Senate Confirms Stephen Goldsmith to National Service Board," News release, 10 May 2001. <www.cns.gov/news/pr/100501.html>

23. The second DiIulio interview.

24. The second DiIulio interview.

25. The second DiIulio interview.

26. Famous Texans, www.famoustexans.com. This site points out that although Rove attended "nearly a half dozen colleges," he never did get a degree.

27. "A Discussion with Karl Rove," 6.

28. Derrick DePledge, "Tristater Helps Manage Bush Transition," *Cincinnati Enquirer*," 15 January 2001.

29. Nina J. Easton, "The Wings of an Idea," *Washington Post*, 27 March 2002, C1.

30. Easton, "The Wings of an Idea," C1.

31. Stephen Goldsmith, "A Little Help from Above," *The Wall Street Journal*, 30 January 2001, A22.

32. The first DiIulio interview.

33. Thomas B. Edsall, "Jewish Leaders Criticize 'Faith-Based Initiative,'" *Washington Post*, 27 February 2001, A4.

34. The Savings Opportunity and Charitable Giving Act of 2001 (S. 592), introduced on 21 March 2001.

35. John DiIulio, "Speech to the National Association of Evangelicals," 7 March 2001.

36. DiIulio, "Speech to the National Association of Evangelicals."

37. John J. Miller and Ramesh Ponnuru, "DiIulio Bully Pulpit," *NPR*, 8 March 2001, 1:45 P.M.

38. Miller and Ponnuru, "DiIulio Bully Pulpit."

39. Mary Leonard, "Faith-Based Plan Gets a New Push, Activists, GOP Lead the Bid for House Approval of Bush Measure," *Boston Globe*, 5 June 2001, A12.

40. Craig Gilbert, "Right Divided on Bush's Faith Plan; Some Fear that Government Funding Will Taint Organizations," *Milwaukee Journal-Sentinel*, 25 February 2001, 1A.

41. For a deeper discussion see Jo Renee Formicola and Mary Segers, "The Bush Faith-Based Initiative and the Catholic Response," *Journal of Church and State* 44, no. 3 (Autumn 2002): 693–715.

42. George W. Bush, "Remarks by the President to the National Leadership of the Hispanic Faith-Based Organizations Community," 22 May 2001. <www.harambee.org>

43. Mike Allen, "Bush Aims to Get Faith Initiative Back on Track; Stricter Rules To Be Added for Use of Funds by Groups," *Washington Post*, 25 June 2001, A1.

44. Allen, "Bush Aims to Get Faith Initiative Back on Track."

45. Allen, "Bush Aims to Get Faith Initiative Back on Track."

46. Foundational and Corporate Charitable Giving Incentives Act of 2001, Introduced into the Senate on 1 August 2001.

47. Marvin Olasky, "A Merciful Resignation," *World*, 1 September 2001, 1.

48. Joe Feuerherd, "Faith-Based Chief Faces Ideological Minefield," *National Catholic Reporter*, 11 October 2002, 3.

49. Doug Brown and Jeanie Stokes, "Losing Faith: Turf Battles Derail Funding," *The NonProfit Times*, 1 February 2002, 4.

50. Brown and Stokes, "Losing Faith," 4.

51. CNCS News, "President Calls on All Americans to Serve and Creates USA Freedom Corps," 30 January 2002. <www.cns.gov/news/pr/013002.html>

52. All information in this section is from a phone interview with Jack Horner, former legislative assistant to Rep. J. C. Watts on 5 December 2002. Herein referred to as "the Horner interview."

53. Horner interview.

54. Horner interview.

55. All information in this section from a confidential interview, herein referred to as "Confidential Interview B."

56. This was an organization in both the House and the Senate committed "to build a partnership between government and the community-based nonprofit organizations in order to promote real solutions to human problems." <www.senate.gov/~santorum> It consults with grassroots groups and promotes legislation for the advancement of communities and low-income families. Other members in the Senate have included Spencer Abraham, John Ashcroft, Sam Brownback, Paul Coverdell, Mike Dewine, Chuck Hagel, Tim Hutchinson, Kay Bailey Hutchinson, John Kyl, and John McCain.

57. "Care Act Sidelined Until September." Information from the Association of Fundraising Professionals, 2. <www.afpnet.org>

58. Horner interview.

59. Laurie Goodstein, "Battle Lines Grow on Plan to Assist Religious Groups," *New York Times*, 12 April 2001, A26.

60. We are indebted to Marvin Olasky who allowed us to summarize and use this piece in its entirety. He is editor in chief of *World*, a professor of journalism at the University of Texas, and a senior fellow at the Acton Institute. All quotes in this section are from Olasky's piece in *World* entitled "Rolling the Dice," 4 August 2001.

61. Steve Benen, "Faith-Based Flimflam," *Church & State*, October 2002, 4. See also Thomas B. Edsall and Alan Cooperman, "GOP Using Faith Initiative to Woo Voters," *Washington Post*, 15 September 2002.

62. Ray Hackett, "Faith-Based Man on a Mission: The Head of the Office of Faith-Based and Community Initiatives Visits Willimantic," *Norwich Bulletin*, 22 August 2002. <www.norwichbulletin.com/news/stories/20020822/localnews/479275.html>

63. Joe Feuerherd, "Faith-Based Chief Faces Ideological Minefield," *National Catholic Reporter*, 11 October 2002, 3.

64. Jim Towey, "A Panel Discussion on Government Funding of Faith-Based Initiatives," Opening Remarks, Seton Hall University, South Orange, New Jersey, 20 November 2002.

65. Joe Feuerherd, "Faith-Based Chief," 3.

66. Operation Blessing, a $66-million-a-year agency, describes its principal goal as "providing short-term relief and development assistance to economically disadvantaged people and victims of disaster throughout the world." Steve Benen, "Pat Gets Paid: Robertson Gets 'Faith-Based' Grant from Bush Administration," *Church & State*, 55, no. 10 (November 2002), 5.

67. Washington Post Staff Writer, "Robertson Charity Wins 'Faith-Based' Grant," *Washington Post*, 3 October 2002, A2. See also Steve Benen, "Pat Gets Paid," 4.

68. In an Executive Order issued in 1941, President Franklin D. Roosevelt directed that any business, agency, or group doing business with the federal government (receiving federal contracts) must not discriminate. This 1941 Executive Order later became the basis of President Lyndon Johnson's 1965 Executive Order 11265 establishing Affirmative Action requirements for federal contractees.

69. Richard W. Stevenson, "Bush to Allow Religious Groups To Get Federal Money to Aid Poor," *New York Times*, 13 December 2002, A34. See also David Gibson, "President Revives His Faith-Based Initiative," *The Star-Ledger* (Newark), 13 December 2002, 1 and 15.

70. Ibid. The 12 December 2002 press releases of the American Jewish Committee and the Anti-Defamation League of B'nai B'rith also criticized Bush for circumventing Congress.

71. Kathryn Dunn Tenpas, "Can an Office Change a Country?" 13–16. For an example of this bureaucratic implementation of the faith-based initiative in the Education Department, see "U.S. Courts Applications by Church Schools for Education Grants," *Boston Globe*, 21 July 2002, A1 and A25.

72. Second DiIulio interview.

73. Ron Suskind, "Why Are These Men Laughing?" *Esquire* 139, no. 1 (January 2003): 97–105.

74. Suskind, "Why Are These Men Laughing?" 105.

75. "Ex-Bush Aide Offers Apology for Remarks," *New York Times*, 3 December 2002, A27.

76. Second DiIulio interview.

77. James Towey to Jo Renee Formicola, 20 December 2002.

78. Christopher Marquis, "Financial Crisis Forces AmeriCorps to Halt Recruiting," *New York Times*, 11 December 2002, A33.

Conclusions

Jo Renee Formicola, Mary Segers, and Paul Weber

𝒜mericans are a curious people. While they have one of the highest rates of religious affiliation and church attendance in the world, the U.S. Constitution has long been interpreted as requiring separation of church and state and forbidding the use of religion as a litmus test for public office. Some observers think these two facts about Americans are related—that the reason they can worship freely according to conscience is *because* government steers clear of organized religion.

President Bush's faith-based initiative, the subject of this book, challenges this American achievement of religious vitality in the midst of church-state separation. Claiming that the social service of churches is not recognized and is not properly supported by taxpayer funds, the president has proposed to "end discrimination against the churches" in order to eliminate barriers to the eligibility of religious charities for government contracts and grants. In this concluding chapter, readers are asked to reflect upon the prudence and wisdom of the president's proposed policy.

To be sure, church-state relations are not the same as the complex linkage between religion and politics that has shaped American history. Religious communities have influenced politics and public policy in the past and in the present. In the history of the United States, religious traditions have often been fertile sources of constructive political action. The antislavery and temperance movements, the drive

161

toward women's suffrage and civil rights, and the antiwar activities of the 1960s were all, at least partly, inspired and motivated by religious values and religious commitment. Social services provided in soup kitchens and shelters through job training, prison ministries, and other services to the needy continue this religious tradition of denominational involvement in building civil society.

Nor should it be forgotten that religiously affiliated organizations have long been awarded "contracts for service" and continue to receive substantial federal and state funding to deliver social services, build hospitals, provide instructional materials, participate in educational voucher plans, provide disaster relief, manage immigration processes, and the like. However, this traditional public funding comes with restrictions. Namely, those receiving funds must refrain from direct or indirect proselytizing, they must provide services to clients irrespective of their religious affiliation or lack thereof, they must keep separate financial records, and they are required to follow all laws in regard to employment discrimination, workplace safety, and the like.

In other words, to oppose the Bush administration's new initiative for funding of faith-based organizations because it violates constitutional church–state separation is not to denigrate religion or deny the valuable role it plays in American public life and in the delivery of social services. Almost everyone recognizes the important part that faith-based organizations have played and continue to play in building ties of community in highly individualistic, and often fragmented, sections of society. And few dispute the rights of churches, temples, and mosques to articulate their views on sound public policy and to contribute to the public debate on major issues such as war and peace, economic justice, healthcare, and social security. As citizens, both believers and nonbelievers have equal rights to participate in the American political process.

But to recognize the role that religious groups have played in building civil society is not to say that the government should become involved in their missions, which are both material and spiritual. By providing public monies that would be channeled to churches to subsidize their soup kitchens, shelters, or after-school literacy programs, it is possible that government would advance religion in violation of the religion clauses of the First Amendment. In so doing, it might support religious preaching, and promote hiring discrimination, thus threatening religious freedom, church-state separation, and anti-discrimination laws. These are some of the concerns that have prompted opposition to President Bush's faith-based initiative.

This book has looked at the first two years of the president's faith-based initiative from the aspects of the good, the bad, and the ugly. And, in so doing, it has provided a brief policy history, described the controversy surrounding the initiative, characterized the positive and negative features of it, and explored the political conflicts that have shadowed the Bush policy from its inception. This concluding chapter summarizes the pros and cons of faith-based initiatives and suggests some future directions for the Bush policy.

It has, however, been difficult to come to consensus in this analysis because the authors began—and have ended—with different opinions on the faith-based initiative. They converge briefly in four areas. First, they all believe that the under-served (the poor, the homeless, the disabled, and the sick) in American society are intrinsically valuable human beings and deserve charitable help. Second, they all hold that the government, social service agencies, foundations, individuals, and religious groups should play a part in providing help to those in need. Third, they agree that the president may have put his finger on two weaknesses in past funding of faith-based organizations—namely, that the groups funded tend to be large, well-organized groups such as Catholic Charities, the Salvation Army, Lutheran Social Services, and the like, rather than storefront and small neighborhood churches in poor neighborhoods. In that context, then, government agencies may well have discriminated against smaller, lesser-known religious groups seeking funding. Fourth, they all view the faith-based initiative as a strategic, presidential attempt to deal with the problems of the under-served in a *new* and often *problematic* way.

From that point on, the authors diverge on almost everything, even on which analytic framework to use to come to some sort of an agreement as to the efficacy and potential effectiveness of the faith-based initiative. Segers argues adamantly that the faith-based initiative must be evaluated in terms of "context." Charitable Choice—and, by extension, Bush's faith-based initiative—are provisions of the controversial 1996 welfare reform act, a major devolution of public responsibility for the poor from the federal government to states and localities. The Personal Responsibility and Work Opportunity Reconciliation Act ended the entitlement status of welfare. It eliminated the AFDC program by replacing it with TANF block grants to the states, required welfare clients to engage in work within two years of receipt of welfare, cut spending on the food stamp program, eliminated benefits to legal aliens, and imposed a five-year lifetime limit on welfare. Therefore, Charitable Choice and, by extension, the faith-based initiative, in Segers's thinking, must always be analyzed in the context of welfare reform. The primary goal of such reform, to her, is to free the poor from poverty, not to "bring religion back into public life," as some commentators and policymakers claim.[1] This implies that Charitable Choice and the faith-based initiative should be evaluated primarily in terms of whether these policies succeed in reducing poverty and placing welfare recipients in decent paying jobs.

Second, Weber wants faith-based initiatives to be evaluated historically, especially seen in the light of the famous Patrick Henry–James Madison struggle over taxation to support religious ministries in Virginia. Segers and Weber both argue that the faith-based initiative must be evaluated in the constitutional context in which it will be implemented. To them, faith-based initiatives must be seen against a backdrop of fifty years of Supreme Court rulings on the meaning of the First Amendment religion clauses, especially the Establishment Clause. The First Amendment both secures religious liberty and protects against governmental establishment of religion. Recent Supreme Court decisions have shifted markedly over the past few decades away from a strict separationist toward a neutrality framework that honors pluralism. This has led law professors such as Michael McConnell to argue that government neutrality toward religion does not mean that government should discriminate against religious groups.[2] However, strict separationists continue to argue that Bush's faith-based initiative is profoundly unconstitutional. Derek Davis, editor of the *Journal of Church and State*, made this clear when he said,

> There are serious problems attending a framework of nondiscriminatory distribution of government benefits to religious institu-

tions. . . . Every distribution of taxpayer dollars to a church, synagogue, mosque, or other religious organization is a violation of the religious liberty of taxpayers who would find objectionable the propagation of the form of religious belief represented by the recipient. In the words of Thomas Jefferson, "to compel a man to furnish contributions of money for the propagation of opinions which he disbelieves and abhors is sinful and tyrannical."[3]

Weber supports the neutralist interpretation of the religion clauses, and argues that proponents of faith-based initiatives are using the language of neutrality but moving toward accommodation—that is, preferring religious providers to secular ones.

Third, Weber also argues that the faith-based initiative must be analyzed in light of tax cuts. He maintains that Charitable Choice putatively rests on four principles: (1) a level playing field; (2) respect for the integrity of faith-based organizations; (3) protecting clients; and (4) maintaining separation of church and state. That may have been the original intent, but he claims that the authors have shown that its implementation is problematic, at best. According to Weber, reality belies rhetoric in this case. He reports that in a recent column, E. J. Dionne wrote that "[President] Bush . . . is doing all he can to benefit the economic elites and, through stealth, to undercut government's commitments to the least fortunate."[4] Dionne, who has written extensively on faith-based initiatives, then continued,

> This is not a liberal fantasy. Conservatives acknowledge that Bush's long-term goal is to reduce the federal government's capacity to act—yes, to spend—without saying so publicly. The large tax cuts the President put on the table this week, conservative columnist Donald Lambro wrote candidly, "are, in effect, Bush's stealth initiative to curb future spending—big time." Exactly. And if you look carefully, most of the spending cuts will be in programs for the poor and near poor. *Stealthy redistribution upward is the theme of Bush's domestic program.* (emphasis added)[5]

Dionne is speaking most directly of the president's tax proposals, not faith-based initiatives, but the impact will be very direct and immediate, although the cause of the difficulties may not be clear so quickly: "The President's program is neither conservative nor compassionate. It is radical in its stealthy way, and it threatens to undermine the federal government's rather modest commitment to helping states and cities assist their poorest citizens. Yet by pushing so many of the fiscal problems so far down the road, Bush hopes to insulate himself from the political costs of his choices."[6] Weber believes that if this book does anything, it looks as thoroughly, sympathetically, and honestly at faith-based initiatives as possible. Then it blows the whistle.

Formicola is on another page. While she looks at the faith-based initiative through the same prism as her colleagues, she concentrates on the context of equity. She questions whether the denial of public funds to faith-based organizations that are providing social services is in reality a matter of subtle or overt *religious discrimination* and part of a larger denial of *equal opportunity*. Indeed, the Supreme Court has recently been deciding that individuals and religious groups have been denied access to funds, space, and protection by actions of the government and other actors. Among those decisions that point to the need for greater neutrality include *Agostini v. Felton,*[7] *Mueller v. Allen,*[8] *Rosenberger v. Rector and Visitors of University of Virginia,*[9] *Lamb's Chapel v. Center Moriches School District,*[10] *Widmar v. Vincent,*[11] and *The Good News Club v. Milford Central School.*[12] This line of reasoning supports free religious speech in a broader number of venues and the right of religious groups to use public school buildings for clubs, parental instruction, and remedial instruction. Neutral programs, which adhere to the *Lemon* test, made by true private choice, and that assist a broad class of citizens, are now being tested in the courts and passing constitutional muster. Formicola believes this will also happen with the faith-based initiative, if and when it is challenged.

Thus, with the positions of each of the authors noted, they reflect on the pros and cons of the faith-based initiative.

THE FAITH-BASED INITIATIVE: THE PROS

President Bush's faith-based initiative is predicated on the idea that everyone should be involved in social/charitable assistance. He perceives help for the under-served as a public and private responsibility that should be carried out jointly, with government and nonprofit resources providing care and to bring about a personal change in the lives of those in need. On this issue, George W. Bush continues to use the presidential bully pulpit—to talk like both a political leader and a preacher. At the 2003 annual convention of the National Religious Broadcasters, he exhorted his audience to "rally the armies of compassion so that we can change America one heart, one soul at a time."[13]

There is no doubt that the president is deeply committed to his faith-based initiative. According to White House spokesperson Ari Fleischer, Bush is personally invested in it "because of his own history of drinking, where faith did result in a change in him."[14] Bush has often said that what led him to stop drinking, and to turn his life around, was a spiritual awakening that began when he was about to turn forty. The evangelical orientation of President Bush toward a policy of social service is what impelled him to incorporate the faith-based initiative into his political agenda and to give it priority status from the beginning of his tenure.

The president's longstanding commitment to faith-based initiatives can also been seen in his actions as governor of Texas, particularly during his first term. Texas was one of the original states to partner with religious groups to achieve common public objectives. The strength of Bush's commitment to the federal initiative should be evident to the readers of this book. Whenever the policy proposal ran into significant obstacles, the president personally revived it—after John DiIulio's resignation, and after the Senate failed to act in 2001, and again in 2002. When Bush encountered significant congressional opposition on constitutional grounds, he simply bypassed Congress and used executive orders to put many of his ideas into operation. What is noteworthy is the strength, will, and commitment he continues to bring to this policy of faith-based initiatives. Equally important is the underlying idea of forging public/private partnerships to help those in need.

Other positive aspects of faith-based initiatives have been noted in preceding chapters. These may be summarized as follows. The faith-based initiative (and its predecessor, Charitable Choice):

- Calls attention to the duties of compassion.
- Recognizes the positive role of religion in society.
- Respects the integrity and autonomy of religious groups.

- Helps to build community, to build the structure of civil society.
- Helps to get the poor onto the political agenda.
- Stops subtle discrimination against religious groups in funding agencies.
- Provides technical assistance to small faith-based organizations, helping them to build the capacity to network and acquire the skills to manage programs and attract future funding. In other words, assistance to faith-based neighborhood organizations helps build social capital.

Structurally, it can be argued that the faith-based initiative can work and is already functioning—to assist those in need, even in light of potential legal obstacles. In practical terms, it is advancing through the political process by executive order and bureaucratic reorganization.

These tactics have been used by previous presidents; indeed executive orders alone have been used successfully by former chief executives to bring about needed change in society many times. FDR used an executive order to end hiring discrimination by companies that did business with the government during the war, and President Lyndon Johnson introduced Affirmative Action by Executive Order 11246 in 1965. He directed the Department of Labor to give preferential treatment to minorities in certain cases in an attempt to eliminate hiring discrimination.

Other public policies have been instituted by the courts as well—for example, busing to end the doctrine of separate but equal treatment of black students, as well as a host of other decisions designed to meet the "compelling interests" of the state on a variety of issues. In this instance, President Bush is using the power of the executive order to eliminate religious discrimination and to foster the compelling interest of the state to eradicate poverty, homelessness, and a number of other essential needs in society. So, although the legislative path appears closed to the faith-based initiative, it is important to point out that it is advancing via the administrative route, and being carried out now by offices within major cabinet agencies and organizations within the federal government infrastructure.

Bureaucratically as well, the president's plan is already functioning. Incorporating the faith-based initiative as part of a larger program of volunteer service, the White House has shifted internal responsibilities, reorganized its domestic policy office, and directed the implementation of the program within the larger context of social action. The White House has been able to foster the establishment of more than 100 state agencies and liaison organizations to start public/private faith-based programs on the state and local level. It has recruited large numbers of individuals to serve in provider capacities, so that it can be said that devolution of the faith-based initiative is already taking place in almost every state of the union.

Pragmatically, the faith-based initiative is also an innovative means to enhance the way that government does business with the private sector. The government must rely heavily on "proxy-networks"—that is on contracting agencies, to offer government services. It cannot carry the burden of welfare alone. Over thirteen million people are engaged in these types of services. They are paid "largely, if not entirely by federal funds. There are more than six government-by-proxy employees for every one federal civil servant."[15] The conclusion is simple: government must provide welfare services though private agencies—and because it has had a history of charitable involvement with a number of faith-based organizations traditionally, this is a natural path to take. To some extent, then, the faith-based initiative is both a continuation of providing social service funding and an experiment in a new way to help the under-served.

In this regard, Formicola argues for a *qualified* faith-based initiative, one that would respect church-state separation, and one that, in the end, would keep its eye on the prize and would help those whom it was intended to serve. It would require the following components.

First, an effective faith-based initiative would have to be based on government payment of vouchers to *individuals*, rather than direct, public funds to private (both religious and secular) organizations, for most social services. Government funding would follow the recipients, who could spend their vouchers where they wanted to, and give them some control and dignity over their lives. Market forces and personal preferences could then be used to determine where individuals would purchase the types of services they needed.

Vouchers would stimulate competition among all types of providers, not just religious ones, leading to innovation and allowing demand to drive supply.

They would also most likely pass a constitutional test if challenged in the courts. Indeed, the Supreme Court has already decided in *Zelman v. Simmons-Harris*[16] that the use of vouchers for tuition, under certain conditions, could be used to pay for education in parochial schools. Therefore, it is reasonable to assume that the court would uphold its precedent in the context of the purchase of social services with vouchers, as well.

Second, the religious organizations participating in the faith-based initiative could only be used as "proxy-networks." This means that they would have to compete with other agencies to receive government contracts to provide services and be required to obey all the federal rules and regulations of all other proxy networks. That is, they would have to keep separate books, obtain 501(3) (c) status approvals, and be willing to submit to the monitoring of their finances and the evaluation of the services that they provide. Those groups who would not want to comply with this requirement would be ineligible to receive faith-based funds.

Third, faith-based organizations would be allowed to hire those individuals who represented their religious views, but only in those positions where their mission required explanation or implementation. This exemption, already allowed within the civil rights statutes, would not apply to nonessential personnel. Constitutionally, the Supreme Court has also previously ruled on this, reinforcing the legal position of religious organizations in *Corporation of the Presiding Bishop v. Amos*.[17] In its finding, the court held that provisions against hiring discrimination do not apply to religious organizations, and do not violate the Establishment Clause. Further, it is also important to point out that the principle of hiring exemptions has been functioning successfully in the private sector as well. A prime example of this is the case of Planned Parenthood, which requires that those who counsel others about family planning be of the same mind as the goals of their organizations.

Fourth, the government must respect the religious nature of organizations but also recognize their proxy-network identity as well.

Therefore, it must be the responsibility of faith-based organizations to provide services to all clients who seek their assistance, and, alternatively, to direct individuals to seek similar services at secular agencies if they so desire. All social service providers, both religious and secular must be treated the same with regard to training requirements, grant writing, and financial records.

Fifth, the government must provide new funds—that is, monies for training and the development of innovative programs that can make a difference. The latter is also critical. There should only be a duplication of worthwhile, efficient charitable programs. The most valuable part of the faith-based initiative lies in the fact that it may be able to reach individuals more quickly and in different capacities than public agencies.

Sixth, there can be no direct funding of organizations, only individuals or services. And there can be no direct funding of any explicitly religious activities such as prayer, Bible study, the singing of hymns, or other actions that may be construed as denominational in any way. All programs must be neutral and provide true choices.

An important qualification should also be made here, however. That is, there is a big difference between the debate among Washington insiders about the constitutionality of faith-based initiatives and what will actually occur at the grassroots in terms of small community and church-based groups that provide desperately needed social services. While there may be some gap between theory and practice, in reality the fears about church-state separation will likely seem overblown when the practical success of these programs is measured.

THE FAITH-BASED INITIATIVE: THE CONS

The negative aspects of the president's faith-based initiative should be evident to the reader at this point. These features may be grouped into three categories: politics, policy, and philosophical assumptions.

As evident from chapter 3, the *politics* of the faith-based initiative has always been controversial and has occasionally become ugly. Indeed, this policy is no exception, and touches upon some of the deepest personal convictions people have—about religious freedom, religious conversion, and the role of religion in society. In a religiously diverse society, religious conviction and religious toleration are challenged by pluralism. While churches, temples, and mosques have the right to articulate their views on sound public policy, they are also constrained by society's need for toleration and respect.

For this reason, it is disturbing that President Bush's faith-based initiative has failed to win congressional approval. Passage of the initiative by both Houses of Congress would indicate that the most egregiously offensive aspects of the policy had been eliminated. The faith-based initiative has failed this test of democratic acceptability. President Bush's imposition of the policy by fiat—through executive orders that circumvent Congress—is regrettable. On such a controversial public policy as this one, the wise and prudent course for a president would be to seek the broadest possible approval from the people's elected representatives in the legislative branch.

As a *policy*, the faith-based initiative leaves much to be desired. Despite claims to the contrary, there is simply no evidence to show that religious organizations engaged in social services deliver these services more effectively than secular organizations. Moreover, although President Bush has issued several executive orders and encouraged cabinet-level agencies to pursue faith-based initiatives, actual new funding has not been significant. In other words, *this is largely an untested policy*. There is no evidence that it will save money or be more effective in changing people's lives.

Moreover, the lack of significant new monies means that the policy will continue to be untested. Indeed, without substantial added money, the faith-based initiative will only create more competition among religions, when what is most needed is cooperation. Americans have made much progress in this direction. As James Madison knew early on, religious competition—especially, if government abets it—leads to violence and civil disturbance. From a Madisonian perspective, the Bush administration is playing with fire.

Without new money, the faith-based initiative will result in resource shifting. Bureaucratic agencies will have to move existing resources from current recipients to newer faith-based organizations. This process is an open invitation to politicization. Indeed, Jim Towey, who replaced John DiIulio as director of the White House

Office of Faith-Based and Community Initiatives, stated recently that he will ask every cabinet faith-based office to give an accounting of where and to whom they have awarded contracts and grants. So faith-based offices in FEMA, USAID, and six cabinet departments will be under scrutiny from the White House (and possibly under pressure as well) to award contracts and funding to minority faith-based organizations, some of which could be groups in the base constituency of the Republican Party. Undoubtedly, revenue shifting will also occur with grant recipients. In other words, there is no assurance that provision of government funding would increase either the quantity or the quality of social services offered by an inner-city church.

Finally, many take issue with the *philosophical and theological assumptions* underlying the president's faith-based initiative. There is a tendency to blame the poor for their poverty. Instead of focusing on structural causes of joblessness, the president's policy focuses on personal responsibility and changes in life direction. It is a given that faith-based organizations should be funded by the government because they are said to be more effective and because they focus on personal conversion and personal transformation. It is assumed that poverty results from immoral behavior—from the personal and family failures of the poor. It is assumed, further, that personal renewal is necessary in order to end poverty and welfare dependency and that faith-based groups can help people achieve renewal and transformation. From these assumptions and premises, the conclusion follows: the government should fund faith-based providers of social services in the struggle to end poverty.

Weber calls such an approach to poverty "evangelism as social service," thus the solution is an evangelical one: find Jesus and life will change. According to him, evangelicals believe "redemption" is essential to any effective social service program. For example, Marvin Olasky insists that Bible reading and prayer cannot be omitted from a successful drug abuse program—precisely because of the need for personal transformation to overcome dependency. However, other groups tend to emphasize spirituality rather than religion. For example, Alcoholics Anonymous (AA), a group that has probably helped more alcoholics than any other organization in America, stresses that the key to recovery is spirituality rather than religion as such. AA strongly endorses the idea of personal transformation but keeps religion at arms' length, neither disavowing nor embracing it.

It may be very important to acknowledge that social problems arise from *both* unjust socioeconomic structures *and* from misguided personal choices. If the assumptions about the roots of poverty are wrong or incorrect, then the conclusions based on those premises should be reexamined. The evangelical approach to poverty is to emphasize personal transformation, something which the churches and faith-based groups can provide. However, if the operations of the larger economy are instrumental in creating poverty, then that cannot be ignored. Critics of faith-based initiatives argue that government must pay attention to the structural causes of joblessness as well as to the need for a social safety net.

The Bush administration claims that faith-based groups are more effective than secular programs because religion changes lives. This concept of life transformation seems to confirm the idea that religious worship, preaching, and proselytization are part of a successful program (a program that effects inner transformation as well as external behavioral change). However, both the Charitable Choice provision of the 1996 welfare reform law and the president's faith-based initiative forbid religious worship and religious indoctrination on the public dollar—in order to comply with the First Amendment and in order to allay the fears of civil libertarians and secularists. So, we seem to be faced here with a faith-based public policy that is inherently contradictory.

In addition to these negative aspects of faith-based initiatives concerning *politics, policy, and philosophical assumptions*, there are other criticisms of the president's initiative. These may be listed as follows:

1. *No shekels without shackles.* Government money brings with it complex forms and restrictive regulations. Will religious groups have to squander their already meager resources on administrative duties? According to the National Congregations Study, a 1998 survey of all kinds of churches, temples, and mosques, half of the congregations in the United States

have seventy-five members or less, and the average number of volunteers in direct social work is only ten.[18] Many of these small churches do not have the personnel and resources to keep up with government bookkeeping.

2. *The law of zero-sum.* Will the amount of funding for welfare and social service programs be increased? Established social service providers such as Catholic Charities USA did not back Bush's original proposal because they saw no appreciable increase in funding and thought faith-based organizations were being invited to compete for a static amount of federal funding. Also, other factors—the Bush tax cut, the recession, the evaporation of the federal surplus, and expenditures for the war on terrorism and the war against Iraq—raise questions about future funding. Finally, a less noticed development is the shift in charitable giving from the wealthy to the middle and working classes. Philanthropy groups have praised President Bush's proposal that nonitemizers be allowed to deduct charitable contributions on their tax returns. At the same time, philanthropy groups see themselves as net losers because the Bush administration and Congress are phasing out the estate tax, which promotes charitable giving by allowing a dollar-for-dollar credit for contributions. According to Gary D. Bass, executive director of OMB Watch, a Washington advocacy group for nonprofit charities, "The scope and dimension of the estate tax is beyond comparison with the new proposal" of the Bush faith-based initiative.[19]

3. *Standards and competence.* It would be naïve to assume that simply being religious makes a program competent. Large service-providing nonprofits that are in fact "faith-based," such as Lutheran Services in America, Catholic Charities, and the Salvation Army, have developed standards of professional competency. These providers of professional services in social work and psychological counseling wonder what small storefront churches will do. The use and training of volunteers, compared with professional social workers, does raise issues of standards and competence. Add to this the capacity to manage funds and staffs for some of these community organizations. In addition,

the pragmatic emphasis placed upon performance-oriented programs by the Bush administration suggests that there is perhaps an almost inevitable bias in funding towards large, well-established programs with proven track records. (DiIulio said: "I'm a civic venture capitalist; I need to see, with data, what works.") This would probably leave the small, storefront churches out of the picture.

4. *Disadvantages for religion.* Some see government-religious partnerships as threatening the integrity, autonomy, and missions of religions. "Filing annual compliance reports, waiving rights of confidentiality, and submitting to government investigation may take a large toll on religious autonomy."[20] Moreover, some core elements of government programs may conflict with religious doctrine. For example, the new welfare law places a heavy emphasis upon personal responsibility and work. This would likely conflict with religious-based convictions that mothers of young children should stay at home. Conscientious religious ministers might find themselves in the awkward position of having to terminate benefits for some charitable recipients and to report violations by others. Clearly, such blurring of ministerial and provider roles could threaten the spiritual integrity and religious autonomy of churches, temples, and mosques. Finally, participation in these new government-religion partnerships fuels the fear that religion's prophetic witness will be silenced—or at the very least diminish the willingness of its members to criticize those in power.

5. *Disadvantages for the poor.* Charitable Choice guarantees potential clients a choice between faith-based and secular service programs. This is a fundamental, constitutional issue of religious freedom. How can noncoercion of participants in such faith-based programs be assured? Indeed, given the insistence of Marvin Olasky and others that personal renewal and transformation are essential to behavioral change, can the proselytizing ethos of some religious groups easily be separated from the touted efficacy of their programs? Who will police and enforce respect for the religious liberty of clients?

Charitable Choice runs the risk of subjecting persons in need to unwanted proselytism.

The original provisions of the 1996 welfare reform law stipulated that recipients of faith-based social services must be provided with a secular alternative (to protect the religious freedom of clients). In large rural areas, such as parts of Texas, there may be only one social service agency for the whole population. If it is a faith-based provider, where is the secular alternative? How is the religious freedom of clients protected?

6. *Hiring discrimination.* Under Charitable Choice, a religious organization retains freedom to hire staff on the basis of religion (see chapter 2). This provision has generated the most significant political opposition to Charitable Choice and the Bush faith-based initiative and remains particularly controversial with civil rights groups who object to any weakening of the antidiscrimination principle. Throughout the brief history of the policy, controversy has erupted frequently over whether faith-based organizations that received government funding could be exempted from state and local antidiscrimination laws. Given pending lawsuits in the courts, this issue will not go away anytime soon. As noted in chapter 2, it would be bitter irony indeed if legislation touted as creating a level playing field provided a wedge to reintroduce discrimination. It would be doubly ironic if such an injustice swept in under the cloak of religion.

7. *Constitutional issues.* Should the federal government fund sectarian social services? According to President Bush, "We recognize that the funds will be spent on social services, not worship services. We respect the separation of church and state." Defenders of the Bush plan argue that tax dollars would go *directly* only to secular social services and that government would not directly subsidize religious worship, sectarian instruction, or religious proselytizing. But critics like Wendy Kaminer argue that government would *indirectly* subsidize such sectarian activities because faith-based groups can either use their own private funds to proselytize, or use money that has been freed up by the government's funding

of social programs. In other words, there really is no distinction between direct and indirect funding. According to Kaminer, the federal government is funding religious, sectarian activities in violation of the Establishment Clause, a basic violation of First Amendment freedoms. She likened it to the president's executive order of January 21, 2001, reinstating the "gag rule" on federal funding of International Planned Parenthood and other international family planning clinics. The Bush administration denied funds to such agencies because they use their own money or private funds to do family planning and abortion counseling. President Bush argued that the federal government does not fund abortions nor does it fund any agencies doing abortion counseling, even if they do it with their own money. In other words, when it comes to abortion and funding of international family planning agencies, the distinction between direct and indirect funding is a distinction without a difference. Kaminer simply took the Bush administration's reasoning on abortion and applied it to the Bush administration's faith-based initiative.[21]

THE FUTURE: WHAT DIRECTION FOR THE FAITH-BASED INITIATIVE?

Obviously most of the questions raised in this study remain unanswered, but many may find resolution in the coming years. One way they will be clarified is through the third branch of government—federal and state courts. There, several legal challenges are already wending their way through the judicial process, as we have mentioned in the introduction to this book. They bear watching to see how questions about the constitutionality of faith-based initiatives will be resolved.

Should any of these cases rise to the level of the U.S. Supreme Court, the composition of the court will be critical. Right now, the Supreme Court is evenly divided on First Amendment religious questions, with Justice Sandra Day O'Connor being the decisive swing vote. If there are any resignations or retirements on the

Supreme Court in the next two years, President Bush may well appoint a more conservative justice who could significantly change the court's jurisprudence on establishment and religious freedom kinds of cases.

Another way that the faith-based initiative will be resolved will be through the Congress. Despite President Bush's efforts to circumvent the legislature, Congress will also have significant input on the future of his program. The president cannot bypass Congress completely. It must reauthorize funding for programs that include Charitable Choice. These include energy assistance for the poor, Head Start, the Community Services Block Grant, and a slew of antipoverty efforts under the TANF program. Welfare reform is up for renewal in the first session of the 108th Congress. So, the debate about faith-based policy will continue in the halls of Congress—a debate, incidentally, that has now become polarized and subject to partisan forces. It is allied with an ideology (i.e., compassionate conservatism), and an individual (the president). Thus, Bush has been portrayed as the "Pastor-in Chief" and as using his bully pulpit to effect a strategic change in social charitable services. However, the initiative lacks broad bipartisan support and is not likely to develop a congressional coalition that will assure the votes needed for legislation in the future. The champions of the original legislation have shifted their own priorities. J. C. Watts is no longer in Congress; Joseph Lieberman has announced for the presidency in 2004; Rick Santorum is moving the notion of charitable choice to care and recovery in the light of September 11.

Finally, of course, the outcome of the presidential election of 2004 will obviously bode well or ill for faith-based initiatives. If President Bush is reelected, he will undoubtedly protect and perhaps expand his policy. On the other hand, if a Democrat wins the White House, it is difficult to say what the future of the policy will be—one of benign neglect, or complete repudiation. Much depends on whether faith-based organizations actually achieve results in their social service activities. It is understandable and perhaps predictable that presidents pay attention to the political dimensions of their preferred policies. However, based on their analysis, the authors agree that Charitable Choice should be viewed primarily as part of a welfare reform designed to free people from poverty, not a political strategy intended to bolster the electoral fortunes of the Republican Party.

While the authors believe that all faith-based groups should have equal access to government funding and services, they approach such a stance from a position of caution. They realize that this represents a stretching of the principle of constitutional neutrality, a stretch that could easily slip into accommodation of religion at the expense of secular groups. This would be problematic for each of them. In the long term, they recognize that Bush's faith-based policy represents a major change in strategic thinking about church-state relations in the United States. Again, however, the point must be stressed: Charitable Choice is part of a welfare reform package designed to free people from poverty, not a strategy to effect major change in church-state relations.

At the same time, the faith-based initiative must also be seen in political context—as a way President Bush can both secure his Republican Party base of conservative evangelicals and expand that base to include new minority and Catholic voters. To speak of its political context is not to minimize the importance of the faith-based initiative as part of Bush's agenda of "compassionate conservatism." It seems clear that Bush sincerely believes in the power of religious groups to effect personal transformation by providing social services to needy persons. But it would be naïve to ignore the political reasons that also drive the Bush faith-based policy. Indeed, the faith-based initiative has created a coalition of strange political bedfellows. The White House is attempting to woo certain constituencies—African Americans and Roman Catholics. In the 2000 election, African Americans preferred Gore to Bush by 9 to 1. Providing governmental assistance to social programs run by small black churches is, presumably, one way for President Bush and the GOP to win more support among black voters. As for Catholics, they voted 50 percent for Gore to 47 percent for Bush (with Nader 2 percent and Buchanan 1 percent). Since Catholics are demographically concentrated in some seventeen states with large electoral votes, no presidential candidate can afford to ignore them. And since the Roman Catholic church is the largest single nongovernmental provider of social services in the country, providing government funding to faith-based service programs has the potential for generating more support for President Bush and the Republican Party among Catholic voters.[22]

So much has happened since research began for this book, much of it discouraging. The economy has been in an extended decline and malaise, resulting in a substantial decline in tax revenue. President Bush has proposed a 2004 budget that includes significant tax cuts and deficit spending of breathtaking reach and depth. The same budget gives no new money for faith-based initiatives, relying instead on the redistribution of resources. The president continues to advance his program through executive orders, and it continues to be turned down by Congress. The war on terror, the conflict with Iraq and the tensions with North Korea lead to an international situation that is dangerous, disturbing, destabilizing, and most certainly distracting from domestic concerns. Nonetheless, President Bush forges ahead on his faith-based initiative. It is clear that he believes strongly in this policy, strongly enough to bypass Congress, and to play political roulette—at least in the short term.

Despite all that has occurred, the authors remain optimistic, yet realistic, about this policy. They see the faith-based initiative as an opportunity, as well as one fraught with partisan pitfalls. They question the wisdom of a policy that has the potential to encourage religious discrimination and competition between religions. But they also recognize the hopes and aspirations of those who proposed faith-based policies as a way to better serve those in need. There will always be differences, dangers, and limitations inherent in this approach to social service delivery, particularly concerning any policy that challenges church-state separation in the United States. It is the authors' hope that the reader will add to the discussion of the faith-based initiative and help those committed to the under-served to find a creative solution to the quandaries it raises.

NOTES

1. Stanley Carlson-Thies, "Charitable Choice: Bringing Religion Back into American Welfare," *Journal of Policy History* 13, no. 1 (2001): 109–32.

2. Michael W. McConnell, "Believers as Equal Citizens," in *Obligations of Citizenship and Demands of Faith*, ed. Nancy L. Rosenblum (Princeton: Princeton University Press, 2000), 90-110.

3. Derek H. Davis, "President Bush's Office of Faith-Based and Community Initiatives: Boon or Boondoggle?" *Journal of Church & State* 43, no. 3 (Summer 2001).

4. E. J. Dionne, "Not Conservative, Not Compassionate," *The Courier Journal*, 8 February 2003, A7.

5. Dionne, "Not Conservative, Not Compassionate," A7.

6. Dionne, "Not Conservative, Not Compassionate," A7.

7. *Agostini v. Felton*, 521 U.S. 203 (1997).

8. *Mueller v. Allen*, 463 U.S. 388 (1983).

9. *Rosenberger v. Rector and Visitors of University of Virginia*, 515 U.S. 899 (1995).

10. *Lamb's Chapel v. Center Moriches School District*, 508 U.S. 384 (1993).

11. *Widmar v. Vincent*, 454 U.S. 263 (1981).

12. *Good News Club v. Milford Central School*, 533 U.S. 98 (2001).

13. Bob Herbert, "Heavy Lifting," *New York Times*, 13 February 2003, A41.

14. Laurie Goodstein, "A President Puts His Faith in Providence," *New York Times*, 9 February 2003, IV4.

15. John DiIulio, "Government by Proxy: a Faithful Overview" (unpublished paper), 2. See also Frank J. Thompson and John DiIulio, "Medicaid and Devolution: A View from the State" (Washington, D.C.: Brookings Institution, 1988).

16. *Zelman v. Simmons-Harris*, 536 U.S. (2002).

17. *Corporation of the Presiding Bishop v. Amos*, 483 U.S. 327 (1987).

18. Kenneth L. Woodward, "Of God and Mammon," *Newsweek*, 12 February 2001, 24-25.

19. Elisabeth Bumiller, "Accord Reached on Charity Aid Bill after Bush Gives In on Hiring," *New York Times*, 2 February 2002, A19.

20. Melissa Rogers, "The Wrong Way to Do Right: A Challenge to Charitable Choice," in Dionne & DiIulio, *What's God Got to Do with the American Experiment?* 138-45.

21. Wendy Kaminer, on the *Lehrer News Hour*, 30 January 2001.

22. Here, it is interesting to note that the Catholic Bishops were very critical of the 1996 Welfare Reform Act and fought vigorously to modify some of the more controversial features of the legislation. However, five

years later, they were among the more ardent supporters of Charitable Choice and the president's faith-based initiative. How to explain that shift? See Jo Formicola and Mary Segers, "The Bush Faith-Based Initiative: The Catholic Response," *Journal of Church and State* 44, no. 3 (Autumn 2002): 693-715.

Bibliography

Allen, Mike. "Faith-Based Initiative to Get Major Push from Bush: President to Use Executive Orders to Implement Some Parts of His Proposed Bill without Hill's Consent This Fall." *Washington Post*, 1 September 2002, A8.

"Amen Corner." *Atlanta Journal and Constitution*, 28 April 2001, 1B.

American Civil Liberties Union. "ACLU Blasts Bush Executive Order Allowing Discrimination in Workplace." Press release. 12 December 2002.

———. "ACLU of Florida Condemns President Bush's Executive Order on Faith-Based Initiatives." Press Release. 12 December 2002.

American Jewish Congress. "Congress Hails Victory in Texas Charitable Choice Case." Press Release. 20 May 2002.

Americans United. "Taxpayer Funding of 'Faith-Based' Social Services Violates Constitution, Says Federal Court." Press release. 9 January 2002. <www.au.org/press/pr010902.htm>

Andersen, M. J. "In the Office of Zeal." *Milwaukee Journal Sentinel*, 26 March 2001, A9.

Anti-Defamation League. "The Case against Charitable Choice: Why Government Funding for Faith-Based Social Services Endangers Religious Freedom." Press release. 24 December 2002.

Ashcroft, John, United States Senator. Letter from materials on Charitable Choice prepared by Stanley W. Carlson-Thies, Director, Project on Government and the Religious Social Sector. The Center for Public Justice, Washington, D.C., December 1996.

Associated Press. "New Faith-Based Initiative Draws Fire." *Star-Ledger* (Newark), 24 January 2003, A9.

Avery, John L. Statement by John L. Avery, LICSW, MPA, Government Relations Director of NAADAC, The National Association for Addiction

Professionals before the Committee on the Judiciary, United States Senate, 6 June 2001. <www.senate.gov/~judiciary/te060601jla.htm> (6 June 2001)

"Bad Bill in the House." Editorial. *Washington Post*, 19 July 2001, A26. <www.washingtonpost.com/wp-dyn/articles/A17730-2001Jul18.html> (19 July 2001)

Baer, Susan. "An Advocate with an Edge." *Baltimore Sun*, 26 April 2001. <www.sunspot.net/bal-te.diiulio26apr26.story>

Balz, Dan. "Democrats Criticize Their Own—and Bush: Centrists Say Party Must Welcome Religious Belief; President Accused of Lurching Right." *Washington Post*, 17 July 2001, A4. <www.washingtonpost.com/wp-dyn/articles/A5138-2001Jul16.html> (18 July 2001)

Banks, Adelle. "African American Churches Assess Their Public Policy Role." *Religion News*, 19 April 2001. <http://pewforum.org/news/index.php3?NewsID=324>

———. "Bush's Faith-Based Initiative Divides Black Community." *Religion News*, 2 May 2001. <http://pewforum.org/news/index.php3?NewsID=354> (3 May 2001)

———. "DiIulio: No Funding for Conversion-Based Social Programs." *Beliefnet*. <www.beliefnet.com> (9 March 2001)

———. "NAE Backs Fed Funding for 'Charitable Choice' Programs." *Reuters News Service*, 6 March 2001. < www.beliefnet.com> (9 March 2001)

———. "U.S. Catholic Bishops Endorse Legislation on Faith-Based Initiative." *Religion News*, 14 June 2001. <http://pewforum.org/new/index.php3?NewsID=467> (15 June 2001)

Baptist Joint Committee. "BJC Attorney Says Faith-Based Order Ignores Constitutional Safeguards." Press Release. 12 December 2002.

Baptist Joint Committee on Public Affairs, and Interfaith Alliance Foundation. *Keeping the Faith: The Promise of Cooperation, The Perils of Government Funding: A Guide for Houses of Worship.* Washington, D.C.

Barnes, Fred. "In DiIulio Bush Trusts." *Weekly Standard Magazine* 6, no. 35 (28 May 2001). <www.weeklystandard.com/magazine/mag_6_35_01/barnes_art_6_35_01.asp> (22 May 2001)

Becker, Elizabeth. "Bill on Church Aid Proposes Tax Incentives for Giving." *New York Times*, 18 March 2001, A20.

———. "Bush Is Said to Scale Back His Religion-Based Initiative." *New York Times*, 14 October 2001, A18.

———. "Democrats Stand on Both Sides of Faith Bill." *New York Times*, 18 July 2001, A16.

———. "Head of Religion-Based Initiative Resigns." *New York Times*, 18 August 2001, A11.

———. "House Backs Aid for Charities Operated by Religious Groups." *New York Times*, 20 July 2001, A1.

———. "Lieberman Joins Bush Bid to Push Aid-to-Charity Bill." *New York Times*, 21 July 2001, A1.

———. "Republicans Hold Forum with Blacks in Clergy." *New York Times*, 26 April 2001. <www.nytimes.com/2001/04/26/politics/26FAIT. html> (31 May 2001)

———. "Senate Delays Legislation on Aid to Church Charities." *New York Times*, 24 May 2001, A22.

Belluck, Pam. "Many States Ceding Regulations to Church Groups." *New York Times*, 27 August 2001, A1.

Benedetto, Richard. "Bush, Republicans Court Catholics." *USA Today*, 21 May 2001, A2.

———. "President Asks Mayors to Back Faith-Based Plan; Bush Seeks to Revive Stalled Program." *USA Today*, 26 June 2001, 11A.

Boyd, Julian P., ed. *The Papers of Thomas Jefferson*. Princeton, N.J.: Princeton University Press, 1950.

Boyer, Dave. "Bush Pushes House GOP on Faith Plan; Tax Provision Passes Easily." *Washington Times*, 12 July 2001, A1.

Broadway, Bill. "Faith-Based Groups Benefit from New Federal Grants." *Washington Post*, 3 August 2002, B9.

Brown, Dorothy M., and Elizabeth McKeown. *The Poor Belong to Us: Catholic Charities and American Welfare*. Cambridge: Harvard University Press, 1998.

Bruni, Frank. "Bush Pushes Role of Private Sector in Aiding the Poor." *New York Times*, 21 May 2001, A1.

Bruni, Frank, and Elizabeth Becker. "Charity Is Told It Must Abide by Antidiscrimination Laws." *New York Times*, 11 July 2001, A15.

Bruni, Frank, and Laurie Goodstein. "New Bush Office Seeks Closer Ties to Church Groups." *New York Times*, 29 January 2001, A1 and A20.

Buckley, Thomas, S.J. *Church and State in Revolutionary Virginia*. Charlottesville, Va.: University Press of Virginia, 1977.

Bumiller, Elisabeth. "Accord Reached on Charity Aid Bill after Bush Gives In on Hiring." *New York Times*, 8 February 2002, A19.

———. "Bush Rallies Faithful in Call for Passage of Charity Bill." *New York Times*, 12 April 2001, A20.

———. "Faith, Politics and One Eye on Heaven." *New York Times*, 13 May 2002, A12.

———. "New Leader Picked for Religion-Based Initiative." *New York Times*, 2 February 2002, A14.

Bush, George W. Commencement Address at the University of Notre Dame, South Bend, Indiana, 20 May 2001. Reprinted in *Origins* 31, no. 3 (31 May 2001): 46–48.

———. "The Duty of Hope." 22 July 1999.

"Bush Meets Catholic Leaders to Push Faith-Based Solutions." *Daily Catholic* 12, no. 28 (28 January 2001). <www.dailycatholic.org/issue/2001Jan/jan28nul.htm>

"Bush on the Creation of a White House Office Tied to Religion." *New York Times*, 30 January 2001, A18.

"Bush Pushes Faith-Based Plans." eMediaMillWorks, *Washington Post*, Monday, 29 January 2001. <www.washingtonpost.com/wp-srv/0npolitics/elections/bushtext012901.htm>

Carr, Rebecca. "Bush Scores Critics of Faith-Based Initiatives." *Atlanta Journal and Constitution*, 26 June 2001, 3A.

———. "Bush's Faith-Based Initiatives; Surprise Attack Hits from the Right." *Atlanta Journal and Constitution*, 11 March 2001, 7C.

———. "DiIulio Driven by Values of His Boyhood." *Atlanta Journal and Constitution*, 3 April 2001, 5F.

———. "'Faith Talks Fuel Support, Opposition." *Atlanta Journal and Constitution*, 26 April 2001, 3B.

———. "GOP Hopes Faith-Based Plan Draws Black Clerics." *Atlanta Journal and Constitution*, 25 April 2001, A4.

———. "House Delays Debate on Faith-Based Bill." *Atlanta Journal and Constitution*, 19 July 2001, 3A.

———. "Racism Alleged among Foes of Faith-Based Plan." *Atlanta Journal and Constitution*, 20 March 2001, 4A.

———. "Talk of Delaying Tax Breaks Upsets Nonprofits; Incentives Play Crucial Role in Faith Initiative." *Atlanta Journal and Constitution*, 7 July 2001, 5B.

———. "White House Denies Aides Pushed Anti-Gay Regulation; Nonprofits Decry 'Backroom' Deals." *Atlanta Journal and Consitution*, 13 July 2001, A10.

Carrasco, Rodolpho. "Hispanic Religious Leaders Back Bush's Faith-Based." *Religion News*, 10 July 2001. <http://pewforum.org/news/index.php3?NewsID=531> (11 July 2001)

Castanon, Eliezer Valentin, Rev. Testimony presented by the Rev. Eliezer Valentin Castanon, General Board of Church and Society of the United

Methodist Church, Hearing before the Senate Judiciary Committee on Faith Based Solutions, 6 June 2001. <www.senate.gov/~judiciary/te060601evc.htm> (6 June 2001)

Castelli, Jim. "Faith Based Social Services: A Blessing Not a Miracle." Progressive Policy Institute. *Policy Report 27* (December 1997): 1–17.

Center for Jewish Community Studies. "Religion as a Public Good: Jews and Other Americans in the Public Square," a national conference sponsored by the Jews and the American Public Square project of the Center for Jewish Community Studies, 12–13 September 2001. <www.cjcs.net/events.htm> (30 July 2001).

"Charitable Choice Policy." *Religion & Ethics Newsweekly*, 11 May 2001. <http://thirteen.org/religionandethics/week437/newsfeature.html> (16 May 2001)

"Charities Are Denied Bias Law Exemption." *New York Times*, 11 July 2001, A1.

Chavez, Mark. *Religious Congregations and Welfare Reform: Who Will Take Advantage of Charitable Choice?* Washington, D.C.: Aspen Institute, 1998.

"Church, State & Money." *Commonweal* 28, no. 4 (23 February 2001): 5–6.

Cnaan, Ram A. "Keeping Faith in the City: How 401 Religious Congregations Service Their Neediest Neighbors." Center for Research on Religion and Civil Society, *Report 2000–1*. University of Pennsylvania, Philadelphia, 2001.

———. and Stephanie C. Boddie. "Charitable Choice and Faith-Based Welfare." *Social Work: Journal of the National Association of Social Workers* 47, no. 3 (July 2002): 224–35.

———. *The New Deal: Social Work and Religion in Partnership*. New York: Columbia, 1999.

Cohen, Richard. "As Buddhas Fall." *Washington Post*, 6 March 2001, A23.

"Compassionate Conservatism Takes a Bow." *Economist*, 1 February 2001. <www.economist.com/world/na/PrinterFriendly.cfm?Story_ID=490796>

Conniff, Kimberly. "Change of Heart." *Philadelphia Magazine* (March 2001): 43–54.

Crime Prevention Association of Michigan. *Program, Practice and Policy Brief*, Issue 9, April 2000. <www.preventcrime.net>

Davis, Derek H. "President Bush's Office of Faith-Based and Community Initiatives: Boon or Boondoggle?" *Journal of Church & State* 43, no. 3 (Summer 2001): 411–22.

Davis, Martin. "Faith, Hope, and Charity." *National Journal*, 28 April 2001, 1228–35.

Debates and Proceedings in the Congress of the United States. Washington, D.C.: Gales & Seaton, 1825–1837.

Diament, Nathan J., Esq. Testimony by Nathan J. Diament, Esq., Director of Public Policy—Union of Orthodox Jewish Congregations of America, United States Senate Committee on the Judiciary with Regard to Faith-Based Solutions; What Are the Legal Issues? 6 June 2001. <www.senate.gov/~judiciary/te060601njd.htm> (6 June 2001)

DiIulio, John, Jr. "The Church and the 'Civil Society Sector.'" *The Brookings Review* 15, no. 4 (Fall 1997): 27–31.

———. "God and the First Amendment." Unpublished paper, 2002.

———. "Government-by-Proxy: A Faithful Overview." Unpublished paper, 2002.

———. "The Lord's Work." In *Community Works, The Revival of Civil Society in America*, edited by E. J. Dionne Jr., 50–58. Washington, D.C.: Brookings Institution Press, 1998.

———. "The Political Theory of Compassionate Conservatism." *Weekly Standard*, 23 August 1999, 10.

———. Speech before the National Organization of Evangelicals. 7 March 2002.

———. "What Is Compassionate Conservatism?" *Weekly Standard*, 7 August 2000, 33–36.

"DiIulio Works on Religious Issues." *Associated Press*, 2 March 2001. <http://jsonline.com/news/nat/ap/mar01/ap-religion-diiulio030201.asp> (19 June 2001)

Dionne, E. J., Jr., ed. *Community Works, The Revival of Civil Society in America.* Washington, D.C.: Brookings Institution Press, 1998.

Dionne, E. J., Jr., and Ming Hsu Chen. *Sacred Places, Civic Purposes: Should Government Help Faith-Based Charity?* Washington, D.C.: Brookings Institution Press, 2001.

Dodson, Debra L., and Laura D. Burnbauer. *Election 1989: the Abortion Issue in New Jersey and Virginia.* New Brunswick, N.J.: Eagleton Institute of Politics, Rutgers University, 1990.

Doerr, Edd. "Faith-Based Folly." Letter to the Editor. *New York Times*, 2 May 2001. <http://query.nytimes.com/search/article-page.html?res=9C02 E1DC1738F931A35756C0A9679C8B63>

Dollinger, Marc. "Religion; Bush's Faith-Based Plan Borrows a Page from FDR." *Los Angeles Times*, 18 February 2001, M1.

Dunham, Richard S., Lee Walczak, and Lorraine Woellert. "When Courting the Right Turns Off the Middle." *Business Week*, 9 July 2001, 37.

Eckstrom, Kevin. "Democratic Majority in Senate Clouds Future of Faith-Based Plan." *Religion News*, 5 June 2001. <http://pewforum.org/news/index.php3?NewsID=439> (7 June 2001)

Edsall, Thomas B. "Bush Aims to Strengthen Catholic Base." *Washington Post*, 16 April 2001, A2.

———. "Jewish Leaders Criticize 'Faith-Based' Initiative." *Washington Post*, 27 February 2001, A4.

Elsasser, Glen. "Many Lack Faith in Charity Plan." *Chicago Tribune*, 16 April 2001. <http://chicagotribune.com/news/nationworld/> (17 April 2001)

Epstein, Gady A. "O'Malley, Churches Unveil Initiative; $1 Million Program Would Aid 900 Youths Considered at Risk." *Baltimore Sun*, 14 February 2001, 3B.

Esbeck, Carl H. "Charitable Choice and the Critics." *New York University Annual Survey of American Law* 57, no. 1 (2000): 17–32.

———. Statement of Carl H. Esbeck, Senior Counsel to the Deputy Attorney General before the Committee on the Judiciary, United States Senate, concerning Sec. 701 (Charitable Choice) of S. 304 Drug Abuse Education, Prevention, and Treatment Act of 2001, 6 June 2001.

"Faith-Based Funding Backed, but Church-State Doubts Abound." The Pew Research Center for the People & the Press Report. 10 April 2001 (released). <www.people-press.org/rel01rpt.htm> (31 May 2001)

"Falwell Remark Sparks Outrage; Religious Leaders Renounce Views on Islamic Faith." *Arizona Republic*, 8 March 2001, A7.

"Few States Giving Welfare Money to Religious Groups." *Associated Press*, 19 March 2001. <www.cnn.com>

"Five Groups Joining Forces to Mentor Children." *CNN.com*, 2 July 2001. <www.cnn.com/2001/ALLPOLITICS/07/02/bush.mentors.reut/index.html> (5 July 2001)

Foer, Franklin, and Ryan Lizza. "The Bushies' Faith-Based Brawl. Holy War." *New Republic*, 2 April 2001. <www.thenewrepublic.com/040201/forelizza040201.html>

Foltin, Richard T. Testimony of Richard T. Foltin, Legislative Director and Counsel, the American Jewish Committee, Office of Government and International Affairs, Hearing of the Senate Judiciary Committee on "Faith-Based Solutions: What Are the Legal Issues?" <www.senate.gov/~judiciary/te060601rtf.htm> (6 June 2001)

"Foreign-Aid Hike Urged; Helms' Surprise Proposal Has Faith-Based Strings Attached." *Arizona Republic*, 20 February 2001, A1.

Formicola, Jo Renee, and Hubert Morken, eds. *Religious Leaders and Faith-Based Politics. Ten Profiles*. Lanham, Md.: Rowman & Littlefield, 2001.

Formicola, Jo Renee, and Mary Segers. "The Bush Faith-Based Initiative and the Catholic Response." *Journal of Church and State* 44, no. 4 (Fall 2002): 693–715.

"From Promise to Policy: A Discussion of the White House Office of Faith-Based and Community Initiatives." Press briefing. The Pew Forum on Religion and Public Life. 30 January 2001. <http://pewforum.org/events/0130/>

Gerstenzang, James. "Some on Religious Right Miffed as Bush Courts Catholics." *Los Angeles Times*, 23 March 2001, 32.

Gibson, David. "President Revives His Faith-Based Initiative." *Star-Ledger* (Newark), 13 December 2002, 1 and 15.

Gilbert, Craig. "'Faith-Based Initiative to Face First Political Test; White House Will Have to Pull Out All the Stops to Help Bill Along, Backers Say.'" *Milwaukee Journal-Sentinel*, 17 June 2001. <www.jsonline.com/news/state/jun01/faith17061601.asp>

———. "Joyce Enlists to Push Bush's Faith-Based Plan; Bradley Foundation Chief to Lobby Congress." *Milwaukee Journal-Sentinel*, 23 May 2001. <www.jsonline.com/news/nat/may01/joyce23052201.asp>

———. "Right Divided on Bush's Faith Plan." *Milwaukee Journal-Sentinel*, 25 February 2001, 1A.

Gilman, Michele Estrin. "Charitable Choice and the Accountability Challenge: Reconciling the Need for Regulation with the First Amendment Religion Clauses." *Vanderbilt Law Review* 55, no.3 (April 2002): 799–888.

Glennon, Fred. "Blessed Be the Ties That Bind? The Challenge of Charitable Choice to Moral Obligation." *Journal of Church and State* 42, no. 4 (Autumn 2000): 825–43.

"God and Man and W." *Wall Street Journal*, 23 May 2001, A26.

"God and Man in Washington." *Economist*, 19 May 2001, 32.

"God and the Governor." *Charisma Magazine* interview, 29 August 2000. <www.beliefnet.com>

Goldsmith, Stephen. *The Twenty-First Century City: Resurrecting Urban America*. Washington, D. C.: Regnery Publishing, 1997.

Goode, W. Wilson, Sr., Rev. Dr. Testimony of Rev. Dr. W. Wilson Goode Sr., Senior Advisor on Faith-Based Initiatives Public/Private Ventures on Senate Bill 304, 6 June 2001. <www.senate.gov/~judiciary/te060601 wwg.htm> (6 June 2001)

Goodman, Ellen. "Can We Keep Public Policy Out of Pulpit?" *Houston Chronicle*, 18 February 2001, 6.

Goodstein, Laurie. "Battle Lines Drawn on Plan to Assist Religious Groups." *New York Times*, 12 April 2001, A26.

———. "Bush's Call to Church Groups Get Untraditional Replies." *New York Times*, 20 February 2001, A1.

———. "Bush's Charity Plan Is Raising Concerns for Religious Right." *New York Times*, 3 March 2001, A1.

———. "Church Group Provides Oasis For Illegal Migrants to U.S. " *New York Times*, 10 June 2001, A1.

———. "Nudging Church–State Line, Bush Invites Religious Groups to Seek Federal Aid." *New York Times*, 30 January 2001, A18.

———. "States Steer Religious Charities toward Aid." *New York Times*, 21 July 2001, A1.

Greem, Steven K. "Charitable Choice and Neutrality Theory." *New York University Annual Survey of American Law* 57, no.1 (2000): 33–48.

Guerricagoitia, Carmen M. "Innovation Does Not Cure Constitutional Violation: Charitable Choice and the Establishment Clause." *Georgetown Journal on Poverty, Law, and Policy* 8, no. 2 (2001): 447–73.

A Guide to Charitable Choice. Washington, D.C.: Center For Public Justice, 1997.

Gushee, David. "Colson's Career Has Become Model for Social Involvement." *Religion News*, 3 June 2001. <http://pewforum.org/news/index.php3?newsID=434> (5 June 2001)

Hamburger, Philip. *Separation of Church and State*. Cambridge, Mass.: Harvard University, 2002.

Hamilton, Marci A. "Separation: From Epithet to Constitutional Norm." *Virginia Law Review* 88, no. 6, at 1433 (October 2002).

Healey, Robert M. "Thomas Jefferson's Wall: Absolute or Serpentine?" *Journal of Church and State* 30, no. 3 (Autumn 1988): 441–57.

Herman, Ken. "Bush's Faith-Based Initiatives; Black Clergy Could Add Surprising Support." *Atlanta Journal and Constitution*, 11 March 2001, 7C.

Hollman, K. Hollyn. "Guides Set the Record Straight on Political Activity by Churches." Baptist Joint Committee. 9 October 2002. <www.bjcpa.org/Pages/Views/2002/10.09.intersection.html>

Hook, Janet, and Ronald Brownstein. "Bush Enters Era of Limits as Agenda Hits Resistance." 26 June 2001.

Hoover, Dennis R. "Faith-Based Ambivalence." *Religion in the News* (Spring 2001): 10–14.

"How Representatives Voted on Religion-Based Initiative." *New York Times*, 20 July 2001, A16.

Huffington, Arianna. "It's Not about Church and State." *Salon.com*, 13 March 2001 <www.salon.com/politics.feature/2001/03/13/faith/index.html> (5 June 2001)

Hutcheson, Ron. "Bush to Bypass Congress on 'Faith-Based' Charities." *Knight Ridder Newspapers*, 11 December 2002. <www.philly.com/mld/philly/4718731.htm?template=contentModules/printstory.jsp> (23 January 2003)

Hutchison, William T., and William M.E. Rachal, eds. *The Papers of James Madison*. Chicago, Ill.: Chicago Press, 1962.

Ifill, Gwen. "Church and State." Transcript of *PBS Newshour*, 29 January 2001.

Jackson, Derrick Z. "A Boost for Faith-Based Bigotry." *Boston Globe*, 13 July 2001, A23.

Joint Committee on Taxation. "Description of Present Law and Certain Proposals Relating to Charitable Giving and Individual Development Accounts." Paper prepared for the Select Revenue Measures and Human Resources Subcommittees of the House Committee on Ways and Means, 14 June 2001.

Joyce, Michael J. "Gotta Have Faith? Wisconsin Showed Way on Faith-Based Initiatives." *Milwaukee Journal-Sentinel*, 17 June 2001. <www.jsonline.com/news/state/jun01/faith17061601.asp>

Kenney, Jane. "Acting Governor Announces $2.5 Million for Faith-Based Groups." Department of Consumer Affairs News Release, 30 October 2001.

Kettl, Donald F. "Having Faith in Faith." *Governing Magazine*, April 2001, 12.

Khan, Muqtedar. "Why Muslims Shouldn't Support Federal Funds for Faith-Based Programs." *Iviews.com*, 4 February 2001. <www.iviews.com>

Kicklighter, Kirk. "Habitat for Humanity Turns 25: First the World, then Americas; Nonprofit Had to Build Trust Elsewhere before Being Embraced in Its Hometown." *Atlanta Journal and Constitution*, 10 June 2001, 1M.

Kiefer, Francine. "Guiding Hands for Kids with Parents behind Bars." *Christian Science Monitor*, 5 July 2001. <www.csmmonitor.com/durable/2001/07/05/p1s4.htm> (5 July 2001)

Kim, Soonhee. "Faith-Based Service Delivery: A Case Study at Ground Zero." *Journal of City and State Public Affairs* 2, no.1 (Spring 2001): 41–52.

Kress, Michael. "Separation of Church and Gay." *Belief Net.* <www. beliefnet.com> (4 June 2001)

Kuo, David. "Poverty 101: Liberals and Conservatives Can Learn from One Another." *Brookings Review* 15, no. 4 (Fall 1997): 36–38.

Kurtz, Stanley. "The Wall's Expansion." *National Review Online*, 22 May 2001. <www.nationalreview.com/comment/comment-kurtz052201. shtml> (24 May 2001)

Lampman, Jane. "Public Wary of Funding Faith-Based Social Service." *Christian Science Monitor*, 11 April 2001, 2.

Laycock, Douglas. Testimony of Douglas Laycock, University of Texas Law School, before the Senate Committee on the Judiciary, Faith-Based solutions: What Are the Legal Issues? <www.senate.gov/~judiciary/ te060601dl.htm> (6 June 2001)

League of Women Voters of New Jersey. *New Jersey: Spotlight on Government.* Montclair, N.J.: League of Women Voters, 1969.

Leahy, Patrick, U.S. Senator. Statement of Senator Patrick Leahy, Chairman, Senate Judiciary Committee, Hearing on "Faith-Based Solutions: What Are the Legal Issues?" 6 June 2001. <www.senate.gov/~judiciary/ pj1060601h.htm> (6 June 2001)

Lebowitz, Holly, J. "The Race Card." *Belief Net.* <www.beliefnet.com> (4 April 2001)

Leonard, Mary. "Backers, Foes Differ on Faith Initiative." *Boston Globe*, 25 April 2001, A2.

———. "Faith-Based Plan Gets a New Push; Activists, GOP Lead the Bid for House Approval of Bush Measure." *Boston Globe*, 5 June 2001, A12.

———. "Many Jews Hit Faith Plan Funding." *Boston Globe*, 28 February 2001, A2.

———. "The Nation: Faith-Based Initiative Is Modified, White House Alters Plan on Eve of Vote." *Boston Globe*, 28 June 2001, A2.

———. "Salvation Army, Catholic Bishops Back Bush Charity Plan." *Boston Globe*, 15 June 2001, A16.

Levy, Leonard. *The Establishment Clause: Religion and the First Amendment.* New York: Macmillan, 1986.

Lichtblau, Eric. "Bush Plans to Let Religious Groups Get Building Aid." *New York Times*, 23 January 2003, A1 and A20.

Lin, Elbert, Jon D. Michaels, Rajesh Nayak, Katherine Tang Newberger, Nikhil Shanbhag, and Jake Sullivan. "Faith in the Courts? The Legal and Political Future of Federally-Funded Faith-Based Initiatives." *Yale Law and Policy Review* 20 (2002): 182–225.

Lipscomb, Andrew A., and Albert E. Bergh. *The Writings of Thomas Jefferson.* Washington, D.C.: Thomas Jefferson Memorial Association, 1905.

Liptak, Adam. "A Right to Bias Is Put to the Test." *New York Times,* 11 October 2002, A30.

Lutton, Linda. "Indy Builds a Front Porch, Gov. Bush Likes the View: City Hall Change Makes a Shaky Porch." *Youth Today,* May 2000, 33.

Magnet, Myron. *The Dream and the Nightmare: The Sixties; Legacy to the Underclass.* New York: William Morrow and Company, 1993.

———. "What Is Compassionate Conservatism?" *Wall Street Journal,* 5 February 1999, A14.

Marshner, Connie. Statement for Distribution at Coalition for Compassion Press Conference. *Free Congress Foundation Online,* 11 April 2001. <www.freecongress.org/press/releases/010411.htm> (16 May 2001)

Matovina, Timothy. "Latino Catholics and American Public Life." In *Can Charitable Choice Work?* ed. Andrew Walsh. Hartford: Trinity College, 2001.

McNeely, Dave. "The Book that Helped Shape Bush's Message." *Austin American-Statesman,* 27 January 1001, A14.

McQuillan, Laurence. "$100 Million Grant Will Go to Religious Groups." *USA Today,* 28 March 2001, 7A

Meckler, Laura. "Bush Moves to Aid Faith-Based Groups." *Washington Post,* 30 January 2001, A1.

Michelman, Scott M. "Faith-Based Initiatives." *Harvard Journal on Legislation* 39, no. 2 (Summer 2002): 475–502.

Milbank, Dana. "Bush Endorses Compromise in Senate on Aid to Charities." *Washington Post,* 8 February 2002, A4.

———. "Charity Bill Compromise Is Reached." *Washington Post,* 6 February 2002, A1.

———. "Needed: Catchword for Bush Ideology." *Washington Post,* 1 February 2001, A1.

Milbank, Dana, and Hamil R. Harris. "Bush, Religious Leaders Meet." *Washington Post,* 21 December 2000, A6.

Miller, John J., and Ramesh Ponnuru. "Faithless California." *National Review,* 5 July 2001. <www.nationalreview.com/daily/nr070501.shtml>

Mitchell. "Bush Draws Campaign Theme from More than 'the Heart.'" *New York Times,* 11 June 2000, A1.

Monsma, Stephen V. *When Sacred and Secular Mix.* Lanham, Md.: Rowman & Littlefield, 1996.

Morano, Marc. "White House Defends Plan for Faith-Based Environmental Grants." *CNSNews.com.* <www.crosswalk.com/new/1180601.html>

Morgan, Edward. Testimony before the Senate Committee on the Judiciary Faith Based Solutions: What Are the Legal Issues?, 6 June 2001. <www.senate.gov/~judiciary/te060601em.htm> (6 June 2001)

Muckleroy, George. "Double Entendre: How the Two Interpretations of the Establishment Clause Will Determine the Future of Charitable Choice." *Texas Tech Law Review* 33 (2002): 1196–1226.

Mutterperl, Laura B. "Employment at God's Will: The Constitutionality of Anti-discrimination Exemptions in Charitable Choice Legislation." *Harvard Civil Rights–Civil Liberties Law Review* 37, no. 2 (Summer 2002): 389–445.

Nakashima, Ellen. "A Management Guru Fails to Make Team." *Washington Post*, 6 March 2001, A21.

Neal, Terry M. "Midwestern Mayor Shapes Bush's Message." *Washington Post*, 5 June 2000, A6.

New Jersey Department of Consumer Affairs. *Annual Report 1998.* <www.state.nj.us/dca/98annual/aisle2.pdf>

Newman, Maria. "Bush Visit Sets Off Debate about Religion and State." *New York Times*, 15 March 2001, B5.

Nicholas, Peter. "DiIulio: For Now a Crusader, Forever a Scholar." *Philadelphia Inquirer*, 5 June 2001. <http://inq.philly.com/content/inquirer/2001/06/05/national/DIIULIO05.htm> (5 June 2001)

Niebuhr, Gustav. "A Point Man for the Bush Church–State Collaboration." *New York Times*, 7 April 2001, A8.

O'Beirne, Kate. "Church(Groups) and State." *National Review*, 19 February 2001. <www.nationalreview.com/19feb01/obierne021901.shtml>

———. "Uncharitable Choice: The President's Way Is the Wrong Way." *National Review*, 9 July 2001, 24–25.

O'Beirne, Kate, and Ramesh Ponnuru. "Great Society II: Will Bush Repeat LBJ's Mistakes and Expand the Welfare State?" *Wall Street Journal Opinion Journal*, 30 April 2001. <http://opinionjournal.com/editorial/feature.html> (30 April 2001)

O'Brien, David. *Constitutional Law and Politics: Civil Rights and Civil Liberties.* 5th ed. New York: W.W. Norton, 2003.

Office of the Press Secretary. "Remarks by the President at Meeting with Catholic Charities." <www.whitehouse.gov/news/releases/20010311 html>

———. "Remarks by the President at National Prayer Breakfast." <www.whitehouse.gov/news/releases/20010201.html>

———. "Remarks by the President in Commencement Address." <www.whitehouse.gov/news/releases/2001/05/20010521-1html>

Olasky, Marvin. "A Merciful Resignation," *World* 1 September 2001.

———. *Compassionate Conservatism*. New York: The Free Press, 2000.

———. "Rolling the Dice," *World*, 4 August, 2001.

———. "The White House Faith-Based Initiative: What's Going Right, What's Going Wrong?" *Notre Dame Journal of Law, Ethics, and Public Policy* 16 (2002): 355–66.

———. *The Tragedy of American Compassion*. Washington, D.C.: Regnery Publishing, 1992.

Oppel, Richard A., and Gustav Niebuhr. "Bush Meeting Focuses on Role of Religion." *New York Times*, 21 December 2000, A37.

Ostling, Richard N. "Bush's Faith-Based Initiative Has Protestant Origins." Associated Press, 9 February 2001. <www.beliefnet.com>

Pasternak, Judy. "Mayor Relies on Faith to Deliver Services." *Los Angeles Times*, 9 April 2001, 4.

Peterson, Barrie. "Working with the N. J. Office of Faith-Based Initiatives; a Case-Study." Paper delivered at the Northeast Political Science Association Meeting, Philadelphia, Pa., November 2001.

Peterson, Jonathan. "Muslims Wary of White House Efforts on Faith-Based Initiative; Politics: Meeting Incident Underscores Tensions and Points to Community's Broader Concerns about Its Status in U.S." *Los Angeles Times*, 13 July 2001, A18.

Pimental, O. Ricardo. "Faith-Based Funding: The Devil with It." *Denver Post*, 23 March 2001, B9.

Post, Robert C. "Subsidized Speech." *Yale Law Journal* 106, no.1 (October 1996): 151–65.

Putnam, Robert. *Bowling Alone*. New York: Simon & Schuster, 2000.

Raspberry, William. "A GI Bill of Faith." *Washington Post*, 19 March 2001, A17.

Ready, Willing and Able—Citizens Working for Change: A Survey for the Pew Partnerships for Change. Philadelphia: The Pew Charitable Trust, 2001.

Reifler, Dr. Burton V. "Faith in Action." Letter. <www.FIAVolunteers.org>

Richardson, Valerie. "The Future of the Faith-Based Initiative." *Philanthropy* (May/June 2001): 10–12.

Robertson, Pat. "Mr. Bush's Faith-Based Initiative Is Flawed." *Wall Street Journal*, 12 March 2001, A15.

Rosin, Hanna. "Charity's Image Shaken by Gay Bias Flap: Salvation Army's Social, Spiritual Efforts Collide." *Washington Post*, 15 July 2001, A5. <www.washingtonpost.com/wp-dyn/articles/A63288-2001Jul14.html> (17 July 2001).

Ross, Thomas W. "The Faith-Based Initiative: Anti-Poverty or Anti-Poor?" *Georgetown Journal on Poverty, Law, and Policy* 9, no.1 (Winter 2002): 167–92.

Sanger, David E. "Bush Asks Mayors to Lobby for Faith-Based Social Aid." *New York Times*, 26 June 2001, A17.

Sapong, Emma D., and Larissa Theodore. "Pulling No Punches." *Buffalo News*, 29 June 2001, C1.

Schleifer, Yigal. "'Completed Jews' Row Leaves Bush Unmoved." *Jerusalem Report*, 18 June 2001, 5.

Segers, Mary. "The Bush Faith-Based Initiative." Unpublished paper delivered at the University of North Florida, April 2002.

———. "New Jersey and the Bush Faith-Based Initiative." Unpublished paper presented at the 2002 annual meeting of the American Political Science Association, Boston, Mass., 29 August–1 September 2002.

Sherman, Amy L. "Little Miracles: How Churches Are Responding to Welfare Reform." *The American Enterprise* (January/February 1998): 64–68.

Sider, Ronald, J. "Why Democrats Should Support Charitable Choice—Including the Hiring Exemption." Evangelicals for Social Action. <www.esa-online.org/faithdem.html>

Solomon, Lewis D., and Matthew J. Vlissides Jr. "Faith-Based Charities and the Quest to Solve America's Social Ills: A Legal and Policy Analysis." *Cornell Journal of Law and Public Policy* 10 (2001): 265–302.

Starr, Alexandra. "A Leap of Faith that May Fall Flat." *Business Week*, 26 March 2001, 104.

Stevenson, Richard W. "Bush to Allow Religious Groups to Get Federal Money to Aid Poor." *New York Times*, 13 December 2002, A34.

Stockman, Farah. "Rivers Walking Turbulent Line." *Boston Globe*, 4 April 2001, B1.

Stoil, Michael. "Matters of Faith." *Behavioral Health Management* 21, no. 2 (March/April 2001): 8–9.

Strode, Tom. "Faith-Based Director Challenges Leaders' Concerns; Land Responds." *Worthy News*, 31 May 2001. <www.worthynews.com/news-features/faith-initiative-6.html> (31 May 2001)

Tenpas, Kathryn Dunn. "Can an Office Change a Country?" Report by University of Pennsylvania scholar at a forum sponsored by the Pew Forum on Religion & Public Life, 20 February 2002.

Texas Department of Community Services. "Philosophy." Updated 24 January 2003. <www.dhs.state.tx.us/about/mission>

"Thirty U.S. Catholic Leaders to Meet with Bush." *Zenit.org*, 30 January 2001. <www.mccw-usa.org/news/article12.html>

Thomas, Cal. "Christians Should Aid Needy without Government Subsidy." *Columbus Dispatch*, 6 July 2001, 2E.

Thomas, Oliver. "Partnership or Peril? Faith-Based Initiatives and the First Amendment." First Amendment Center Publication. *First Reports* 2, no. 1 (May 2001): 1–20.

"Twenty Five Faith-Based Organizations Call on President to Restore Benefits to Legal Immigrants." *Catholic Charities Online, News Release,* <www.catholiccharitiesusa.org/media/releases/2001/020801html>

U. S. Census Bureau. *Statistical Abstract of the United States: 2001.* Washington, D. C. 2001.

U.S. Department of Health and Human Services. The Center for Faith-Based and Community Initiatives. "What Is Charitable Choice?" 12 December 2002 (last revised). <www.hhs.gov/faith/choice/html>

———. "HHS Releases Fact-Sheet on Compassion Capital Fund." *States News Service*, 5 June 2002.

VandeHei, Jim. "Bush Turns to Corporations to Help Fund Faith-Based Plan." *Wall Street Journal*, 24 May 2001, A24.

Waldman, Steven. Interview with George W. Bush. October 2000. <www.beliefnet.com>

———. "Town Meeting." Columbia, South Carolina, 12 February 2000. <www.beliefnet.com>

Wall Street Journal, 01 September 1999, C1.

Wallis, Jim. "Acting in Good Faith." *Sojourner*, 30 no. 3 (May/June 2001): 27ff. <www.sojo.net/home/magazine/index/cfm/action/sojourners/issue/soj0105/article/010510.html>

Walsh, Andrew. *Can Charitable Choice Work? Covering Religion's Impact on Urban Affairs and Social Services.* Hartford, Ct.: Trinity College, 2001.

"Watts' Faith-Based Bill Passes House Committee." *Associated Press*, 12 July 2001. <http://web.lexis-nexis.com> (12 July 2001)

Weber, Paul J. *Equal Separation: Understanding the Religion Clauses of the First Amendment.* Westport, Ct.: Greenwood Press, 1990.

———. "James Madison and Religious Equality: The Perfect Separation." *Review of Politics* 44 (1982): 163–86.

———. and Dennis Gilbert. *Private Churches and Public Money: Church–Government Fiscal Relations.* Westport, Ct.: Greenwood, 1981.

Weisberg, Jacob. "Leap of Faith." *Slate Ballot Box*, 1 February 2001. <http://slate.msn.com/code/BallotBox/BallotBox.asp?Show=2/1/2001&idMessage=6995>

Welch, Aimee. "Charitable Choice for Washington?" *Insight on the News*, 8 January 2001, 16.

The White House Office for Faith-Based and Community Initiatives. "Faith-Based and Community Initiatives: Rallying the Armies of Compassion." Foreword by President George W. Bush. January 2001. <www.whitehouse.gov/news/reports/faithbased.html>

———. "Unlevel Playing Field: Barrier to Participation by Faith-Based and Community Organizations in Federal Social Service Programs." August 2001.

"White House and Senate Agree on Church Charities." *New York Times*, 2 June 2002. <www.nytimes.com/2002/02/06/politics/06faith.html>

Wilson, James Q. "Why Not Try Vouchers?" *New York Times*, 27 April 2001, A25.

Witham, Larry. "Amendments Kill CARE in Senate." *Washington Times*, 15 November 2002. <www.washtimes.com>

———. "Towey Says Faith-Based Bill 'Held Hostage' by Reed." *Washington Times*, 24 October 2002. <www.washtimes.com/national/20021024-3491772.htm>

Working Group on Human Needs and Faith-Based and Community Initiatives. "Finding Common Ground: 29 Recommendations of the Working Group on Human Needs and Faith-Based and Community Initiatives." January 2002.

Zapor, Patricia. "Two D. C. Newcomers Get Acquainted over Dinner." *Daily Catholic*, 28 January 2001. <www.dailycatholic.org/issue/2001Jan/jan28nul.htm>

Zwiebel, David. Testimony of David Zwiebel before the Senate Judiciary Committee in support of the proposed expansion of the Federal "Charitable Choice" Program, 6 June 2001. <www.senate.gov/~judiciary/te060601dz.htm> (6 June 2001)

WEBSITES

www.esa-online.org (Evangelicals for Social Action)

www.isaiahhouse.org (Isiah House, an organization for assisting the homeless in New Jersey)

www.lutheranservices.org (Lutheran Services in America, a joint program between the Evangelical Lutheran Church and the Missouri Synod)

www.newcommunity.org (New Community Corporation, an organization established to develop safe, decent and attractive housing for poor residents in a new community within New Jersey's Central Ward)

www.welfareinfo.org/faithbase.asp
www.whitehouse.gov/infocus/Faith-Based (White House Office of Faith-Based and Community Initiatives)
www.workinggroup.org

INTERVIEWS

John DiIluio, former Director of the White House Office of Faith-Based and Community Affairs.
Jack Horner, former legislative assistant to Congressman J. C. Watts.
Confidential Interview, "A"
Confidential Interview, "B"

COURT CASES/LEGISLATION

Public Law 104-193, the Personal Responsibility and Work Opportunity Reconciliation Act of 1996, enacted 22 August 1996, Sec. 104.
Agostini v. Felton, 521 U.S. 203 (1997).
Bowen v. Kendrick, 487 U.S. 589 (1988).
Cantwell v. Connecticut, 310 U.S. 296 (1940).
Corporation of Presiding Bishops of Church of Jesus Christ of Latter-Day Saints v. Amos, 483 U.S. 327 (1987).
Everson v. Board of Education of Ewing Township, 330 U.S. 1 (1947).
Lamb's Chapel v. Center Moriches Union Free School District, 508 U.S. 384 (1993).
Lemon v. Kurtzman, 403 U.S. 602 (1971).
Mitchell v. Helms, 530 U.S. 793 (2002).
Reynolds v. U.S., 98 U.S. 145 (1879).
Rosenberger v. The Rector and Visitors of the University of Virginia, 515 U.S. 819 (1995).
Rust v. Sullivan, 500 U.S. 173 (1991).
Serbian Orthodox Diocese v. Milivojevich, 426 U.S. 696 at 713 (1976).
Watson, v. Jones, 80 U.S. 679 (1871).
Zelman v. Simmons-Harris, 536 U.S. (2002).
Zorach, v. Clauson, 343 U.S. 306 (1952).

Index

About the Authors

Jo Renee Formicola is professor of political science at Seton Hall University in South Orange, New Jersey. She is the author of *John Paul II: Prophetic Politician* and *The Catholic Church and Human Rights*. She is the coauthor with Hubert Morken of *The Politics of School Choice* and the coeditor of *Religious Leaders and Faith-Based Politics: Ten Profiles* and *Everson Revisited: Religion, Education and Law at the Crossroads*, also with Hubert Morken. Her areas of research include church-state issues and Catholic politics.

Mary Segers is professor and Chair of the Department of Political Science at Rutgers University in Newark, New Jersey. She is author and editor of *Piety, Politics, and Pluralism: Religion, the Courts, and the 2000 Elections* (Rowman & Littlefield) and is the coauthor with Ted Jelen of *A Wall of Separation: Debating the Public Role of Religion*. She is also coeditor with Timothy Byrnes of *Abortion Politics in American States*, and *The Catholic Church and Abortion Politics: A View from the States*. Her special interests include church-state matters, Catholic politics, and feminist issues.

Paul Weber is Distinguished Teaching Professor of Political Science at the University of Louisville, senior fellow of the McConnell Center for Political Leadership, and executive director of the Grawemeyer Awards. He is the author or coauthor of several books on the

Constitution and church-state relations, including *Private Churches and Public Money; Equal Separation: Understanding the Religion Clauses of the First Amendment; Unfounded Fears: Myths and Realities of a Constitutional Convention;* and *U. S. Religious Interest Groups: Institutional Profiles.*